MOVEMENT AND THE ORDERING OF FREEDOM

PERVERSE MODERNITIES

A Series Edited by Jack Halberstam and Lisa Lowe

MOVEMENT AND THE ORDERING OF FREEDOM

On Liberal Governances of Mobility | HAGAR KOTEF

DUKE UNIVERSITY PRESS   DURHAM AND LONDON   2015

© 2015 Duke University Press
All rights reserved

Designed by Natalie Smith
Typeset in Quadraat by Copperline

Library of Congress Cataloging-in-Publication Data
Kotef, Hagar
Movement and the ordering of freedom :
on liberal governances of mobility / Hagar Kotef.
pages cm—(Perverse modernities)
Includes bibliographical references and index.
ISBN 978-0-8223-5843-5 (hardcover : alk. paper)
ISBN 978-0-8223-5855-8 (pbk. : alk. paper)
1. Liberalism. 2. Freedom of movement. 3. Social mobility.
4. Liberty. I. Title. II. Series: Perverse modernities.
JC585.K68 2015
323.44—dc23
2014033900
ISBN 978-0-8223-7575-3 (e-book)

Cover art: Miki Kratsman, Erez #3, 2003 (Erez checkpoint,
Gaza). Digital print, 70 x 100 cm. Courtesy of the artist.

CONTENTS

Preface vii

Acknowledgments xi

Introduction 1

1 / Between Imaginary Lines: Violence and Its Justifications at the Military Checkpoints in Occupied Palestine
Hagar Kotef and Merav Amir 27

2 / An Interlude: A Tale of Two Roads—On Freedom and Movement 52

3 / The Fence That "Ill Deserves the Name of Confinement": Locomotion and the Liberal Body 61

4 / The Problem of "Excessive" Movement 87

5 / The "Substance and Meaning of All Things Political": On Other Bodies 112

Conclusion 136

Notes 141 *Bibliography* 203 *Index* 217

PREFACE

There is a camera at the airport's gate. Often, it is left unnoticed, but if one is asked she would probably know to say it is there. Many of us are by now familiar with such cameras and various security apparatuses that are installed in public spaces—airports, streets, pubs, train stations, shopping malls, or elevators. Most of the readers of this book are probably also familiar with the many critiques of the growing expansion of such mechanisms, their uses and abuses. But what does the camera monitor? Some cameras today can identify faces (to match the profile of a runaway), body heat (to trigger an alert when detecting an anxious—and thus presumably a suspicious—person) or logos of cars (to identify the economic status of a person, in order to prompt the appropriate advertising on a billboard). But the vast majority of security apparatuses today monitor *movement*.[1]

These security apparatuses are based on algorithms that analyze the data accumulated via a variety of sensors. The algorithms are used, first, to identify regular patterns of movement and then to flag movements that deviate from this identified norm. The norm thus becomes a pattern of movement deduced from sets of natural and social phenomena.[2] Once established, every deviation from this norm is defined as a problem or a potential threat. We therefore have "*normal*" and "*abnormal*" movements: the movements of airport travelers (and the airplanes themselves), of the business people or shoppers in their daily routines, of subway passengers; but also the movements of those who seek to kill them or themselves (suicides on railways are apparently a major economic hazard for transit companies),[3] to steal, or perhaps simply to reside in a nonresidential space of movement (homeless people whose presence is undesired by municipal, governmental, and economical authorities). The first (normal) movement is to be maximized; the second (abnormal movement), to be eliminated, or at least minimized.

Monitoring movement began as a solution for a technical difficulty: the need to separate an object from its background. A security threat is often imagined as an object (usually a bag that is an index for the bomb presumably hidden within it). Yet while the human eye can identify objects, the first learning algorithms could not. Like primitive brains, they could only see movement.[4] Objects could thus be identified by these algorithms only once they moved, were moved, or stopped moving. Hence, questions had to be revised: suspicion could not be ascribed to objects but to the *irregular movements* that brought them to their suspicious location. This was the technological requisite that placed movement at the forefront of contemporary security apparatuses. However, we will see that the tie between the two—movement and security—has a long history. Whereas these surveillance technologies undoubtedly create new desires for regulation and reframe old questions, the regulation of movement was the object of political desires at least since Plato. This book sets to trace these desires, as well as the different—and differentiated—bodies they seek to capture, but also produce and shape in this process. It is a book about movement—about motion, locomotion, and mobility as physical phenomena, images, myths, and figures, and first and foremost about movement as an axis of difference.[5]

The story of these technologies, however, does not end here, with a pervasive regulation of movement that is founded on parting normal from abnormal patterns of movement or modes of being in space. Irregular movements are, after all, quite common, and these systems therefore trigger alerts constantly. So the question had to shift again. "The question is no longer how to identify the suspicious bag," said a CEO of a large security company whom I interviewed for this project. "Rather, the question is how to stop evacuating the airport every other week." The objective was accordingly altered: neither identifying a suspicious object nor detecting suspicious movements, but securing the regular movement of goods, passengers, and airplanes. "Bombs don't go off that often," he remarked, "so it makes no sense to stop the activity of the airport so frequently for this statistically negligible chance."[6] This may bring to mind the attribute of liberal security/biopolitical regimes identified by Foucault: an integration of threats—albeit minimized—into the normal order of movement. This integration rests on the assumption that any attempt to completely eliminate threats would bring to a stop the circulation of things and people whose furtherance is perceived as the most essential goal of politics.[7] Movement *is* the order of things.

ACKNOWLEDGMENTS

This book, perhaps like any book, is not simply my own. My thoughts seem to always be a segment of a collective endeavor, and over the years, I had the privilege of belonging to several wonderful intellectual communities that were absolutely essential to my never-ending struggles to find words and arguments, to formulate and curve ideas, to write, to think.

More specifically, and personally, I would like to thank several people: Adi Ophir, for agreeing to be my teacher; for teaching me, as if for anew, how to think, how to read, and how to approach a problem; and for creating some of the assemblages with which and through which this book—among other texts—took form (assemblages of concepts, projects, and above all people). I'm also grateful to Merav Amir, for thinking with me so intimately—indeed a truly rare experience; and for giving me the first chapter. Judith Butler made a certain life-course possible, and I'm forever indebted to her for that, as well as for many other things: for giving me many of my questions; for always pushing me further when I thought I was already "there"; for including me within her wonderful community; and for providing me with an intellectual home. (There is both an academic and a personal home here, which I would not have been able to inhabit without her.) To Yves Winter I thank for so much, really, but above all for always being unsatisfied with what I say—or write—and for, at the very same time, providing me a network of security that caught me and restored my confidence every time I was dissatisfied with myself; and for his friendship. Gil Anidjar meticulously read so many drafts of this text and provided his most insightful comments; it took me months to understand most of them, but eventually they have contributed to this text more than I could have ever asked for. Anat Biletzky made me fall in love with philosophy, and has since then always reminded me—without even knowing—why it is still valuable. For this, and for teaching me the art of writing as my PhD adviser, she will always have my deepest gratitude. My many thanks also to the various friends and colleagues who were kind enough to read, listen, ask, and demand more: Ariel Handel, Nima Bassiri, Amir Engel, Niza Yanai, Uday Mehta, Elisabeth Ladenson, Annika Thiem, George Ciccariello-Maher, Neil Roberts, James Ingram, Josh Dubler, Emily Ogden, Dana Fields, Adam Smith, Roy Wagner, Yoav Kenny, William Walters, Ann Stoler, Jack Halberstam, Étienne Balibar, Liz Donnelly, Deborah Aschkenes, the members of the lexicon groups in Tel Aviv as well as NYC—early versions of this work were published in the Hebrew, as well as the English journals of these groups: *Mafte'akh* and *Political Concepts*, the fellows and board members of Columbia's Society of Fellows, the participants of Columbia University's "Seminar for Social and Political Thought," those who took part in the workshop "Moving Towards Confinement," and several anonymous reviewers of several journals, who may be able to identify their most helpful feedback in this text. There are probably many others.

The manuscript was largely written during a three-year fellowship at Columbia University's Society of Fellows. To the people who brought me there, who gave me the institutional, academic, and personal support that I never dared even dreaming of, and who became dear friends, colleagues, and interlocutors, I am grateful. Above all I want to thank those who made it a true home: Eileen Gillooly, Chris Brown, David Johnston, Elizabeth Povinelli, Melissa Schwartzberg, and Hilary Hallett.

I completed the manuscript during a dual appointment in the Minerva Humanities Center, Tel Aviv University, and the Department for Politics and Government, at Ben Gurion University. I thank these institutions and the people (specifically Dani Filk and—again—Adi Ophir), for the rare gift of time they have given me.

There are not enough words of appreciation to thank Courtney Berger from Duke University Press, who understood from the first moment what I am trying to do in this somewhat untraditional project, and who made this happen (and so smoothly and pleasantly so), as well as the two readers of the manuscript, whose comments, thoughts, and suggestions were indispensable and immensely productive.

Finally, to Maya, who already at two tried to teach me that playing with her is more important than sitting at my desk. I hope I learned this lesson well enough. And to Lavi, for tolerating all this.

INTRODUCTION

> People have always moved—whether through desire or through violence. Scholars have also written about these movements for a long time and from diverse perspectives. What is interesting is that now particular theoretical shifts have arranged themselves into new conjunctures that give these phenomena greater analytic visibility than ever before. Thus we . . . have old questions, but also something very new. —LIISA MALKKI

"Of all the specific liberties which may come into our minds when we hear the word 'freedom,'" Hannah Arendt once argued, "freedom of movement is historically the oldest and also the most elementary. Being able to depart for where we will is the prototypical gesture of being free, as limitation of freedom of movement has from time immemorial been the precondition for enslavement."[1] Accordingly, Arendt claims that freedom of movement is "the substance and meaning of all things political."[2] This book aims at unpacking this claim by proposing an inquiry into the politics of motion.

We live within political systems that have an increasing interest in physical movement, or perhaps just an increasingly effective control over it. These systems are, to a great degree, organized around both the desire and ability to determine who is permitted to enter what sorts of spaces: Who may enter a national state, a gated community, a particular street, a playground? Who is permitted to reside in such spaces and for how long? The "guest" worker, for example, may stay, but only on the condition that she will leave when no longer needed. The "undocumented" immigrant, however, who is effectively in the same social position, is always already "illegal" by her very act of staying. These political systems also operate by determining who (or what) should be contained and constrained: young African American men in prisons, asylum seekers in detention camps, demonstrations within tightly policed enclaves. These political systems determine for which circulating good (or capital) a tax must be paid; the exportation of what sorts of goods (or capital, or people) should be hindered or promoted. They also control which segments of borders, public spaces, and particular estates should be entrenched and which segments should be left breached.

As Foucault demonstrates throughout his work, these systems are the substance through which the modern subject emerges. From their early establishment as systems of confinement,[3] to more complex modes of distributing bodies in space that Foucault identifies as the essence of disciplinary power,[4] and to a later attentiveness to circulation that eventually becomes according to him "the only political stake and the only real space of political struggle and contestation,"[5] these systems have functioned as the transmission medium for the formation of modern subjectivity. In other words, both subjects and powers take form via movement and its regulation. Different technologies of regulating, limiting, producing or inciting movement are therefore different "technolog[ies] of citizenship,"[6] as well as of colonization, gender-based domestication, expropriation, and exclusion.

This book seeks to map several modes of configuring movement into different forms of subject-positions, and thus, into the production and justification of different schemas of governance. For this purpose, I will primarily consider movement *as physical change in the locations of bodies*. And even though I will allow this meaning to stretch and expand in ways that will eventually necessitate us to revisit not merely this concept of movement, but also the concepts of "bodies" and "location," I nevertheless focus here mostly on motions of individual bodies.

The following pages wind between two main routes, which—I hope—can thereby be woven into a single one: (I) a reading in political philosophy, whose main foci are Thomas Hobbes and John Locke, but which circulates around many other protagonists, including Plato, William Blackstone, Elizabeth C. Stanton, John S. Mill, and Hannah Arendt; and (II) a spatial analysis of contemporary spaces. This scope means that the path I wish to follow here is bound to be full of gaps. It is my hope that these gaps will not turn into abysses, but will leave spaces for other contexts, texts, and political orders to echo. If the book has only one argument, it can be summarized—somewhat reductively—as follows: In a long tradition, that in political theory is often termed "liberal," and within which we largely still live today, movement and freedom are often identified with each other. Movement, that is, is the material substance of a long-standing concept of freedom. Yet for movement to become so tightly interlaced with freedom, an entire array of mechanisms, technologies, and practices had to be put in place so that this movement would become moderated enough (one could say tamed or domesticated). Movement had to become the order of freedom rather than a chaotic violation of order itself. Slightly more elaborately, I propose here four main arguments.

First, I argue that subject-positions (or identity categories) and the political orders within which they gain meaning cannot be divorced from movement. We cannot understand, for example, the formation of gender categories without understanding the history of separate spheres and the history of confining women of certain races and classes to the home. We cannot grasp poverty without thinking about a history of vagrancy, migratory work, or about homelessness (as a concrete situation or as a specter). We cannot account for racial relations in the United States without considering, on the one hand, the practice of mass incarceration and, on the other, the history of slave trade and the middle passage. We cannot explain the current legal situation of Bedouins in Israel—the repeated acts of house demolition, of expropriation, the systematic denial of tenure rights—without understanding the myth of nomadism. The history of movement as well as its images, the practices of controlling it as well as the fear of it, the tradition of cherishing it as a right as well as the many exclusions that are embedded into this tradition, all are crucial in understanding social and political hierarchies, practices of rule, and identities.

Second, I examine this claim in regard to one, historically privileged, subject-position: the liberal subject. The particular features of this subject have changed through history (including and excluding different groups), and there is little agreement in the literature on where this subject—and the discourse of liberalism more broadly—begins and ends. I have no stakes at this moment in marking these changes and disagreements. For the current purpose it is sufficient to say that this subject is nonetheless often characterized via endeavors to mark him as "universal," and often as an abstract entity. In other words, it is a subject who is a mere anchor for rights and liberties, and whose essence is rationality or "mind." Through a reading of liberal freedom as pivoting around free movement, I argue—counter to this understanding of liberal subjectivity—that at least until the end of the eighteenth century, the liberal subject was largely configured as corporeal. My point here is not merely to rehearse the well-established critique according to which this figure was in fact—despite efforts to pretend it is universal—racialized, classed, or gendered. My point is rather that in the seventeenth and eighteenth centuries, even *within the logic of liberalism*, the subject at the core of liberal theory had a corporeal dimension: the capacity of locomotion (and the relations between this particular bodily facet and the other aforementioned facets—whiteness, masculinity, propertiedness, but also maturity and others—will be explored throughout this book). Moreover, even after the liberal subject underwent processes of abstractness, roughly at the turn of the nineteenth century, it nevertheless appeared as an embodied entity whenever it could be imagined as a moving body. Indeed, whereas after the eighteenth-century movement might no longer explicitly be proclaimed as one of the most important rights of liberal subjects, freedom of movement remains at the heart of liberal conceptualization of freedom. Albeit in different ways, throughout the history of liberal thought movement functions as *a pivot of materialization for the liberal body*.

Asking the question of the political meanings of movement is, perhaps above all, asking how our bodies affect, are affected by, become the vehicle of, or the addressees of political orders, ideologies, institutions, relations, or powers. Asking this question in regard to liberal discourses directs us away from the prevalent reading of this political tradition, contending that liberalism perceives and produces subjects as essentially reasoning judicial entities whose corporeality is constantly repressed or excluded from the domain of political relevance. Therefore, at its second layer, this book offers an alternative reading of liberal subjectivity, that does not simply bridge the Cartesian model with a later (predominantly nineteenth and twentieth century) understanding of the subject as reducible to its will, reason, decision-making processes, or a juridical status (a bridge that thereby erases alternative models of subjectivity). My purpose, however, goes beyond proposing a more nuanced understanding of the liberal subject. Eliding the moving body from liberal subjectivity obscures major modalities of the exercise of liberal power. Accordingly, the aim of this analysis is to bring these forms of power to the surface. It is done here not merely in order to show their historic operations, but also to echo contemporary political orders, to point to a political rationale that still governs contemporary political trends, and to expose some building blocks of our own forms of governing and of being governed.

For this purpose, I show how this liberal concept of freedom emerged in tandem with other configurations of movement, wherein movement was constructed as a threat rather than an articulation of liberty. Here we arrive at the third argument at the core of this book. The movement through which liberal subjectivity obtained material presence and through which liberty became a physical phenomenon was not unbound, unrestrained movement. Rather, this movement was given within many constraints and was secured by many anchors that provided it with some stability. Beyond questions of volition and intention that themselves constrain movement, movement has been conceptualized and has materialized within sets of material, racial, geographic, and gendered conditions in a way that allowed only some subjects to appear as free when moving (and as oppressed when hindered). The movement (or hindrance) of other subjects has been configured differently. Colonized subjects who were declared to be nomads, poor who were seen as vagabond or thrown into vagrancy as they lost access to lands, women whose presumed hysterical nature was attached to their inability to control bodily fluids, all were constituted (or rather deconstituted) as unruly subjects whose movement is a problem to be managed. This configuration was the grounds for justifying nonliberal moments—and spaces—within liberal regimes.

This argument has two opposite trajectories whose causal relation to each other is not completely clear. On the one hand, we see *an inability to conceive* some movements as a manifestation of freedom, and on the other hand, an *active effort to deny* and thwart this freedom. There is a certain coproduction between these two directions but its nature changes across different discursive fields, ideologies, and times. By providing a reading of several means through which movement is produced as freedom or as a threat, as an iconography of self-regulation or as a proof of the impossibility to discipline this person or that group, this third layer also offers a critique of the modes of governance that crystallize around these two main configurations of movement: surveillance, enclosure, eviction, imprisonment, and siege.

The fourth layer of this book is an endeavor to show how this split in the configuration of movement, as well as the modes of governance that are formed alongside this split, are mapped into contemporary spaces. Within this mapping I focus on the regime currently at place in the occupied Palestinian territories (oPt). This regime's focal point of interest (and major political technology) is the movement of people and goods. In other words, it is a regime of movement. As one of the most perfected and elaborate systems of controlling a population via controlling its movement, this regime offers a condensed laboratory for examining technologies of regulating movement and the subject-positions emerging through these technologies. While abnormal in its radicality, this particular context is by no means privileged, but is rather one manifestation of a global trend that is far from new, but that has been critically intensifying in recent years.[7] Thinking on and from this particular context is a way of marking some of the contemporary stakes of my theoretical analysis. As the argument unfolds, this context supposes neither to circumscribe these stakes, nor to suggest we can see here a single political structure extending from seventeenth-century England to twenty-first century Israel/ Palestine, or even a certain continuum. This context aims, rather, at opening many other points of resonance, that eventually demonstrate how different configurations of motion partake in justifying different modes of governing populations within the frame of liberal democracies.[8]

Finally, subtending these four arguments is an endeavor to understand the political bearings of movement; to chart the operations, roles, doings, and meanings of movement within our political lexicon(s). Hence, my account in this book is lexical more than phenomenological. Rather than examining the essence of movement, I analyze the political syntax within which the concept circulates and through which it takes form.

Regimes

Different forms and technologies of ordering movement were always central to the formations of different political orders and ideologies. From the tethering of serfs to the land under feudalism, to the modern territorial state and its demarcation of borders, political orders are in many ways regimes of movement. The modern state—to take what is perhaps one of the most relevant examples—especially after the invention of the passport,[9] and increasingly with the evolution of technologies of sealing and regulating borders, is to a great degree a system of regulating, ordering, and disciplining bodies (and other objects) in motion.[10] Adi Ophir further defines the sovereign state as an apparatus of closure: sovereignty is what consolidates (and then unravels) in efforts of closure—actual or potential, successful or failed.[11] It is important to note, already here, that alongside these apparatuses of closure and controlling movement, an elaborated ideology and theory of the state was developed that ties these modes of confinement to freedom. Enclosure, hindrance (or other modes of slowing things down), and hedges of various types, were seen as preconditioning freedom, rather than standing in an opposition to circulation, flow, and above all liberty. Most of the great thinkers of the state could not conceptualize freedom without the possibility of its management, without some form of closure that would render movement a principle of order rather than chaos.

This understanding of the modern state is perhaps most explicit in John C. Torpey's work. If Max Weber sees the formation of the modern state as a function of monopolizing the legitimate means of violence, Torpey follows this formulation to propose that the modern state consolidated also by monopolizing the "legitimate means of *movement*."[12] While Torpey presents his analysis as parallel to Weber's, I propose these two processes or ideologies are inextricably linked, and seek to explore how they work in tandem. Did one of these processes of monopolization condition the other? Is one a means for the other? Does one serve to justify the other? Can one be thought of in terms of the other (violence as movement; movement as violence)? Was violence but another movement to be monopolized?

State violence, moreover, has its own movements: invasion, infiltration, and conquest. And these often rest upon other movements—or myths thereof. John Stuart Mill provides a very lucid manifestation of this structure that will be delved into in the following chapters. For Mill, Europe is a site of motion. It has a "remarkable diversity" that constantly facilitates movement: "the people of Europe," he writes, "have struck out a great variety of *paths*, each leading to something valuable; and although at every period those who *traveled* in different paths have been intolerant of one another, and each would have thought it an excellent thing if all the rest could have been compelled to *travel his road*, their attempts to thwart each other's development have rarely had any permanent success."[13]

Mill's Europe is a space in which people are in perpetual nonhomogeneous movements (to varied locations, using myriad roads and paths) that facilitate (perhaps produce) one homogeneous movement of society as a whole: progress. This progress is precisely what justifies Europe's expansion to the "greater part of the world," which has "become stationary."[14] "The tutorial and paradigmatic obsession of the empire and especially imperialists are all part of the effort to move societies along the ascending gradient of historical progress," argues Uday Mehta. Accordingly, "the liberal justification of the empire" relies on the argument that since most of the world has lost its own capacity of movement, without Europe's mobile (almost motorist) powers, the rest of the world would not be able to move (read: improve). Progress in its global articulation "is like having a stalled car towed by one that is more powerful and can therefore carry the burden of an ascendant gradient."[15]

The combination of Europe's movement and Asia's stagnation stands at the base of Mill's justification of the imperial project. This stagnation, which is perhaps best marked by the image of the bound feet of Chinese girls,[16] threatens Europe itself. Mill warns us that "unless individuality be able successfully to assert itself against this yoke, Europe, notwithstanding its noble antecedences and its professed Christianity, will tend to become another China." Europe may, in other words, "become stationary."[17] To avoid this fate, Europe has to endure in its motion—an endurance Mill seems to simply assume. (And it is quite striking that this assumption is made concurrently with his terrified warning that this endurance is about to fail.)[18] One may speculate, perhaps, that the motion into the East was one way to guarantee Europe's freedom-as-movement. This motion might be conceived of in general terms—terms so wide they might seem figurative or abstract: the movement of the entire body-politic (a movement that often takes military form—war—as we know from Plato[19] or Hobbes[20]). Alternatively, this motion might be detailed via the minute particularities of imperial administration.

Earlier in the seventeenth century, the portrayal of America as a site of excessive movement served to justify similar projects of expansion. The movements of armies, trading companies, private military powers, settlers, capital, and goods, constituted zones that were characterized by their own regimes of movement: the colonies. The colony—which Ann Stoler defines as a nonstable space for the management, retaming, confinement, containment, disciplining, and reforming of movement—came to *address*, but also *demonstrate*, and thereby construct, the presumably dangerous and wild movements of the colonized. As Stoler argues, this regime of movement was established in opposition to "the normative conventions of 'free' settlement, and [to] a normal population."[21] Hence, these oppositions embedded into movement were given within a wider regime of movement, that is often taken to mark a much later epoch but that, as Étienne Balibar reminds us, has a long history: "The process of globalization, which has been occurring for several centuries, has not simply been 'capitalist' in the abstract sense of the term—a mere process of commodification and accumulation. It has been capitalist in the concrete political form of colonization."[22]

If we are to understand regimes of movement, we have to examine also the subject-positions they simultaneously assume and constitute. Such an examination reveals that the above opposition, between settlement (stability, sedentarism, normality) and unbound movement, operated on two levels. The first was not a global, colonial setting, but rather the individual body itself. Within this level this "opposition" emerges rather as a balance: a balance between movement and stability that is also a balance between freedom and security. At stake, for liberalism, has always been the reconciliation of its concept of freedom with social order. The idea of the autonomous individual who must not be controlled despotically (who *no longer* needed to be controlled despotically) rested upon the assumption that this individual can control and self-regulate herself. Foucault's work is a notable venture point from which to study the articulations of this idea, but already in Hobbes, before the technologies of power explored by Foucault were put into effect or even systematically theorized, we find its kernel. Reading Hobbes's defense of absolutism via the prism of movement enables us to see that for him, the subject within the commonwealth is free even under the most tyrannical power not just since he is part of this power (this would be Hobbes's argument against republican notions of liberty). The subject's freedom is also a function of his willingness to control and confine his movements: once he agrees "not to run away"[23] and submits his actions to the will of the sovereign, the shackles imprisoning him can be removed, and this is precisely the meaning of his freedom. Given that Hobbes defines freedom as unimpeded movement, freedom emerges as the outcome of its very limitation, as long as this limitation is internal. Locke can be read as putting forth a different model that nonetheless obeys a very similar principle: freedom—as movement—is possible only within a system of enclosures. Ultimately, this combination of stability and movement enabled liberalism to craft the idea of an ordered freedom. The liberal subject was carved within "a certain 'epistemology of walking'": he was a subject "walking on his two feet" in a stable, and firm manner;[24] a subject whose stability came to define his body, as well as his social and material backdrop: a home, a homeland, an owned domain.

On the second level of the imagined balance between settlement and movement, we find that these notions are superimposed, time and again, on spatial divisions. Home, location, rootedness, and other factors that render movement desirable and free are in various ways preserved to very particular subjects. Notwithstanding varied models of localization, Africans, indigenous Americans, or Asians, as well as women and paupers, keep appearing in the texts of liberal thinkers as either too stagnant or too mobile. Thus, the balance presumably achieved within the body of the liberal subject becomes a schism, a contrast, between those who can control their movements, and thus rule, and those whose movement is hindered or excessive, and thus cannot. This mapping bisects the freedom of the movement of white, male, and propertied bodies, from the presumed threat carried by colonized ("savages"), poor ("vagrants"), or female (seen as either confined to the domestic sphere or as hysterical—or both) bodies.

Significant parts of this book return to the seventeenth century to explore this duality. This temporal focus has to do with three major developments converging roughly around this era: the body of work that would later become the foundations of liberalism begins to take shape;[25] the state begins to consolidate the contours of its body by imagining a growing control over the movement of people into, out of, and within its borders (even if the bureaucratic apparatuses that could effectively control those movements were yet to be established);[26] and finally, the hands, as Hobbes would phrase it, of the stronger European states reach farther and farther out, expanding into territories beforehand unimaginable. The seventeenth century thus also marks some of the earliest systematic theoretical engagements with colonized subjects. But the pattern within which free movement is conditioned upon some assumption of stability—that is either presumed to be lacking in the case of colonized subjects and/or systematically denied from them—remains prevalent long after we have seemingly entered the postcolonial era. Tim Cresswell shows that this binary splitting movement stands at the core of liberal citizenship. Whereas the mobility of citizens is almost sanctified as a right, and is taken to construct "autonomous individual agents who, through their motion, [help] to produce the nation itself," there are always "unspoken Others [who] are differently mobile"; others whose mobility is "constantly hindered": "Arab Americans stopped at airport immigration, Hispanic Americans in the fields of American agri-business or African Americans 'driving while black,'"[27] and we can add here Palestinians at checkpoints, but also anticapitalism demonstrators arrested on bridges.[28] Accordingly, even today, as a matter of general rule, the subject who is most mobile is the (Western) "citizen": a subject-position that is often tied to stability and sedentarism.[29]

In her *Walled States, Waning Sovereignty*, Wendy Brown identifies a similar tension between an ideology of open borders and an exponential increase in technologies of managing borders; between an ideology of free movement across borders and a reality of growing restrictions of movement: "what we have come to call a globalized world harbors fundamental tensions between opening and barricading, fusion and partition, erasure and reinscription. These tensions materialize as increasingly liberated borders, on the one hand, and the devotion of unprecedented funds, energies and technologies to border fortification, on the other."[30] These tensions do not form as a result of two competing logics of governance.[31] On the contrary, globalization must be seen as "government of mobility,"[32] rather than as simple openness of borders.[33] "The reduced significance of the state border" should not be taken as the outcome of "a freer movement of people." Rather, as Didier Bigo observes, "a differential freedom of movement (of different categories of people) creates new logics of control that for practical and institutional reasons are located elsewhere, at transnational sites."[34] "Mobility gaps" is Ronen Shamir's apt term for the outcome of this logic.[35]

Liberal democracies have always operated in tandem with regimes of deportation, expulsion, and expropriation, as well as confinement and enclosure, implementing different rationalities of rule to which colonized, poor, gendered, and racialized subjects were subjected, thereby "drawing a categorical distinction between those who should be granted the benefits of citizenship, however meager, and those who must be managed authoritatively, even despotically."[36] Therefore, these tensions or oppositions are integral to a single order that couples within it different regimes of movement.[37] In a similar vein, we cannot simply contrast a "sedentarist metaphysics of rootedness" to a "metaphysics of movement."[38] Indeed, rather than competing metaphysics, we have here complementary processes: First, citizenship has to rely on a process of "taming mobility,"[39] which serves to support the sedentarist ideology of the nation-state within a factuality wherein people are, and were, always mobile.[40] Second, once this image of stability is established for particular categories of now-"rooted" people, it serves to facilitate their growing mobility. Movement and stability thus precondition each other. Finally, these particular categories are formed vis-à-vis other groups, which are simultaneously presumably less rooted and yet constantly hindered. The immigrant, the nomad, and certain modes of what we have come to term "hybrid-subjectivity," all represent subject-positions that are configured through their mobility, but that more often inhabit spaces of confinement: detention and deportation camps, modern incarnations of poor houses, international zones in airports.[41] The flux that is frequently celebrated as subversive[42] has repeatedly served to restrict movement-as-freedom, to facilitate nonfree movements (expulsion, slave trade, denial of land tenure), and ultimately to preclude movement.

Movements

Early in the twentieth century, in one of the first reflections on liberal theory, L. T. Hobhouse defined liberalism as a political critique whose main "business" is "to remove obstacles which block human progress."[43] While liberalism also imposes *restraints*,[44] those are but means for a greater goal: the construction and sustainment of a liberal society, which is conceived by Hobhouse as an organism moving forward. It is not simply, adds Michael Freeden, that "concepts such as civilization, movement, and vitality turn out to be inextricably linked to liberal discourse and the liberal frame of mind"; what "sets liberalism aside from most of its ideological rivals, whose declared aspiration is to finalize their control over the political imagination," he argues, is tolerance, which "suggests a flexibility, a movement, a diversity—of ideas, of language, and of conceptual content."[45] It does not matter, for the current purpose, whether this diagnosis is correct or not. It is enough to argue that there is a liberal-imaginary seeing itself as a moving body of thought which facilitates the movement of the political space itself.[46]

Yet despite this appeal to movement as a defining criterion, "setting liberalism aside from most of its ideological rivals," these rivals, too, have often appealed to the same phenomenon to define themselves. In his juridical account of the structure of the Third Reich, *State, Movement, People*, Carl Schmitt defines the National Socialist state as composed of three elements: the state (a static element), the people (a nonpolitical element), and the movement (which he later identifies with the party): the "dynamic political element," which "carries the State and the People, penetrates and leads the other two."[47] There are three crucial attributes of "the movement" in Schmitt's account. First, it is the only political element in the trio. Both the state and the people may be political only through it. Second, it is the "dynamic engine" in it—the force vitalizing politics by moving it,[48] and perhaps we may say: the force that is political by virtue of its moving capabilities. Finally, it is the bearer of unity: through it the trio becomes a whole. This unmitigated nature of the movement, that comes to encompass the entirety of the political structure, is, Schmitt argues, precisely what distinguishes the German National Socialist state (together with its Fascist and Bolshevik allies) from liberal democracies.[49] Indeed, according to Giorgio Agamben, the systematic use of the term *movement* to refer to what we have come to term "political movements" emerged with Nazism.

Whereas Agamben merely notes that we begin to see the concept in the eighteenth century, around the French Revolution,[50] Paul Virilio shows in great details how movement—the mobility of the masses until nations themselves are conceived as movable, moving, and even obliged to move—runs as a thread from the revolutionary moment in France (if not earlier), to the Fascist regimes and to Communist dictatorships. Beginning with a revolt "against the *constraint to immobility* symbolized by the ancient feudal serfdom . . .—a revolt against arbitrary confinement and the obligation to reside in one place," these revolutionary movements turned freedom of movement to "an *obligation to mobility*." The "*freedom of movement* of the early days of revolution" was quickly replaced by "the first *dictatorship of movement*": war, colonization, production, and trade.[51] All these forms of violence—mobilization into battle, into labor, an expansion of a state and a nation, circulation of capital, commerce and credit—"can be reduced to nothing but movement," Virilio seems to be arguing.[52]

Nazism and liberalism are therefore not unique in this appeal to movement as a defining criterion. I cannot survey all other orders, ideologies, or political strands here, but can briefly point to Marx's identification of modernity with a powerful movement[53] and his effort to explain the operation of capital by delineating its laws of motion[54]; to postmodernist appeals to notions of hybridity and to the image of the nomad as symbolizing modes of movement that work counter to modernist ideologies;[55] or to frameworks seeing globalization as a system typified by a growing flow of capital, culture, information, and above all people.[56] The point here is not to argue that these competing ideologies/orders share similar attributes. The point is rather to illustrate the appeal of the notion of movement to politics and to political thinking.

Some of these movements have quite different meanings. The physical motion of (individual) bodies is not the same as "the fascist movement" or the "flexibility, movement, diversity" to which Freeden refers when he talks about liberalism. Whereas I believe it is important to allow these meanings to sustain their differences, ultimately I will try to show that these differences are less stable than what may seem at first. To begin accounting for this fluidity of the term itself, we should perhaps begin by wondering about its wide appeal. It is not sufficient to dismiss the widespread use of movement by claiming that all these are, indeed, political or social movements. First, this would merely beg the question and call up another question: How did the term "movement" emerge to describe this particular social and political phenomenon? But more important, movement is used in many of the examples above as a defining (and hence supposedly unique) attribute: it supposes to create a distinction, to mark a difference, and not to point to a quality of taking part in a shared category: social/political movements.

Why "movement" then? One way to begin to form an answer would be to think of politics itself qua movement. Standing as an opposition to nature, to stable power structures, to a static state bureaucracy, politics brings the potential carried by instability: the potential of change, of widening the gaps allowing our agency, redistributing resources, and realigning power. A set of different (even if tangent) traditions of thinking about the meaning of "the political" conceptualizes it as that which moves, as the moment of movement, or as that to which movement is essential. The political is the domain in which and upon which humans can act, which humans can change, and which is thus defined as inherently instable. Movement can take here the form of an earthquake—a radical and rare upheaval (as in the case of Rancière[57]); of a repetitive, potentially slower, and more local operation of undoing in which the movement of the individual body produces a movement of categories—troubling the assumption of giveness and stability (as in the case of Butler[58]); or of a space wherein the world is revealed as movable, a space in which and through which the world emerges as the substance, product, and target of action (as in the case of Arendt[59]).

If we think of these social/political movements *as movements*, then movement appears in a multiplicity of meanings. These meanings are at times folded into one another and operate together, and include physical movements of individual bodies as a part of a social/political struggle for change (movement); as a site of (and act of) transgression that may have political meanings; as a particle in large-scale movements of political bodies: states, armies, trade. Accordingly, Schmitt and Hobhouse (but also many others, including Mill, Hobbes, and Hardt) see the political sphere as a moving body almost literally. It is a body of bodies that become a collective body. If we situate these particular moving political bodies (of Hobhouse, Schmitt, and Hobbes) within a historical, global context, we see that the movement of these collective bodies is, indeed, a movement in space: an expansion.

Earlier I argued that movement serves as a surface, a grabbing point for different forms of control; that its ordering and circulation are the organizing principle of different regimes; and that it is a privileged mode through which bodies and powers operate on and through one another. Now we can add that movement is also an iconography, an imaginary as well as a physical phenomenon that allows different bodies to take form.

Subjects/Bodies

Disability studies have long called our attention to the relation between ability and citizenship; between particular assumptions regarding the "normal" manners of carrying our bodies in space, and the construction of democratic spaces, which are, ultimately, spaces of accessibility of possible and impossible movements. Accordingly, the process of subject formation is, to a great degree, a project of "normalizing" movements. Indeed, a reading in political theory reveals almost an obsession with this need to educate the body in "proper" modes of movement.[60] So strong is this obsession that, according to Andrew Hewitt, by the nineteenth century, walking became what embodied a "bourgeois self consciousness."[61]

"How subjects move or do not move tells us much about what counts as human, as culture, and as knowledge," argues Caren Kaplan.[62] Indeed. But this is only part of the story. How the movement of subjects is described or imagined tells us almost as much. Movement is a technology of citizenship or subjectivity, as I noted above. Through the production of patterns of movement (statelessness, deportability, enclosures, confinement), different categories of subjectivity are produced. Regimes of movement are thus never simply a way to control, to regulate, or to incite movement. Regimes of movement are integral to the *formation of different modes of being*. But movement is also a lens through which to trace the models within which subjectivity is framed. Tracking reports on movement, the role of movement in political theories, the attempts to emphasize or sideline images of mobility or immobility, may teach us a lot about how subjectivity is—and was—perceived and constructed. Finally, movement is a perspective from which to think about subjectivity. In Erin Manning's words, "A commitment to the ways in which bodies move," is a commitment to thinking about the subject in particular ways. Manning, as many before her, proposes that such a commitment is a way to think against a stabilization of the body within "national imaginaries."[63] As I briefly suggested earlier, I think this claim is somewhat rushed. The tendency to celebrate the deterritorialization effects of movement often "overlook[s] the colonial power relations that produce such images in the first place."[64] Manning, however, makes another claim regarding this commitment that is worthy of further exploring: to think bodies through movement, she argues, is to think the subject against the nexus of identity, since "a moving body . . . cannot be *identified*."[65] The question of movement is thus also the question of the contours and limits of subjects/bodies.

If movement is a way of thinking about a certain openness of these contours; if it eventually comes to contain a plurality of people in which, as Arendt portrays it, "each man moves among his peers";[66] if it is through movement that a plurality becomes a body (a social movement, an empire, a state as an orchestrated collective movement), then a commitment to thinking on and through movement is more than a commitment to thinking of the flexibility, if not impossibility, of identity. It is also (and the two are intimately connected) a commitment to thinking the possibility of nonindividual bodies and to be attuned to the moments in which the impossibility of individual bodies is revealed. At times, movements injure us. Some movements open wounds in our bodies. Others open wounds in our wills. Melville's Ishmael, the narrator of *Moby Dick*, probably describes it best. Situated on the deck of the ship, tied to Queequeg with a rope, he watches the motions of fellow crewman becoming his own: "my own individuality was now merged in a joint stock company of two . . . my free will had received a mortal wound," he describes it. At this moment he understands that we are all tied to "a plurality of other mortals" in some "Siamese connexion" that renders one's movements also the other's movements; that breaks the ties between individual volition and action;[67] but also: that opens up volition itself. At times movements fortify us. They enhance our own movements with a cohesive motion of other bodies, of a body larger than us. A collective movement of people—a march, a war, an occupy movement such as the ones we have seen recently from Tahrir Square to Occupy Wall Street—charges our individual movement with a meaning and power it could not inhabit and produce on its own. Importantly, movement also occurs between these two poles, injury and fortification. The wounds to our will and bodies (whose bleeding is a form of movement in and of itself—a flow) demonstrate the degree to which others can affect us, the fragility of our bodily boundaries or our individual volition. These wounds, and this affect, the undone volition, are the unavoidable effect of the opening of the bodily boundaries of individuality. However, therefore, they are both the outcome of and the precondition for the formation of collectivities. A plurality as a political body produces—or is produced by—the Siamese ties that render one's actions also the other's. In a more Arendtian formulation: this plurality is the substance through which action appears as something that happens *in between* people.

Nevertheless, thinking of subjects as moving bodies does not necessarily produce political ontologies that work counter to models of autonomous individualism. This book shows that whereas such models can be opened by thinking of and through movement, the autonomous subject of liberal discourse emerged as a figure of corporeal mobility.

A Brief Genealogy

In the seventeenth and eighteenth century it was the denial of free movement that was—and was thought of as—the primary negation of liberty. This was probably a function of two interlaced limitations: the limited technologies of monarchical power (which were largely limited to imprisonment and execution), alongside a limited comprehension of the modes through which power operates or may operate. Accordingly, we have both a mode of power and a mode of thinking about power for which movement is quintessential. Thus, until the turn of the nineteenth century, liberty was largely seen as the freedom from unjustified external restraints that limited one's power of locomotion. While liberal freedom emerged as freedom of movement, while liberty is still tied to movement when freedom is attached to the body, and while the movements of some groups (that we can identify as standing at the core of shifting liberal and neoliberal discourses) is still maximized and largely protected, the idea of freedom as movement has been for the most part sidelined in liberal thinking.

Chapter 3 outlines in more details the first moments of this genealogy. Here I would like to very briefly and partially sketch the stages that follow the point with which that chapter concludes: an initial process of abstraction occurring roughly at the end of the eighteenth century, through which the will becomes the main bearer of freedom. What is significant about this process is not merely that the element within man to which freedom is attached changes; the important difference is that for many later liberals "man's will is himself."[68] The subject becomes reducible to will, rationality, or judicial status (or in other words: abstracted). Once again, Mill provides a telling example. In chapter 1 of *On Liberty*, Mill proposes a typology of power, whose contours would later be filled by Foucault. According to this typology, power has shifted its operation from the body to the soul. The power of the sovereign (imprisonment) can no longer be thought of as the single, even primary, threat for our freedom, he argues. As we are now faced with a more pervasive "social tyranny," our soul is subjugated to the yoke of public opinion and it is the freedom of ideas and thoughts that we must secure.[69] Significantly, movement remains attached to freedom even within this framework. However, this movement is only marginally the physical movement of bodies. Movement in Mill's account is first and foremost the movement of ideas, whose free circulation creates venues for a potential escape from the yoke of custom.[70] Second, as we saw, it is the movement of progress.[71] And third, physical movement appears as a manifestation and illustration of freedom—or the lack thereof—in the case of women, whose oppression is often described by Mill via the metaphor of chains. At the margins of the discourse, describing those who are yet to obtain an equal, universal, perhaps abstract status, movement once again emerges as the meaning of freedom.

Already with Kant, the problem of freedom is attached to questions of autonomy, of judgment, and decision making, rather than to one's ability to execute an action once chosen. This framework would become more and more central to liberal thinkers in the twentieth century. Yet while with Kant, as we shall later see, movement nonetheless plays a role in the configuration of political freedom, by the twentieth century his leading successor would replace the emphasis on movement with a craving for stability. John Rawls repeatedly declares throughout his second treatise that stability is precisely what is at stake in *Political Liberalism*. As far as possible, he aspires to take both time and change out of the equation and "fix, once and for all, the content of certain political basic rights and liberties."[72] According to Freeden, in so doing, Rawls joins Ronald Dworkin[73] in "prioritiz[ing] rules as stasis, equilibrium and consensus over rules of change."[74] Both join in an attempt to bring to a halt (almost literally) the movement Freeden sees as essential to liberalism. Rawls sees freedom as resting not on one's ability to move her body, but "on persons' intellectual and moral powers."[75] Indeed, Rawls is a paradigmatic example of the liberal configuration of the subject as largely abstract—or in his formulation: as a "basic [unit] of thoughts, deliberation, and responsibility."[76]

The freedom Rawls seems to have in mind is not a freedom that "can only mean . . . that if we choose to remain at rest we may; if we choose to move, we also may"[77]—the concept of freedom so prevalent in the seventeenth century. Such a notion of freedom-as-movement does appear in *Political Liberalism*, yet it is not situated under what Rawls defines as "basic rights and liberties." Rather, together with other "matters of distributive justice," freedom of movement takes part in securing "institutions of *social* and *economic* justice" (in contrast to "just *political* institutions").[78] Within the "basic list of primary goods," freedom of movement appears in conjunction with "free choice of occupation against the background of diverse opportunities."[79] The phenomenon that served as the kernel of freedom, if not formed freedom as such, is thus reduced to "occupation." Movement, in other words, is depoliticized and becomes subjected to free market principles.

This reduction to free market logic is not just a reduction to principles of money, occupation, or trade. As Foucault identified in his 1977–78 lectures, this logic is entangled with questions of security (that can be translated, in their turn, to questions of circulation and movement). Ultimately, with this reduction and depoliticization, some movements become the hallmark of threat rather than freedom. "There are two chief reasons why movement of persons across borders can be more problematic than movement of products," explains Loren Lomasky. These two reasons are "security concerns and financial entitlements. A widget purchased from abroad is inert; it lies there until put to service that widgets perform. But immigrants exercise agency. As no one needs to be reminded post-September 11, 2001, some intend harm to the country they have entered."[80]

Two splits bisect movement-as-freedom in this account: a split between things and people, within which the second split is already assumed—that between residents (or citizens) and immigrants. Those who move—unlike the things that simply "lie there" (but we can add, also unlike those who remain within their own boundaries)—carry with them security hazards. Their agency itself appears as a risk in the quoted paragraph. And while Lomasky later admits that "it is simply not credible to maintain that the vast bulk of immigration poses any significant security threat," poverty becomes a complementary facet of danger: "*as with the potentially hostile*, [the poor's] exclusion is justified on grounds of self-interest."[81] Lomasky simply ignores the potential risks to our "self interest" that the movement of goods may carry. Unlike "poor, tired huddled masses" who attempt to cross borders of "well-off states," things that can move freely across borders, enabling the relocation of manufacturing and jobs, the global robbery of natural resources, the impoverishment of entire classes or countries, the poisoning of soil by tainted produce, or cross-pollination through the introduction of new seed to previously pristine environments, do not enter Lomasky's equation of fear.

Indeed, as many recent accounts of globalization have noted, it is commodities and capital, alongside a small group of privileged people, which are increasingly mobile—and hence "free."[82] What interests me in this equation, however, is not just the circulation of movement, as it were, but also the deployment of fear. Adriana Cavarero calls us to notice that the two are interlaced. Cavarero proposes that fear is a physical state: it is "the act of trembling," the "local movement of the body that trembles," as well as "the much more dynamic movement of flight." In other words, "terror moves bodies, drives them into motion."[83] At the same time, movement itself is often seen as the bearer of terror. Probably needless to say, this is not merely Lomasky's approach. In the post–September 11th United States "any and all matters of immigration law enforcement, as well as all procedures regarding migrant eligibility for legal residence or citizenship, have been explicitly and practically subordinated to the imperatives of counter terrorism and Homeland Security."[84] This subordination was institutionalized in 2002, with the move of the Immigration and Naturalization Service (INS) to the Department of Homeland Security. "Despite little evidence of the connection," Brown writes, there is a routine identification of "unchecked illegal immigration with the danger of terrorism."[85] Nevertheless, as we can see with Lomasky, surprisingly, this securitization of movement does not detach movement from questions of freedom—almost as if the tie between the two is too deep to fully break. Rather, freedom—or in the above quote agency—is itself depoliticized with the depoliticization of movement, and becomes a threat. To return to the site that had initiated this project, the regime of movement in the occupied Palestinian territories (oPt) provides us with a striking manifestation of this process. The regime of movement, which drains movement into a security hazard to be tightly managed, is interlaced with the securitization of liberty. Indeed, it is almost inconceivable for most Israelis to imagine the Palestinian struggle for independence as anything but brute aggression. The regime of movement—the notion that control over land and population can be almost fully accomplished by regulating the circulation of people and goods—is the primary political technology of a regime that can see a struggle for self determination and national liberation only as "terror."[86]

Technologies

The logic I trace in the philosophical inquiry is both demonstrated by, and serves to explain, predominant trends in contemporary politics. This logic is further developed and refined by a close analysis of several sites in which movement is presently regulated, focusing especially on the checkpoints deployed by Israel in the Palestinian West Bank. This particular test case is to a great extent a function of my own intellectual—and personal—history. It was my endeavor to contribute to the understanding of this political order that set off my interest in the political significance of movement. My experience in several years of activism at and across the Israeli checkpoints in the oPt has shaped my understanding of movement as a central component within the formation of different modes of governance. Nevertheless, this test case is not idiosyncratic and enables us to see clearly what other cases may blur.

At a more general level we might say that the aim of projects such as this book is to rethink the relations between the abstract and the concrete; between the conceptual and theoretical on the one hand, and the particularities, the small details of reality on the other. Within this frame, the regime of movement in the oPt functions as the local field on which I look and from which I draw the matters that not merely enrich, but also provide the substance—as well as the method and orientation—for the theoretical analysis. In other words, the checkpoints are not merely where I find "materials" to be theorized, or where I examine "reality" vis-à-vis theory. Rather, there is an attempt here, to propose a mode of inquiry that does not yield to these distinctions.

The "regime of movement" Israel employs in the oPt is an extensive bureaucratic system of permits, backed by a dense grid of physical and administrative obstacles, which fragments both the space and the social fabric, pervasively regulates the circulation of people and goods, and manages the Palestinian population by the means of this regulation. Since these many obstacles are situated also within Palestinian territories (and not only on some imaginary, nonexistent border between the oPt and Israel), this system prevents—or at least severely hinders—what many see as mundane, daily life: going to work, attending a relative's wedding, shopping at the market, or going to school. All are simple routines for most people, but they are denied to most Palestinians or are purchased with the cost of valuable time; time that is robbed, as Amira Hass puts it, and "cannot ever be returned. . . . The loss of time, which Israel is stealing every day from 3.5 million people, is evident everywhere: in the damage it causes to their ability to earn a living; in their economic, family and cultural activity; in the leisure hours, in studies and in creativity; and in the shrinking of the space in which every individual lives and therefore the narrowing of their horizon and their expectations."[87]

In other words, "scarcity of time disables space."[88] It narrows the land and disables the possibility of forming a political community. What thus emerges is a mode of controlling the space and the population inhabiting it by controlling the temporality and continuity of the movement within it.

Jeff Halper has termed this system "the matrix of control." "It is an interlocking series of mechanisms, only a few of which require physical occupation of territory, that allow Israel to control every aspect of Palestinian life in the Occupied Territories. The matrix works like the Japanese game of Go. Instead of defeating your opponent as in chess, in Go you win by immobilizing your opponent, by gaining control of key points of a matrix so that every time s/he moves s/he encounters an obstacle of some kind."[89]

Writing in 2000, Halper could have seen only the seeds of the dense grid of checkpoints that would become the predominant component within this matrix. The checkpoints are valves wherein, first, individual moving bodies are inspected and allowed (or denied) passage; and second, the circulation of an entire population, as well as the goods it consumes and produces, is managed. Yet, I would like to propose that the regular operation of the checkpoints entails, in addition, particular and peculiar disciplinary practices. In one of their facets, the checkpoints are part of a network of *corrective technologies* that *are meant to fail*. These quasi-disciplinary practices constitute the Palestinians moving through the checkpoint as the always-already failed products of a system that operates within a disciplinary logic, that has a disciplinary form, yet that is built to fail precisely because at stake is not the construction of normalized, self-governing subjects. What is at stake, rather, is the possibility of bridging nondemocratic modes of governance (occupation) with a framework that insists on its democraticity. A genealogy of circulation and of the political technologies regulating it may become, accordingly, a genealogy of the regimes and powers circumscribing it.

A genealogy of the "administration of movement" within Israel and the oPt reveals a change in the directions and circulation of people (labor force in particular) and in the technologies managing this circulation. From 1967, and for roughly two decades, two undertakings intersected that assumed (and were conditioned upon) the same project. The first was the "enlightened occupation"—the presumed improvement, triggered by the occupation, in the quality of life of the Palestinian general population.[90] The second was a change in the intra-Israeli labor market that became dependent on the cheap labor force of Palestinian noncitizens.[91] Both projects relied on establishing disciplinary institutions (such as vocational schools to facilitate Palestinians' integration to the Israeli labor market), as well as on the deployment of a biopolitical lattice that is similar, in many ways, to the one described in Foucault's 1975–78 works: a multifaceted lattice that takes as its points of interest reproduction and mortality rates, diseases and vaccinations, quality of water, and so forth.[92]

However, in the last ten years—and in a process that can be traced back to 1989[93]—the operation of this biopolitical system has completely changed. Neve Gordon identifies in this transformation a shift from what he terms politics of life to politics of death.[94] I maintain that this shift can also be explained as a shift from politics of circulation—a liberal project, which is intertwined with disciplinary and biopowers[95]—to a politics of halting, in which the subject of interest is no longer precisely the population, but a new entity of subjects-in-motion, which comprises single-dimensional, subject-like positions with the sole attribute of locomotion.[96] Most of the literature concerning the control over movement in the oPt sees this new form of control as working primarily at the level of population. Following the claim that contemporary Israeli power in the oPt has abandoned its complex disciplinary endeavors and is focusing on controlling the population as a moving body, this literature, too, seems to have abandoned the relationship between subjects and power.[97] This theoretical trend goes beyond the analysis of power in the oPt. One of the pioneers of the field of mobility studies, William Walters, makes a similar argument regarding the camp. The camp, according to him, is no longer a disciplinary site, since states are no longer interested in producing a "positive kind of subjectivity" in regard to the populations inhabiting them: the deportable.[98] Similar arguments can be found in many other contemporary analyses of different regimes of movement. Departing from this literature at this point, this book endeavors to understand how a population that is controlled via movement is produced by technologies of subjectivation. In other words, I ask about the local and concrete apparatuses through which subjects become moving bodies that can be ruled primarily by managing their location and circulation.

The focus on checkpoints, closures, sieges, walls, deportations, and other measures regulating movement in the occupied Palestinian territories may be taken to be but one manifestation of my claim regarding the conjunction of freedom and movement. If movement is indeed the manifestation of liberty, and, moreover, is interlaced with notions of liberal subjecthood and thus citizenship, as this book sets out to argue, then it is almost trivial that a state of occupation—which is by definition an elimination of citizenship and a denial of most political rights—would incorporate a control over movement into its political technologies. Yet this case enables us to see much more. While de facto, the limitations upon movement in the West Bank are limitations upon the freedom(s) of Palestinians, free movement is given in this context primarily within the paradigm of security (as it is in contemporary assumptions regarding immigration and international traveling in general). Put in the words of the Israeli human rights organization B'Tselem, "Palestinian freedom of movement has turned from a fundamental human right to a privilege that Israel grants or withholds as it deems fit."[99] Here we return to where the previous section ends: freedom itself becomes a security concern. This book, then, can be seen as an inquiry into the constant coupling and decoupling of freedom and security (or order), mediated by changing modalities of movement. The normalizing project through which disciplinary subjects appear; the technologies of movement through which such subjects are deconstituted; the maritime map through which both order and its disruptions are globalized.

The book's structure aims at opening up a wider span, both historically and philosophically, through which the argument takes form and within which it echoes. It therefore moves (the pond may prove itself unavoidable) between different contexts and fields. Whereas some anchors organize the book's argument around repeated themes and pivots (both in terms of the theory considered and in terms of the contemporary context from which the theoretical investigation emerges), the book digresses, at times, to what may seem as more eclectic assemblages. These digressions seek to point to the ubiquitousness of a particular logic, grammar, or a structure of movement and of thinking about movement, as well as to delineate variations within different articulations or implementations of this structure.

Chapter 1, "Between Imaginary Lines" (cowritten with Merav Amir), focuses on Israeli checkpoints in the occupied Palestinian territory as a condensed microcosm for examining the relations between movement, violence, and the construction of different subject-positions. In discussions following talks, or in responses to the previous publication of this chapter, people have often referred to its analysis as part of an anthropological study. I was never trained as an anthropologist, and I have no pretense of reflecting on the boundaries of this discipline, but I believe that if there is anthropology here, it is an anthropology of power. The object of my inquiry is not Palestinians. In fact, one may say that the perspective of Palestinians is almost completely erased from my analysis, and to some degree at least, this would be correct. In the collective mosaic of theory concerning this subject matter, I feel I should not presume to represent the Palestinians' voice—being an integral part of the power occupying them. The object of my inquiry is rather the mechanism of justifying the form of rule imposed upon Palestinians—a form of power that by no means leaves its addressees passive, that by no means determines their subject-positions, and that by no means forecloses the possibility of resistance.

The chapter seeks to understand the mechanisms by which violence can present itself as justifiable (or justified), even when it materializes within frames presumably set to annul it (such as "liberalism," "democracy," or "peace process"[100]). It is organized around two lines: an imaginary line, that pretends to organize, but in effect disrupts, the ordered movements of Palestinians at the checkpoint; and a white line, whose addressees are human rights activists, primarily Jewish, Israeli, upper-class women. These two logics of space-demarcation simultaneously assume and constitute two subject-positions: an occupied subject, external to the law regulating it, and a citizen, whose movement is freedom and can therefore be constrained only under particular limitations. Succeeding chapters are set to mark some points in the long history of the formation of these two subject-positions. After a short interlude, whose role is to situate the argument of chapter 1 within a wider genealogy of ideas, chapters 3 and 4 are split, to a great degree, according to the positions contrived by the two lines at the focus of chapter 1. Both chapters seek to show how different assumptions regarding movement (as well as different modes of producing particular patterns of movement) are essential to the formation of these two subject-positions. Chapter 3, "The Fence That 'Ill Deserves the Name of Confinement,'" focuses on the subject at the core of liberalism, and on the role of movement as freedom within this discourse. It shows the modifications in early liberal conceptualizations of movement, and with them, the changes in the assumptions regarding subjectivity, corporeality, and freedom. I show first, that movement was the materialization of freedom within this framework; second, that it was the privileged mode by which the liberal subject was embodied; and third, that it was also the corporeal condition for rationality.

The moving body, especially when it appears as a certain mode of corporealized rationality, both destabilizes and reproduces established dichotomies. It calls into question the accepted mind/body schism, yet at the very moment that it forces us to take the body into account even when we consider classic liberalism, it also renders the body insignificant. Within this frame, the body appears in a narrow, diluted form that is produced, precisely, by reducing it to a change of position between given coordinates. Hence, the centrality of movement also shows that "embodiment" alone does not guaranty attentiveness to particularity and difference (as many critical theorists seem to assume). Indeed, a further analysis of some canonical, liberal texts shows that the moving, "rational" body was of a particular kind: it was an able, firm (masculine?), target-oriented (rational?), and predominantly European body.

It is by now a common, established argument that liberalism and colonialism emerged together. The West has constituted itself by an "othering" process: it affirmed itself as civilized by the barbarization of colonized, sometimes enslaved (and in a different cross section, female) subjects, so that we can only speak of "an intrinsically *colonial* modernity."[101] Yet what is striking here is that this process of distancing took place by pushing to the extreme the very attribute that serves as a hinge of the enlightened, free, liberal subject: movement. Movement was at one and the same time the paradigmatic corporeal form of the abstract universal subject, and its edge, even its beyond. Chapter 4, "The Problem of 'Excessive' Movement," focuses on this othering process. It follows changing conceptualizations of bodies in motion to show the production of differences between the liberal subject and "othered" subjects/populations. The argument is not merely that movement had to be restrained, and that to be reconciled with freedom it had to be, at least to some extent, *self* restrained. It is also not merely that such an ability of self-regulation was not assumed to be the share of all subjects. The argument is that some patterns of movement were constantly produced as unruly by the circulation of both images and concrete apparatuses that rendered movement excessive.

America serves here not just to examine the writings of seventeenth-century theorists on colonial spaces, but also to resonate with the analysis of the movements of Palestinians in chapter 1. Indigenous Americans are portrayed in these texts much like the configuration of Palestinians within the frame of Israel's occupation: their attachment to the land is at one and the same time denied and feared, in what seems to be a contradiction but is actually a coherent justification mechanism of projects of ongoing expropriation and occupation.

Chapter 5, "The Substance and Meaning of All Things Political," expands this relation between imperial violence and movement—or confinement. It also seeks to begin moving from the analysis of power that is at the focus of the first four chapters to an analysis of action and resistance, which is only partially developed in chapter 1. Looking at both the movement of the body politic itself and the meaning of movement within other collective bodies, this chapter analyzes movement as a collective political undertaking. The many different types—perhaps different meanings—of movement that circulate in this chapter (from *emotions*, to social *movements*) allow me to make more explicit some of the themes underlying this book in regard to the flexibility and spread of the concept. Movement ultimately appears as the material substance of political life, action, and association.

1 / Between Imaginary Lines

Violence and Its Justifications at the Military Checkpoints in Occupied Palestine

Hagar Kotef and Merav Amir

> Then he [the soldier] saw a large group of women, those still waiting for their men who are being kept inside.... He went over to them and stood with his foot marking the soil. Over there, he signaled, showing them the way with his foot, his hands in his pockets. Over there, he signaled with his chin in the general direction behind them, and they started to move back.... Among them was a young woman holding three plastic bags. The soldier approached her and kicked her bags. She looked, waiting for him to say something; to signal. Over there, he said, or perhaps didn't even talk, and anyway, when he talked it was only in Hebrew. But she got the point and retreated with her bags beyond the line he had marked. A line that represents nothing but the true purpose of the checkpoint... — harassment for its own sake. All the rest are clichés that the fictive history one learns here, the brainwashing and the ever-hovering racism offer, for harassing without the slightest movement of a butterfly's wing another people, merely for being the other. —MahsanMilim.com, 2007

Israeli checkpoints are positioned throughout the West Bank as a web, capturing, regulating and often prohibiting movement. They are a component within one of the most material, most efficient, and most destructive means of the contemporary modes of the Israeli occupation, a mode commonly referred to as "the regime of movement." Gradually developed from 1991 (the first general closure of the occupied Palestinian territories), this regime subjects to Israeli control the circulation of people, goods, and services—and with them the economy, society, and polity—in the West Bank.[1] Together with a wide variety of obstacles (ranging from ditches, to metal gates, to walls) and accompanied by a complex and convoluted system of permits, the checkpoints

1.1 Huwwara Checkpoint, 2003. ©Machsom Watch.

form a dense grid, fragmenting both the space and the Palestinian social fabric living within it. Most are not located between "Israel" and "Palestine," but rather inside the Palestinian territories: on the entrance roads to towns and cities, restricting the movement of vehicles entering or leaving them; enclosing the cities, separating them from the surrounding villages that depend on them; and fracturing the few roads on which Palestinians are allowed to move. They inhibit and, in fact, prevent any real possibility of maintaining the mundane aspects of daily lives (getting to work, school, the doctor, the market, or visiting family members or friends); they impede—almost completely paralyze—the economy (hindering the circulation of goods and labor power); and they prevent the establishment of a viable, independent Palestinian political entity (as they prevent maintenance of a political community and territorial continuity).

These checkpoints are elements of a political technology aimed at securing a particular mode of control over the occupied Palestinian territory (oPt). They are also particular sites that can be seen as a condensed microcosm of this political technology. The form of control to be found at these sites—indeed, the form of control I seek to decipher here[2]—was consolidated some time between the Oslo Accords (1993—the formal beginning of the ongoing "peace process") and the years following the El Aqsa Intifada (2000). At this juncture, a growing appeal to the logic of security constantly countered (and still continues to counter) the language of political compromise. Yet the two opposite trajectories—the discourse of reconciliation and its constant undoing by growing securitization, which often takes the form of eruptive violence—keep working in tandem. In fact, I argue that the mediation of the two, which is necessary for the simultaneous sustainability of both, is what gave rise to the new modes of control that form the current stage of the Israeli occupation. To reconcile these contradictory logics a justification mechanism is needed: one that would enable a regime of occupation to be sustained amid peace negotiations and vice versa. Such a mechanism may be obtained by proving that the Palestinians cannot govern themselves. If this were to be the case—and I argue that Israel keeps producing the conditions to (at the very least) simulate that this is indeed the case—it would be justified to continue controlling them (always temporarily, only until they could do it themselves; a date always deferred precisely by mechanisms such as the one in question).[3]

This chapter proposes that movement and its regulation are essential to both the logic of security and the above justification mechanism. Not only has movement become fundamental to Israel's control, and to its understanding of the threat posed by Palestinians, as demonstrated by the technological developments of the regime of movement. Movement is also a key to understanding the production of Palestinians as unruly subjects. This chapter focuses on one local example of such a mechanism; a particular technique of marking the space of the checkpoints—and more accurately, of unmarking it. Merav Amir and I named this technique "the imaginary line." The imaginary line joins other political technologies—such as sets of contradictory orders, obscure and constantly changing regulations and instructions (that sometimes even change on an hourly basis), or a system of permits that is impossible to abide by and that sometimes renders people illegal residents even in their own home—to form a new mode of population management: one that is based on concealment rather than knowledge, on confusion and irregularity rather than regulation.[4] In the first part of the chapter, I describe the operation of this technique of (un)marking. In the second part I further explore the particular subject-position produced by this line by comparing it to another line, and by comparing the Palestinians at the checkpoints to other regular inhabitants of these sites. I examine a tangible demarcation of the space allocated to the activists of the human rights organization that regularly operates at the checkpoints: Checkpoint (Machsom) Watch. This enables me to identify the particular subjectivization processes occurring at the checkpoints and to argue that the checkpoints are part of a corrective system that is meant to fail. Finally, I move to examine a new form of checkpoint: the terminals. Analyzing the emergence of these sites I question the liberal impulse to appeal to regularity and regulation to counter eruptions of violence that induced failure facilitates.

On Imaginary Lines and Technologies of Power: The Checkpoints

The imaginary line is a line drawn (metaphorically, abstractly, in thin air) by Israeli soldiers at the checkpoint. It is a line that delimits the permitted movement of Palestinians within the space of the checkpoint, yet a line that exists only in the minds of the soldiers standing in front of them. As such, the imaginary line is a technique and a symbol of a particular form of controlling a given space, which not only relies on controlling the rules applying to this space, but also, and most important, on controlling the knowledge of those rules.

Let us examine its operation in detail. The density and location of the checkpoints mean that all Palestinians have to pass through at least one checkpoint—and most often through several—whenever they need to move beyond the boundaries of their villages, towns, or cities.[5]

The near impossibility of receiving a permit of passage for one's private vehicle forces most people to cross most checkpoints on foot. Therefore, during rush hours, the major manned checkpoints are packed with long lines of hundreds of people waiting to cross, most of whom are tired and eager to continue on their way. Sometimes they wait in the long, closely packed lines for hours, often exposed to the burning Middle Eastern sun in summer or the winds and rain in winter. This experience, which has become an integral part of most Palestinians' routine since 2000, ends in a thorough and degrading security check upon reaching the security-check booth, in front of drawn and loaded guns. First, a bodily search is conducted; then personal belongings are rudely and invasively checked, sometimes scattered on the dirt paths; and finally, the person's papers are inspected, and sometimes the person also has to go through a short interrogation: "Where do you live? What are your parents' names? Where are you going? For what purpose?" Since the security check progresses slowly, the tension in the line quickly builds. Everybody is pressed against one another so that the people at the front of the line are constantly being pushed forward by the crowd behind them, violating what the soldiers see as the appropriate distance between the head of the line and the security-check booths. Then the imaginary line makes a sudden appearance: "Irja La'wara!" (Go back!) the soldiers shout in what is most often the only phrase they know in Arabic. "Go back" behind the line—the line that cannot be seen, the line that is never marked, the imaginary line.

In his book *Yearning in the Land of Checkpoints*, Azmi Bishara describes this routine:

> "Go back!" shouts the soldier to the crowd whenever the crowd moves forward a few steps because of the shoving, because it is crowded, because of the wish to get to the shade or because of the commotion.... "Go back" is the phrase that leads to pushing in the direction contrary to the direction of movement. How many wars has this phrase instigated between all those who are pushed back while they are trying not to lose their place in line!... Whenever the soldier feels like playing the role of the teacher and educator at the checkpoint, or just to have fun, or when he wants to make sure that the situation is under control, he yells "Go back" in a definitive manner which does not leave room for debate.... "If anyone crosses this line you will all go home." At that instant, with no prior warning, being at the head of the queue turns from a blessing into a curse. The person at the head of the queue is now the protector of the line, and needs to be careful not to cross it.[6]

Because of its invisibility, and since its exact location is completely contingent and frequently changes, the imaginary line is bound to be transgressed. Perhaps needless to say, although this line is never publicly and visibly marked, its transgression carries penalties. Most often these penalties take the form of disciplinary punishments, such as detaining the "transgressors" for hours, sending them back to the end of the line, or denying them passage. Other times the disciplinary punishment is enforced on everybody waiting to cross the checkpoint by slowing down the security-check procedure or completely shutting down the checkpoint for periods of time. But every so often, the reaction of the soldiers is violent, sometimes with the result that whomever is found transgressing the nonexistent demarcation is badly injured or even killed.

The notion of punishment is not altogether foreign to the perspectives through which Israel perceives its relations with the Palestinians. Rationalizing many of its actions in accordance with a proclaimed carrot-and-stick logic, military incursions, bombarding towns, closures, and a six-year blockade (so far) of the 1.5 million residents of Gaza are all explained as corrective responses to successive transgressions by the Palestinians, by their leaders, or by militants among them.⁷ This notion of punishment brings to the fore a predicament that is, to some extent, the quandary subtending this chapter: Can we see the radically oppressive subjection of Palestinians by the Israeli regime as intertwined with subjectivization processes? And if so, how may we understand them? Or, to somewhat rephrase this question in the terms already set in the introduction: How is a population that is controlled as if it were merely moving dots (controlled by controlling movement; killed from above and afar) produced at the level of the subject? Ultimately, this coproduction of populations and subjects, to which, I argue, the incitement and restraint of movement are quintessential, runs as a thread through this book's arguments.

As many contemporary analyses of the occupation have noted, Israel has no interest in the Palestinians as its own subjects and has therefore withdrawn all the disciplinary and biopolitical arrays that were deployed in the first years of the occupation.⁸ Ariella Azoulay and Adi Ophir further argue that "the Palestinian uprising has virtually destroyed Israel's capacity to employ ideological or disciplinary means for governing the Palestinian population."⁹ Without contesting these claims, I maintain that different Israeli controlling apparatuses (including the checkpoints) have a crucial role in constituting a particular subject-position that Israel designates for the Palestinians, even if this is no longer an extensive, or even a coherent one.

In a different geopolitical context, Pradeep Jeganathan has read the checkpoints in Sri Lanka as anthropological sites, aiming at deciphering the identity of those passing through them. Moving through a checkpoint, he argues, is a process in which the soldier has to solve the question that is posed by the very presence of the checkpoint: "What is your political identity?"—a question entangled with another question: "What is your social/cultural identity?" and whose answer may be derived from factors such as areas of residency, place of birth, language, and other attributes on the identification papers.¹⁰ In the oPt, most of these classifications are performed outside of the checkpoint; those who are subjected to the checking procedure (the West Bank Palestinians) are *already* categorized as belonging to a particular ethnic and national group. Furthermore, at the checkpoint itself, the procedure by which the identity of those who pass through them is checked is supported by an extensive and elaborate database collected by the Israeli secret service, detailing the history, familial affiliation, and any other factor that might render the person a potential political enemy of the Jewish state. I further argue that the checkpoint operates not only in an attempt to *read* identities, but also to *produce* them.

It is important to emphasize that the checkpoints were not built for disci-

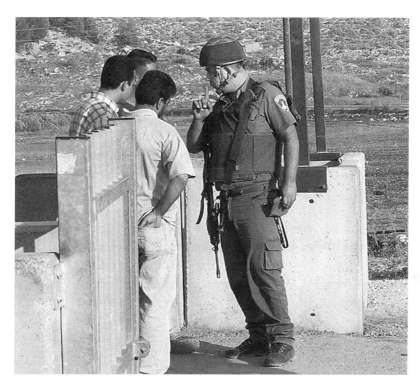

1.2 A lesson at the checkpoint, Huwwara Checkpoint, 2004 [TBC]. The soldier holds the green IDs of the three Palestinians to secure their detention. He will leave them at the confined space for a while (usually between half an hour and two hours), until they "internalize" the lesson. Photo ©Merav Amir. Courtesy Merav Amir, Machsom Watch.

plinary purposes and are lacking many of the attributes of disciplinary sites (although they do include some, in particular the rigorous distribution of individual bodies in space). But the soldiers, successful products of two highly structured disciplinary apparatuses—the school system and the army—identify the disciplinary potential of the checkpoints. Accordingly, they often see their role as educational and attempt to discipline the "child-like" Palestinians who "misbehave." Caught transgressing, the Palestinians are punished so they will learn not to repeat the "bad behavior." Many times, the act of punishment (usually in the form of detention—much like in school) is followed by a lecture in which the soldier makes sure that the lesson has been learned. But when the lines not to be transgressed are imaginary, the operation of discipline is set up to fail.

Between Imaginary Lines / 33

Presumably, all that is at stake is a deficiency in the structure of the checkpoints, an insufficient demarcation of space that can easily be solved. After all, one only needs to mark a line, perhaps also post a sign saying: "please wait here." Yet although this malfunction could have been addressed and eliminated, the imaginary line is an obstinate component of the checkpoints. It shows surprising perseverance over time and space, appearing at practically all checkpoints—from the temporary and primitive to the highly elaborate ones, in which the spatial arrangements are strictly marked by signs, gates, fences, and other measures.

Perhaps more surprisingly, it retains high degrees of permanence in a system that is typified by its flux and inherent arbitrariness.[11] Even as checkpoints became more well constructed and permanent; even after lines were visibly marked; even after turnstiles were installed, separating the crowd of waiting people and the security-check booth; even after these turnstiles were replaced by electric turnstiles activated by remote control, ensuring that the progress of people was fully controlled by the soldiers; even while all these technological apparatuses were put into operation, imaginary lines kept appearing at different areas of the checkpoints. They appeared either before or after the turnstiles—keeping the crowd of people at a distance from the turnstiles or having them wait after going through the turnstiles, before being allowed to approach the soldiers. They emerge in the parking lots or on the roads, determining the point at where the cars waiting to go through the checkpoint should stay until they are signaled by the soldiers to enter the security-check area, or limiting how near taxis waiting to pick up people from the checkpoint can park.[12] And they are occasionally (un)marked in other zones of the checkpoint, setting the distance the people who were already checked should keep from the checkpoint. The stubborn persistence of the appearance of imaginary lines should serve as evidence of the significance of their role.

I propose that the imaginary line is, in fact, an intrinsic failure that is built into the spatial configuration of the checkpoints in their function as disciplinary-like apparatuses. This failure produces Palestinians passing through the checkpoint as undisciplinable, and hence as subjects whose occupation is justifiable, if not necessary. It also (and not unrelatedly) opens a breach within the regular function of the operation of the checkpoints that enables violence to make an appearance, and, moreover, provides a justificatory framework for its appearance. The imaginary line produces movements that can be presented and perceived as unrestrainable and thus threatening, thereby enabling their configuration as "terror."[13] This should be understood

1.3 The not-to-be-crossed line marked with a stick on the ground, Azzun'Atmah Checkpoint, January 2010. Lines were drawn with chalk, marked by wires or by sticks found on the ground, and later enforced through the use of obstacles and fences. Photo ©Tom Kellner. Courtesy Tom Kellner, Machsom Watch.

within the larger framework of a constant search for legitimacy by a regime insisting upon its moral superiority despite more than forty-five years as an occupying force. The Israeli regime therefore constantly seeks justification for its violence. At the level of population control, the ever-existing threat of violent resistance on the part of the Palestinians provides this justification; yet concrete and random acts of violence by the Israeli army, which target people who obviously are not engaged in combat in any way, often seek justification through other means. The imaginary line is one such means.[14]

It may seem that this paradoxical formation, in which the system's success is precisely at the point of its failure (or vice versa), is not paradoxical at all; after all, failure and success occur at two different levels. While at the concrete level of the checkpoint's regular operation we have a self-failing mechanism, success is achieved at an external level from a perspective taking into account the entire regime of occupation and its modes of both operation and justification. It is precisely the local failure, which by means of the failure itself gives rise to the materialization of power as arbitrary. This—as I will aim to show

1.4 Waiting in line in front of the electric turnstiles, Huwwara Checkpoint, 2006. Photo ©Esti Tsal. Courtesy Esti Tsal, Machsom Watch.

here—can be seen as success according to what I understand to be the logics of the system as a whole. However, the separation between the two levels is the privilege of one looking from the outside; at the level of the people having to go through these checkpoints—those who actually have to accommodate their behavior to protect themselves from the looming violence held in store for them—the paradoxical effect of the checkpoint is felt in the most immediate sense.

The violence that emerges with this paradox as justifiable violence is at some level rather paradoxical in itself. Violence tends to have a disruptive effect on the organization of space. Temporarily at least, the appearance of pure violence has a ripple effect on its surroundings; it blurs distinctions (between participants and bystanders, between the threatening and the benign), overriding any other order, and is difficult to contain. Yet, when witnessing violence at play in the particular case of the checkpoint, it is striking to see how quickly the checkpoint resumes its regular operation. How is it that even in those cases when someone who crosses the imaginary line gets shot, the edifice does not collapse into a shooting zone, into a site at which only violence presides? Why do people resume passing through within a matter of minutes, the soldiers return to the standard security check, and order seems to be re-established? It seems that while the mechanisms producing order produce also their own failure (a disorder justifying the appearance of violence), violence facilitates the reinstitution of order. This abnormal symbiosis suggests that we have here a mode of governance/control that is different from the one we encounter in normalizing regimes, and accordingly, a different set of assumptions regarding the subject-position of the governed.

That this position and this mode reveal themselves when examining the checkpoints should come as no surprise. Control over movement was always central to the ways in which subject-positions are formed and by which different regimes establish and shape their particular political orders. As chapter 3 will show, early liberalism saw freedom predominantly as freedom of motion: it configured autonomous subjects as moving beings, it imagined freedom primarily through the metaphor of moving bodies, and it limited the power of the state and the law above all by maximizing free movement of individuals. Chapter 4 further proposes that colonialism constructed its subjects as either commodities or animal-like humans also by producing and foregrounding particular types of movement (as slaves they could *be moved rather than move freely; as indigenous populations* they moved *too much*, presumably lacking proper attachment to a land).[15] Later colonial regimes were largely regimes of movement. The apartheid regime in South Africa, for example, was based on thousands of entries and crossings that were structured to secure political separation in a reality of economic dependency wherein black bodies were needed to nurse white children, to clean white homes, to labor in white industry, and to work in white mines. It was only when the political separation started to be dismantled that space was restructured by closures and checkpoints.[16] Finally, historical patterns of colonial domination can be traced in current patterns of transnational movement of people and goods. Specifically, these patterns are key players in the order that has been given the name "globalization," a reorganization of movement (of capital, labor, culture, and/or information) that still largely reflects colonial maps.[17] Examining the current stage of Israel's occupation, and the checkpoints more specifically, we find another form of subjectivity and another mode of governance founded upon (or at the very least leaning against) particular modalities of controlling movement. These modalities form unique relations between (im)mobility, violence, and subject formation. In their condensed operation and concentration, they can serve as a laboratory for examining movement as a political technology.

I argued above that the checkpoints can be seen, in some of their operations, as entailing aberrant disciplinary (or subjectivization) processes. Yet unlike fully functioning disciplinary sites, which endeavor to produce the subject as a unitary entity, at the checkpoints these processes aim, precisely, at *undoing* this unity. It is not simply that, for the Israeli governing apparatuses, the potential byproduct of the checkpoints as disciplinary sites—the construction of the Palestinians as subjects in the full meaning of the concept—is negligible; rather, Israel has a real interest in a specific subject-position, to which the failure of the disciplinary process is crucial. Accordingly, even when more traditional disciplinary practices are undertaken, it seems that their actual success is of no great concern, if not structurally undesirable. When "lessons" such as I described above are conducted, for example, they are conducted in Hebrew—a language often not spoken by Palestinians. This failure enables the construction of the persons having to go through the checkpoints as subjected to a foreign power, a foreign omnipotent sovereign, to which they can never have access and, potentially speaking, for whom they are the enemy. In other words: it produces them as *occupied subjects*, namely, subjects who are never included within the power to which they are subjected (as opposed to the citizen), nor completely expelled from it (as opposed to the foreigner, or even more so, the enemy). The occupied subject is, thus, in an ever-lingering state of potentiality, as if within a *fata morgana* of partial citizenship, but in fact is always on the verge of (and occasionally even collapsing into) enmity.

Thus, the thin—yet pervasive—shell of disciplinary and biopolitical interest Israel once had in the lives of Palestinians was replaced by a narrow mode of control, which manages to regulate a strikingly wide spectrum of aspects in Palestinian lives simply by controlling their movement. To an extent, from the perspective of Israeli control apparatuses, the Palestinians are reduced to one-dimensional subjects: moving subjects.[18] This thin, or potentially always-already subjugated subject-position construed at the checkpoints appears more clearly in relation to a second subject-position, that of the fully included subject: the citizen. The comparison between these two positions is the focus of the next section.

On White Lines and Full Subjectivity: Checkpoint Watch Activists

At the checkpoints the position of the fully included subject is embodied by Israeli activists and, in particular, the activists of a human rights organization that has a regular presence at the checkpoints: Checkpoint Watch (CPW). The organization was founded in 2001 by a small group of Jewish, Israeli women who became aware of the expansion and growing significance of the checkpoints in the ongoing occupation. It is an all-women organization, currently including about four hundred activists, who stand in small groups at more than forty checkpoints (the main, manned checkpoints throughout the West Bank). The primary goal of CPW is to protest against the occupation and, in particular, against the checkpoints.

The presence of the activists, monitoring, documenting and sometimes even intervening, is only barely tolerated by the army and by the soldiers at the checkpoints. Nevertheless, most of the time and in most places, only sporadic attempts have been made to restrict their access to the checkpoints or to delimit their allowed movement within them.[19] Every once in a while an angry, frustrated, or simply strict soldier would indicate a point in space and ask—or shout—"Don't cross this line! You're too close, move away!" Yet even when such imaginary lines appeared to delimit the allowed movement of the Israeli activists, these spatial limitations were most often not enforced by the soldiers. And then, one day, toward the end of 2006, a line was drawn at some of the checkpoints, nicknamed "the Watch Women line" (Watch Women being a quasi-derogatory name used by the soldiers to indicate the activists of the organization) or "the white line" (as it was drawn using white paint). Once the white line appeared, it became a permanent obstacle, limiting the allowed movement of the activists within the checkpoint, distancing them from the places where the Palestinians were checked, and restricting their ability to witness and document the behavior of the soldiers at the checkpoint. Many activists did not accept this restriction and some of them, who did not hesitate to confront the soldiers, often ignored this limitation and frequently crossed that line. In close to ten years of activity, which included thousands of annual shifts—on a daily basis, at any type of checkpoint throughout the West Bank, including countless encounters with hostile soldiers in delicate situations—the only incidents during which soldiers laid a hand on an activist were when the latter crossed the white line.

This is not to argue that any and all lines drawn in the space of the checkpoints potentially facilitate the appearance of violence. There are fundamental differences in the forms of violence, the conditions under which the two lines operate, and their consequent effects. Even in its initial stages, before it was actually marked, the "Watch Women line" never functioned as an imaginary line; not only because its coordinates were often clearly indicated and were not arbitrarily defined anew according to the whim of the soldiers, but also, and more important, because it functioned under a completely different set of assumptions concerning rules, their manifestations, and the subject-positions they address and constitute.

First, it is important to note that while these instances of violence were a sharp divergence from the range of possible reactions toward activists available to the soldiers before the line was drawn, these violent reactions—however inconvenient to the activists in question—never amounted to life-threatening situations and mostly took the form of soldiers forcibly pushing activists back beyond the line. A second difference can be marked as follows: since CPW activists are citizens in a self-proclaimed democratic regime, even when they go to the checkpoints they are included under what liberalism perceives as the shield of law. This is not merely a formal position granted by citizenship, but perhaps, and more important, a function of being identified by the power operating on them as rational beings, with the ability and authority to interpret the law. Therefore, the Watch Women line had to materialize into a clearly demarcated white line before it could incorporate the effects of the law and, in particular, before it could justify the use of force against its transgressors. As long as a line was not marked, it lacked two of the basic principles of the law in the liberal imaginary: accessibility and regularity, and thus could not function as law. If the liberal subject can indeed be defined as the subject who can recognize, decipher, and rationally act according to the law, then the law must, in principle, be accessible to the subjects to whom it applies, and needs to show stability and regularity.

But when the law is always-already uninterpretable, which as I suggested earlier is the mode by which Israeli law relates to Palestinians, simply marking the imaginary line would not undo its effects and logic. Marking it becomes redundant, if not meaningless. What is striking about this redundancy is that, in the eyes of Israeli rule, the Palestinians passing through the checkpoint inhabit, at one and the same time, two contradictory subject-positions, whose shared denominator is their opposition to the attributes of the classic liberal subject. On the one hand, they are assumed to be alienated from the law—a law that relentlessly constructs itself as indecipherable for them: all signs and commands are in Hebrew; regulations are most often random, change frequently and contradict other regulations; orders are not made public, and are a patchwork of multiple legal systems.[20] Yet, on the other hand, the law is assumed to be inscribed in them: they presumably *already know* all the rules, laws, and regulations. "They know" is one of the most common justifications used by Israeli soldiers to rationalize their harassment of or violence toward Palestinian "transgressors": "they know where the line is," "they know that they should not be here," "they know they are not allowed to drive on this road." And "they" indeed (presumably) "know" all this without any sign, mark, or clear indication of what is forbidden or allowed. This highly prevalent justificatory formulation is possible only if, from the standpoint of the Israeli army as it functions as the law-maker and the law enforcer in the oPt, Palestinians have a shared, almost omnipresent collective consciousness: once one person has been told that a specific road is for Jews only, "they" all supposedly know immediately not to drive on it; once a soldier has pointed to an imaginary point in space for the first person in line, almost miraculously (so the soldiers seem to assume) everyone else in line can identify the line not to be crossed. Marks and signs then become redundant because the orders they provide are, at one and the same time, always already a shared knowledge of what can only be seen as some form of collective consciousness and can never be understood (and therefore obeyed) by a specific individual who is forever racially alien to the rule. While these two assumptions may seem to be contradictory, they form a single subject-position that can be characterized as being concurrently totally foreign to the law and immersed within it, thereby depriving the subject of the ability to be positioned in the (assumed) proper proximity between the individual and the law.

Third, while marking the white line was necessary to punish the activists who transgressed it, the transformation from a roughly marked unseen line to a marked line opened up a field of possibilities for CPW members: the white line marked not only the areas of the checkpoints that were forbidden to them but at the same time, also the areas in which their presence could not be prohibited. If a soldier wanted to expel an activist from a checkpoint, all that she had to do to dispute it was to point to the line and assert—"I am allowed to be here," or "I am standing behind the line." In other words, as long as the subject in front of the law is recognized by that law as possessing it to some extent, the transparency of power enables some range of negotiation that is available to the liberal subject, and may also include additional legal and civil means for appealing it, such as turning to the courts, the lawmakers, the media, public opinion, and the like. This chapter can, therefore, be read as a liberal tale calling for more regularity and the visibility of rules. Yet our story does not end here. To complete it, I would like to examine a new form of checkpoint, which appeared toward the end of 2005: the terminals.

On Lines, Signs, and the Evolution of Checkpoints

Shouldn't lines be marked then? Does the regularity and signifiability of the law always render it somewhat less oppressive? If, time and again, people were detained for hours, beaten or sent back to their homes, guns were drawn and checkpoints completely shut down (so no one was allowed to pass) because someone took one extra step beyond what appears to the eye as nothing, wouldn't it be better to publicly mark the lines that one must not pass? As they witnessed numerous occurrences wherein Palestinians were punished—from being shouted at to being shot at—for transgressing nonexistent demarcations, the answer of many CPW activists to the above question was yes. Presumably, a well-marked line would reduce the instances of "transgression" at the checkpoints, by allowing Palestinians to obey the rules and protect themselves from the violence of the soldiers.

Consider, for instance, the following report from Huwwara, a checkpoint at the outskirt of the city of Nablus, from Monday, August 8, 2005: "We explain to A. [the soldier] that it is impossible to forbid people to cross over a line that is nowhere to be seen. He is convinced that everybody knows the line and is just pretending, and adds that even when there is a drawn line, there are some who cross it. But he promises to prepare a signpost that will indicate the line. We shall look for this signpost next week."[21]

The demand of CPW activists to mark lines joined other demands and suggestions they expressed, aimed at increasing the regularity and the visibility of the rules governing the checkpoints (demands to post signs or to provide instructions in Arabic), all ensuing from the recognition that arbitrariness is a predominant feature of power—of violence—at the checkpoints. These demands and suggestions were supported by others of a humanitarian nature: a demand to supply water to the people having to stand in line for hours, to build shelters to protect them from the sun and rain, and to provide toilet facilities at the checkpoints.[22] To the surprise of the activists, many of these demands were accepted: lines were marked, which were later enforced through the use of obstacles and fences. Signs were put up: initially provisional ones, on cardboard, written in Hebrew only; later official signs using Arabic appeared; and eventually, at the newer checkpoints, electronic signs in Hebrew, English, and Arabic. In response to humanitarian demands, shelters were erected, toilets installed, and water tanks were brought in. The checkpoints thereby expanded; their material presence became more dense and solidified. What was once a cement cube on a dirt path, a provisional obstacle behind

1.5 An electronic sign at Qalandia checkpoint (terminal), 2006. The sign says in Hebrew and Arabic: "Welcome to Atarot Passage-Point. Have a Pleasant Stay." Photo ©Hagar Kotef.

which the soldiers stood, turned into a permanent and elaborate construction. The bigger among these edifices look very much like regular border crossings and are, accordingly, termed "terminals."

Elsewhere Amir and I discussed different rationales for the materialization of the terminals. We focused on the humanitarian discourse (partly brought to the checkpoints by CPW) and argued that it was incorporated by the occupying forces and, peculiarly, in an almost literal manner, became building blocks for the terminals.[23] Here I want to consider another rationale, subtending the process of terminal building; a rationale, which once again, was partly introduced to the checkpoints by CPW. The organization whose main goal is to annul the checkpoints, unwillingly has found itself a contributor to their entrenchment. I want to examine the logic of signification underlying the above evolution of the checkpoints.

Looking at the process through which checkpoints were built and ensconced, we can see that when the army wanted to make sure that people in

1.6 Qalandia Checkpoint, 2002. Lines in front of the checking booths were fixed using concrete blocks. Photo ©Tamar Fleishman. Courtesy Tamar Fleishman, Machsom Watch.

line kept a certain distance from the security-check booth, for instance, it did not simply mark a line (as in the case of CPW activists' white line) or put up a sign: "please wait here"; rather, it built an iron turnstile, sometimes even an electric turnstile controlled from afar by the soldiers. And when a queue was to be marked, it was not marked by some drawing on the floor, or one of those ropes tied to small pillars one finds at banks, government institutions, or airports; rather, high fences were erected. It was not assumed, for one moment, that a symbolic marking of space would suffice. Indeed, since (as with the presumption underlying the imaginary line), the (nonliberal) subject-positions of the Palestinians at the checkpoints were assumed to lack the ability to follow the demarcation of space through the use of instructive signs, order at the checkpoint had to be enforced by material obstacles. Slowly, but with great regularity, these obstacles kept appearing at checkpoints, which gradually became complex structures, until many of them made way for terminals.

When Amir and I started writing this article, several years ago, Israel envisioned transforming most of the central checkpoints into terminals. In accordance with a policy of borders-ambiguousness, what defined a terminal was *not* its location but its structure. In the years since, this project was abandoned

1.7 Qalandia Checkpoint (terminal), 2010. Long, narrow, cage-like iron corridors were installed to ease the pressure on the turnstiles. These corridors are not simply unpleasant; they make passage difficult and at times, impossible. When anyone within them needs to leave the line for some reason, the entire row behind the person has to retrace their steps to let him or her out. This task, if possible at all, creates confusion and chaos. When large crowds are present, it is virtually impossible to leave the line. Photo ©Tamar Fleishman. Courtesy Tamar Fleishman, Machsom Watch.

and all terminals are now situated along the separation wall, presumably as transitions into areas that the state sees as its own territory. Yet, the geopolitical situation, as well as Israel's continuous efforts to annex at least some of the land behind the Green Line, ultimately led to the construction of most terminals *within* Palestinian territory (even if closer to the 1967 borders of Israel), separating Palestinian communities from one another and families from their land. Therefore, I want to avoid reproducing the rhetoric of borders the terminals are supposed to simulate, and focus rather on the layout of these constructions.

Unlike the other checkpoints, terminals are meticulously built through and through. Equipped with an array of monitoring and control apparatuses—from electric turnstiles made of iron to security cameras and biometric identification devices—the terminals enable the soldiers to control the checkpoints from an isolated edifice, always absent but present, often hidden from sight, thus concealing the violence of the checkpoint, making it seem more civilian.[24] They are roofed constructions, surrounded by concrete walls and fences; their lines are marked, signed, and numbered; and they are built so densely they leave almost no room for hidden demarcations. On the contrary. In a way, they are the grotesque manifestation of the overflow of signification. I will further consider this grotesque and its meanings in what follows, yet first I should emphasize that, while the use of signifying indicators is indeed far from lacking at the terminals, and while, accordingly, concrete imaginary lines were almost eradicated from the terminals (or, more accurately, marginalized to their edges), the logic of an order that is never accessible or possible to abide by, is an integral part of their operation. This self-undoing of the organizing techniques and principles is evident when crossing these checkpoints: the army personnel operating them are completely inaccessible and cannot be approached even when there are malfunctions or a need for assistance; the intercom communication systems that were supposed to enable a two-way communication never work; and orders are shouted over almost-indecipherable loudspeakers in a language that most people who go through the checkpoints do not speak.

True to this logic, most often any technological addition, any attempt to enforce order at the terminals proves to be another obstacle and another factor that eventually creates havoc. The turnstiles, which were introduced to most of the permanent checkpoints by the end of 2004 and are to be found in all terminals, are one such example. The turnstiles "attempted to slow, regulate and organize the crowded mass of Palestinians seeking to cross the checkpoints into sequenced and ordered lines in which one Palestinian at a time would face the soldier checking his permit and baggage," describes Eyal Weizman.[25] Yet the turnstiles at the checkpoints are tighter than the acceptable standard and have very little room between their metal arms,[26] and therefore, they eventually produced more chaos than order. "People got stuck, parcels got crushed, dragged along and burst open on the ground. Heavier people got trapped in the narrow space, as were older women and mothers with small children," Weizman cites a report of CPW and summarizes: "It is hard to imagine the cruelty imposed by a minor transformation of a banal, and otherwise invisible architectural detail, ostensibly employed to regulate and make easier the process of passage."[27]

This cruelty, I argue, is not merely a cruelty for cruelty's sake. It is part of a mode of control—a mode of control that subtends a significant portion of the

1.8 A woman trying to go through a turnstile with a stroller, Qalandia Checkpoint, 2006. The narrow turnstiles often necessitate the separations of parents and children—a separation many of them are quite reluctant to accept. The narrow turnstiles make it almost impossible to pass with luggage or in a wheelchair. Later, special "humanitarian gates" were built to allow the passage of people using wheelchairs, but more often than not these gates remain locked. Photo ©Hava Berfman. Courtesy Hava Berfman, Machsom Watch.

controlling apparatuses in the oPt. The most striking support for this claim has been officially named by the army "changing the routine." Changing the routine consists of a variety of abrupt changes in the regulations according to which the checkpoint operates, as far as the imagination of the soldiers allows. It was first discovered by CPW activists in the Qalandia terminal:

> "To change the routine," a soldier revealed [the reason for sending] the Palestinians from line to line, close up the turnstiles in their face, or catch them within them [the turnstiles], and make them suddenly wait for long spans of time. . . . To "change the routine," that is a suggestion (or a command) from higher up than this soldier. Somewhere, at some place, a group of people got together and thought up the idea that, from the security standpoint, the routine should change. . . . Therefore, those waiting in line were shifted around some 15 times from line to line for 45 minutes, and one time [they] changed the routine even more when they closed line 3 and yelled over a loudspeaker to go to line 2 and immediately after they reached there, they were sent back to line 3.[28]

Such direct commands are rare and usually routines such as this come not from calculated planning at the headquarters but from the creative minds of the soldiers themselves. They become part of the normal operation of the checkpoint as a matter of habit. And yet it is startling to see the variety of measures, whether or not they are planned and precalculated, by which the very apparatuses that aim at introducing order, constantly undo it.

But, as I suggested earlier, the terminals are not only sites in which the intrinsic failure to maintain regularity we see at the checkpoints is reproduced through other, more sophisticated means; the terminals entail—indeed *are*—another inversion. By professing to be normal border crossings, even as most are built in the midst of the Palestinian territory, the terminals create the illusion of the occupation's end, while maximizing and stabilizing its techniques and effects. Separating a town from its outskirts, they hoist digital "welcome" greeting signs, as if the people passing through are visitors, and not people who need to cross the checkpoint attempting to go about their daily routine. Preventing people from maintaining their social life, their communities, and their commerce, they are decorated with murals displaying big slogans asserting hope and peace. Called terminals, they mask the fact of occupation, camouflaging control as absent-presence—as if they demonstrate the retreat of Israel from the West Bank; as if by such an act of signification, the occupied territory behind them becomes an independent sovereign state.

What enables this grotesqueness is thus precisely an excess of signification, which serves not to eliminate violence but rather to conceal it. In a way, the story of the terminals reveals the critical side of the liberal story encapsulated within the example and the allegory of the imaginary line. In a way, it is a story about the predicaments of employing signs; a story about how, by making power transparent, making law visible and accessible, violence seems to disappear while, in actuality, it changes form, conceals itself and, thereby, becomes more permanent and sustainable. First, violence becomes less erratic and more structural. It no longer brutally erupts in episodic incidents, but is rather a perpetuated structure of exploitation, expulsion, and oppression.[29] Second, episodic, eruptive violence is marginalized, and for the most part, it no longer occurs in the main area of the checkpoint, but is pushed out to the parking lots, roads, or the areas surrounding them. Most important, the violence of the checkpoint, that Sari Hanafi adequately described as spaciocide,[30] is itself concealed; the demolition of the land, the destruction of people's lives, the shredding of the social fabric the checkpoint entails simply by being there are veiled and denied.

It may seem that what is called for here is simply some balance between the terminals and their oversignification on the one hand, and the imaginary lines and their insufficient signification on the other. Seemingly, it is precisely about obtaining the balance to which I pointed out in the previous section, precisely about producing the assumed proper distance between the liberal subject and the law. Yet, while this liberal impulse may now appear to provide a solution to the violence I have portrayed here, it carries within it two crucial problems—one almost circumstantial and the other more fundamental. First, this solution has potential consequences for which the Jewish-Israeli regime cannot reckon. If this balance is indeed intertwined with assumptions regarding the liberal subject—the subject who can recognize, interpret, and eventually become the authority of the law (partial and imagined as this authority may be)—then at the edge of this solution resides full citizenship for the Palestinians. However, the Israeli regime is structured to impede such an option, which would bring about an integration of the Palestinian population of the West Bank and Gaza as coherent political beings under a liberal notion of this term, either as Israeli citizens—which a state self-defined as Jewish cannot accommodate—or as foreign citizens (as citizens of a Palestinian state)—which the geopolitical conditions make merely impossible.[31] However, this problem reveals another, deeper crisis within the above liberal impulse and liberal impulses in general. Even if the "proper" balance were to be found, and even if it were maintained, and even if all appearances of violence were to be eliminated, still the checkpoint would remain, the dispossession would subsist, and the occupation would remain the structural oppression that it is. Within conditions of radical expropriation, rights deprivation, and ongoing abuse, a liberal impulse that seemingly (and sometimes also actually) provides some alleviations of violence often (also) provides a cloak, enveloping the violent structure with legitimacy. The violence of the structure itself is hidden by the reduction of the more obvious and conspicuous violent incidents, a process that paves the way for normalization and hence, also, the persistence of the conditions of deprivation.

The story of the imaginary line and the terminals is not just a story about specific technologies of occupation, about violence, and about liberal strategies of resisting them; it is also a story about subjectivity and its production within a logic that radically deviates from that of normalizing regimes. It is a story about a corrective system that relentlessly endeavors to situate its objects (subjects) as uncorrectable; about a subjectivization system that is calibrated to fail, and a violence-reducing means that facilitates the occurrence of violent eruptions and, more important, which makes the occupation sustainable within its own logic of justification. If they can never identify the rule, if they can never be disciplined, Palestinians can never control themselves. The imaginary line and the overconstructed terminals thereby join other failure-inducing factors in the occupation, from the inaccessibility of the legal system to the ever-shifting regulations, in order to produce such unruliness, which then justifies external control. In other words, it justifies the occupation—always "temporarily,"[32] presumably, until the Palestinians can prove that they can control themselves, yet always perpetuated by rules that can never be abided by, the transgression of which serves as evidence of Palestinians' inherent inability to do so.

Yet, while within the liberal framing of this article the imaginary line and the terminals serve as figures in a parable, within a story of subjectivization processes, they are but a fraction. While I argue that checkpoints also function as sites of subjectivization, while I argue that the subjects they aim at producing are the always-already failed product of (meant-to-fail) disciplinary processes, and while I understand what the stakes are in these processes, I also maintain that subjectivity does not begin or end at the checkpoints. To understand the operation of power at the checkpoints (and within the occupation), it is crucial that we understand the objects of these technologies of power, that is, the subject-positions they both assume and endeavor to produce; yet, it is no less crucial that we remember that these endeavors are never fully successful. "At best," the checkpoints have momentary success in constructing those who pass through them, at the moment of passing, as undisciplinable subjects. This chapter begins and ends with this moment, and is also confined within a limited perspective: that of (an external, occupying) power. It is only this perspective I aim at examining and deciphering. In important ways, giving voice to this perspective reproduces it. Such a framework of analysis considers the Palestinians as mere objects (even if victims) of an array of Israeli apparatuses. It thereby erases (even if only momentarily during the time of the argument) their agency, experience, voice and, most important, strategies of resistance. Still, I believe—I hope—that within a larger mosaic of perspectives, the one I have provided here may also begin to undo these same apparatuses in some small way.

Finally, the story of the imaginary line is also a small example, a manifestation of a much more widespread mechanism that—so this book sets to propose—is embedded into the structure of liberal law. The task is, therefore, to trace back much more slowly the formation of this structure of law and its relation to space and to movement. We must further examine the idea that self-regulation of movement is inextricably linked to freedom and citizenship, on the backdrop of which we see the dual inversion of the system of which the imaginary line is both a component and an emblem (a denial of freedom that has drained into the control over movement and the meant-to-fail apparatuses of order). This is the aim of the next chapters.

2 | An Interlude

A Tale of Two Roads—On Freedom and Movement

> Mobility climbs to the rank of the uppermost among the coveted values—
> and the freedom to move, perpetually a scarce and unequally distributed
> commodity, fast becomes the main stratifying factor of our time.
> —ZIGMOND BAUMAN, *Globalization, The Human Consequences*

Images

There is an image that has become an icon in various accounts of Israel's occupation (be they scholarly, political or, even if less often, news reports).

This image is of road number 60, connecting in this particular segment Jerusalem with the settlements of Gush Atzion. This segment (figure 2.1) is also known as the "Tunnels Road," since, as this picture barely shows, parts of the road were tunneled under the mountains, beneath Palestinian villages, thereby securing quick, direct, and protected,[1] passageway. Yet, there is not one road here but two. As the image shows, underneath road 60, which is limited to Israeli citizens and tourists only (a somewhat strange definition that sets out to include all potential travelers other than Palestinians who live in the occupied area),[2] there is a second, winding, unpaved road for the movement of Palestinians.[3] In a single frame the image captures the logic of separation governing the Israeli regime over the oPt. Here movement is at one and the same time a symbol, a *technology* and the *object* (or matter) of separation. Movement is the main thing that is separated, and it is via this separation that populations are separated. Movement is the target of control (that is, the element to be controlled, the object of regulation), which thereby becomes the substance (the matter) of a mode of governance whose main attribute is separation.[4] Within the entire territory subjected to Israeli rule, there is a parted regime[5]

2.1 Tunnels Road, wall and a Palestinian road, between Beit Jala and Gilo (Jerusalem).
©Ian Sternthal. Courtesy Ian Sternthal.

whose governing logic is split. One logic governs citizens and one governs the occupied; one governs Jews and one Palestinians.[6] Indeed, the image in figure 2.1 has become iconic precisely because movement is so central to the rules and modes of operation of the Israeli occupation.

But this image shows more than the fact of separation (as an example among many instances) and its primary tool (the control of movement as the political technology through which separation takes place). It also shows the nature of this separation, and what happens (to movement, to people, to space) with this separation. Israeli movement is fast. It has priority. It is this movement that has to be protected. It is direct, straight, and perhaps even rational (target-oriented).[7] It is part of progress, of man overcoming nature, of the achievements of technology, engineering, and construction. Palestinian movement is not. It is slow and meandering.[8] The road on which it takes place (or the road that symbolizes it) is out of date, or at least seems this way. Whereas the movement above is facilitated and maximized, Palestinians' movement is hindered by various means. It is also controlled, both symbolically and concretely, through the horizontal hierarchization of roads. Finally, Palestinian movement is also made invisible from the point of view of Israelis. Those traveling on the top road cannot see the road below them. Since the above road is meant for Jews only, it also lacks any exits to the Palestinian towns and villages next to which it passes. (The assumption is that the two populations do not—and should not—mix. This is of course not merely an assumption—it is a reality that is shaped and constructed by such organization of the space Jews and Palestinians share.) Accordingly, the upper road also lacks any signs indicating the existence of Palestinian towns or villages. Since the road is high above the ground, often the villages themselves become hidden from sight.[9] The visual field of a traveler on these roads is thereby cleansed of Palestinian presence. We can conclude then: The free movement of some limits, hides, even denies the existence of others. Moreover, the movement of some is further maximized by this effacement of others and their need to move.[10]

And yet the others are still there; and thus their movement must be controlled so as not to interrupt the movement of the former. What the picture does not reveal is the degree to which road 60 partakes in a grid that dissects the land to the extent that "a mound of earth became sufficient for blocking access from the village to the road."[11] Parallel to Reviel Netz's account of the use of barbed wire in South Africa during the Boer war,[12] Ariel Handel shows how the settlements and the road system in the oPt were built in a way that creates isolated land cells. Since Palestinians are not allowed to travel on them, and often even to cross them, they become a technology of separation, even if they were originally built for other purposes.[13] Once they were in place "'a topological inversion' occurred, so that the lines connecting the stations [in the South African case to which Netz points, or the settlements in the Israeli/ Palestinian context] became lines separating one area from another."[14] The regime of movement described in the previous chapter became possible precisely through this fragmentation of Palestinian space into land cells. So there is a larger schema of controlling movement at work that this image cannot quite capture. But there are more layers here. Another image then, of another road:

Figure 2.2 illustrates a junction at the exit of Beit Furik, a Palestinian village next to Nablus. To understand this seemingly trivial depiction of an intersection a map is required: The picture is taken from the point of view of a person exiting the village Beit Furik (in dark gray), looking at the intersection with road 557 (which crosses the picture horizontally.) The Beit Furik checkpoint, which is marked on the enlarged map (figure 2.3) is located a few feet to the right of the intersection, and cannot be seen in the image. Turning left on road 557, following the arrow on the road at the center of figure 2.2, leads to several

2.2 A junction outside Beit Furik, July 2009. Photo ©Yudith Levin. Courtesy Yudith Levin, Machsom Watch.

other Palestinian towns and villages, but also to the Jewish settlement Itamar and several other outposts in its vicinity. Therefore, this segment of road 557 is forbidden to Palestinians. Palestinians are only allowed to turn right at the junction. That is, the image captures the point of view of a Palestinian leaving a Palestinian village who is not allowed to turn left at this junction—the direction in which the arrow painted on the road is pointing. If this somewhat convoluted explanation requires more clarity it can be put more bluntly: on a road only Palestinians use, an arrow points in a direction toward which Palestinians are not allowed to travel.

Following the previous chapter, it may not come as a surprise that this restriction is not marked anywhere and Palestinians are presumed to know it without any indication. This pattern obeys the logic of the imaginary line as explained in chapter 1: a failure embedded into the regulation of space facilitates unlawful movement, hence configuring the Palestinians as always-already transgressors of the law, undisciplinable subjects who must therefore be tightly controlled, and justifies some forms of violence in the cloak of pun-

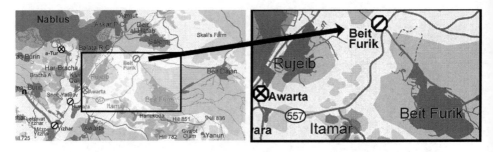

2.3 A map of Beit Furik and surroundings. Checkpoints are marked in crossed circles. The road crossing the map from the bottom left to the upper right of the small map is road 557. Detail of map of the West Bank, settlements and the separation barrier, btselem.org

ishment. While in the case of the imaginary line this failure was introduced by rendering space indecipherable, by introducing irregularities, and by leaving regulations unmarked, here, the system of regulating movement subverts its own operation in a much more direct way. The forbidden left turn is not merely unmarked, it is marked as legitimate. Once a Palestinian follows the mark on the road (obeying what seems to be an official indication of permitted movement), she violates the law, and a sanction is justified. More than once Palestinians have been shot at for driving on such roads.[15]

On December 9, 2008, a shift of Checkpoint Watch encountered six people from Nablus, who were delayed in Beit Furik, for accidentally traveling on this road:

> This was the first time in seven years [these people] were allowed to exit Nablus and visit their relatives in Beit Furik [which is located a mere couple of miles away]. Obviously, they were not familiar with the new regulations [which change frequently], and they accidentally [traveled on the forbidden road]. They did not see the sign stating that Palestinians are not allowed to travel on the road, *evidently because there is no such sign*. So they were caught by the [soldiers] and now they are being punished. "The checkpoint was removed but it doesn't mean they can do whatever they want," a soldier explained. The punishment: detaining the group for three whole hours. Not a single minute less. It does not matter that it is freezing outside, that it is a holiday, or that there is no sign and they are unfamiliar with this road.[16]

We should already be familiar with the mechanism.[17] We are also familiar with the explanation:

First Lieutenant A. arrives at the checkpoint. He does not care that it is forbidden to detain people for the sake of punishment or to educate them. "This is the only way they can learn," he states, talking about three men whose age probably ranges from the age of his father to that of his grandfather. We ask how they are supposed to know they should not be on the road in the absence of a sign. "They know," he says and repeats the mantra again and again, "they know and do it intentionally"; as if "they" are little rebellious kids, who can learn only through physical punishment.[18]

The physical punishment is justified because there is a transgression, but the transgression could have been easily prevented. In fact, it is not prevented because the Israeli army, as well as the government and public opinion, need these transgressions. If the Israeli control is to be sustained, but if Israel is to continue preserving and presenting itself as peace-seeking,[19] then the Palestinians must be constantly produced as "non-partners."[20]

At this point the different layers meet: an efficient matrix of control; a maximization of the movement of settlers as well as of the army's violence (the two main types of movement of non-Palestinians in the West Bank); a hindered movement of Palestinians; and a justification mechanism rendering some movements transgressive thereby justifying, precisely, the limits set upon them.

This bifurcation between movements, that also stood at the foundation of the difference between the white line and the imaginary line in the previous chapter, is mapped into the division of the next two chapters. The next chapter focuses, if I may stretch the analogy opening this chapter, on the movement of those traveling on the top road: the subjects/citizens of liberalism. The following chapter, "The Problem of 'Excessive' Movement," analyzes the history of perceiving and producing some movements, primarily the movement of colonized subjects, as a problem, much like the movement of those following the arrow marked on the road in figure 2.2. In the remainder of this chapter I will try to show the degree to which the two configurations of movement are entangled. The logic that will emerge is quite simple. To understand the idea of "transgressive movement," whose history dates far earlier than the establishment of the regime of movement in the oPt, we need to understand the model of movement on whose backdrop transgression emerges as such: the notion of moderated, self-regulated movement.

A Genealogy of Self-Regulation

The regulation of movement (again: as a symbol, a metaphor, an image, a technology, an instance, a means, a goal) was central to the emergence of liberal ideology and liberal models of subjectivity, power, and freedom. This claim goes counter to many common understandings of liberal subjectivity, hence I unfold it gradually in the next chapter. The conclusion, however, can already be given here: the liberal subject is essentially a moving subject, and her first and most fundamental freedom is freedom of movement—at least as far as political freedom is concerned. The main challenge of liberalism was to craft a concept of order that was reconcilable with its emphasis on freedom. As Otto Mayr shows, a model for addressing this challenge was found within a set of discoveries in natural science that demonstrated that under certain conditions dynamic systems can regulate and maintain themselves.[21] This model—which proliferated in the second half of the sixteenth century and peaked, mostly among British writers, after the revolution of 1688—allowed liberalism to imagine an ordered freedom. As we shall see in the next chapters, before this model became available, and on the margins of this model still today, liberty (at least as long as it was conceived in relation to movement) has been identified with chaos, and seen as destructive to politics. With the emergence of the model of self-regulation, however, liberty could become the hinge on which political space can be organized. For Mayr, key to the strong appeal of this model to emerging liberal conceptual frameworks was the lack of external intervention. I propose that no less crucial was the possibility, through this model, to conceive of moderated, self-regulated movement.

This was not merely a mechanical model; it was also an organizational model that stood at the foundation of modernity's concepts of law, state,[22] population,[23] international relations,[24] and subject[25]—or at modernity's foundation of new modes of power.[26] Eventually, such a model of movement would compose the liberal concept of freedom we will encounter in the next chapter. With it, movement no longer manifested "a restless and inassimilable alterity busily working both within and against state power's most cherished idea: social order";[27] rather, it was conceived as the manifestation (and precondition) of a free social order.

Foucault identified this mechanism most accurately and explicitly in his 1977–79 lectures when he became more and more interested in liberalism. Liberal freedom, Foucault tells us, is "not exactly, fundamentally, or primarily an ideology." It is "first of all, and above all, . . . a technology of power."[28]

This technology of power is a technology of movement, and more specifically, of self-regulating aggregates. The underlying presupposition of liberalism is that the world is in flux. It flows. And things must be allowed to flow in their course (the flow of capital that Marx distinguished as the crux of the matter is but one, even if pivotal, movement to be maximized[29]). This flow—again, as Marx argued—entails its own internal crises, but crises, too, must be allowed to take their course. Perhaps taking his cue from Marx, Foucault points to this logic of self-regulating crises, in which only by allowing a crisis to flow, will the crisis be minimized. For example, "there will no longer be any scarcity in general, on the condition that . . . there was some scarcity . . . and consequently some hunger, and it may well be that some people die of hunger after all. But by letting these people die of hunger one will be able to make scarcity a chimera and prevent it occurring in this massive form of the scourge typical of previous systems." Thus, "a sort of 'laisser-faire,' a certain 'freedom of movement (laisser-passer),' a sort of '[laisser]-aller,' in the sense of 'letting things take their course' . . . will itself entail precisely its own self-curbing and self-regulation."[30]

This, in short, is the liberal technology of freedom. According to Foucault it emerges in the eighteenth century, and he accordingly dates the emergence of liberalism to this time. Yet if we follow Mayr we can see that the quintessential elements of this technology consolidate already in the sixteenth century. Even if the population, as the target and product of this technology, is constituted only in the eighteenth century (Foucault's argument), the core logic of the technology is at play, in regard to other complex systems, already in the sixteenth century (Mayr's periodization). My book adds an intermediate link to this genealogy, whose detailing is the objective of the next two chapters: in the seventeenth century, the model of self-regulation becomes the model through which individual freedom is conceived.

To recapitulate: in the sixteenth century, a model of self-regulation through which movement is moderated develops in natural science and makes its way into thinking about political models (to the extent that these were two distinct disciplines at the time; and the claim that they were not distinct, as Foucault or Shapin and Schaffer have argued in different ways, does not undermine, but rather supports my argument). Then, in the seventeenth century, we see the notion that the individual—itself a product of the time—can and must regulate his own movement. This notion entails two stages: first, the idea that movement is freedom. What Foucault sees vis-à-vis the population appears here earlier, vis-à-vis the individual body. Second, that this freedom should be "ballasted" (in Foucault's terminology[31]) if it is to manifest the exercise of freedom. Chapter 3 excavates the identification of freedom and movement. By examining their presumed absence, chapter 4 points to property or land as rudiment means of such ballasting. By the turn of the seventeenth century, property and land would be augmented by disciplinary apparatuses that much more meticulously, locally, and densely, regulate the movement of the individual body. And finally, in the eighteenth century, freedom becomes "nothing else but the apparatus of security": it is "but the possibility of movement, change of place, and process of circulation of both people and things," in which governance is organized as if within a particular "physics of power." Government protects "no longer the safety (sûreté) of the Prince and its territory, but the security (sécurité) of the population" by "allowing circulation to take place . . . ensuring that things are constantly in movement . . . but in such a way that the inherent dangers of this circulation are canceled out."[32] Movement—synthesizing politics and nature, individual bodies and collective ones—completes a full-fledged arrival into the political imagination and becomes the anchor and object of myriad political technologies.

The goal, therefore, is to retrace how the liberal subject was formed in the image of moderation. Once we see the degree to which this model is based on particular patterns of movement, we can also understand how and why movement becomes so pivotal in the de-constitution of liberal subjectivity and citizenship. This is the role of chapters 3 and 4, which should, accordingly, not be read as a systematic analysis of movement, but rather, as an analysis of the concept (as a category, an image, a metaphor, an understanding of physical phenomena) in the history—in a specific history—of political thought.

3 | The Fence That "Ill Deserves the Name of Confinement"

Locomotion and the Liberal Body

> I can think of no more fitting image for the ideal of social conduct than an English dance, composed of many complicated figures and perfectly executed. A spectator in the gallery sees innumerable movements intersecting in the most chaotic fashion, changing direction swiftly and without rhythm or reason, yet *never colliding*. Everything is so ordered that the one has already yielded his place when the other arrives; it is all so skillfully, and yet so artlessly, integrated into a form, that each seems only to be following his own inclination, yet without ever getting in the way of anybody else. It is the most perfectly appropriate symbol of the assertion of one's own freedom and regard for the freedom of others. —SCHILLER, *On the Esthetic Education of Man*

This chapter traces the role of physical movement as a political phenomenon within the core corpus that would become the framework within which liberal theory develops. Indeed, as the epigraph suggests, as a "symbol" of a notion of freedom in which one presumably asserts her "own freedom" without "getting in the way of anybody else." The liberal subject, I argued in the previous chapter, is a self-regulating subject. This, of course, is not a new claim, but when conceived in terms of movement it poses a theoretical problem. Often, this self-regulation is thought of as the doing of reason in its relation with desires, passions, and other inclinations: self-regulation as the reign of reason (for instance in Kant; but we must remember that also in Plato, and at this moment we see that the historical and theoretical demarcation here is questionable, and I shall return to this point soon) or as the moderation of sentiments (in Hume, or Smith, or Burke, and once again the demarcation is stretched[1]). This understanding, that has both political and epistemological articulations, is rooted in a particular ontology of subjectivity in which an element within the subject (be it mind, reason, or some other component) takes priority over other facets of subjectivity in the delineation of the "self." The "I" thus "also" "has" feelings, desires, inclinations, and even a body; but this "I" is somehow prior to them. Consider as an illustration, a ship sailing on the seas, as a scene of movement. It is the ship of Odysseus, and there are some sirens swimming around. Gerald Dworkin's description of the scene in which Odysseus requests to tie his body to the boat so not to be lured by them is telling. For Dworkin this self-imposed limitation of movement is an act of imposing impediments upon one's liberty. Significantly, liberty is still imagined here via the figure of mobility, yet the fact that the act is an act of limitation merely demonstrates according to Dworkin that liberty itself should be sidelined and replaced with a theory of autonomy. This act, after all, shows that Odysseus "has a preference about his preferences, a desire not to have or to act upon various desires. He views the desire to move his ship closer to the sirens as something that is not part of him."[2] A desire that "is not a part of him," latently means that there is a "him" that goes "beyond" (deeper? Or perhaps above?), and is not shaped by the sets of preferences, desires, decisions, or corporeal acts of the person. It is precisely this entity that can be identified by ordering preferences to higher and lower levels, that then becomes the autonomous subject.

We know this structure too well of subjectivity that Nietzsche saw as the (bad) fruit of modernity. Perhaps above all, it is associated with Descartes and the model of Cartesian subjectivity. It is this very structure that has led critics of liberalism to identify liberal subjectivity with the figure of "the eye from nowhere," in Donna Haraway's famous formulation: a disembodied, juridical configuration, occupying no space (and thus universal),[3] and consequently, a figure without any physical movement, or at least a figure to which movement is politically insignificant.

The purpose of this chapter is to revisit this reading of liberal subjectivity in order to create a theoretical foundation for the argument of the previous chapter. I set to call attention to the fact that even within the grammar and logic of liberalism itself (rather than the point of view of a critique), the body was significant, even if it took a specific—quite narrow—form: locomotion. The chapter thus presents two central arguments. The first, pursuing a claim made in passing by Hannah Arendt,[4] proposes that at least until the eighteenth century, freedom of movement was the materialization of the liberal concept of liberty. The second proposes that movement was a primary mode of corporealization of the subject situated at the core of liberal theory. In other words, the liberal subject appeared as a concrete, embodied being in the moments in which she can be configured, as a moving body.

By situating freedom of movement at the heart of the early conceptualizations of what would eventually coalesce as the liberal notion of freedom, I aim to show that the much-criticized notion of abstracted subjectivity was not essential to the conceptual core of the liberal logic, but was rather a function of a later marginalization of movement. The idea of "freedom as a phenomenon of the will," which in Linda Zerilli's words, "we . . . have inherited from the Western philosophical and political tradition,"[5] was not intrinsic to early liberals. In its earlier stages, liberalism still recognized that the free subject was necessarily an embodied subject, even if its embodiment was different from the diversified modes of embodiment that critical theory has subsequently postulated. Yet this crystallization of the body of the liberal subject around movement, or as a moving body, is not a mere history. The moving body, which stood at the core of liberal subjectivity, liberty, and law, was not completely erased from the political scene of liberalism even in succeeding decades. It left traces—even if at times latent—on later moments of this discourse. The focus on movement in the early sources of liberal theory allows us to excavate this hidden theme that should then become the hinge of the differentiation we saw in the previous chapters: a contemporary split organized around mobility between (I) the citizen (often as a racialized, classed, ethnically marked, and gendered entity more than a juridical one), as a figure of "good," "purposive," even "rational," and often "progressive" mobility that should be maximized; and (II) other(ed) groups, whose patterns of movement are both marked and produced as a disruption, a danger, a delinquency.

My point here is not to express a yearning for early liberalism. The limitations of the early concept of freedom-as-movement, its normalizing functions, its exclusionary practices, and its partaking in colonial logic and projects, will become apparent as the argument unfolds. Furthermore, we should keep in mind that the focus on movement-as-liberty was, to a large extent, a function of a limited understanding of political powers: when they are reduced to the power to take lives or imprison the living,[6] liberty becomes reducible to the ability to move. As Foucault (but already Mill[7]) shows us, since the early modern incarnations of sovereignty, the models and technologies of power have become more complex and multifaceted, and so has the understanding of power. With this change in both the operation and conceptualization of power, the object of freedom has become more multifaceted as well. My purpose here is therefore twofold. First, I seek to propose a more nuanced understanding of the liberal subject who has become something of a strawman in contemporary critiques of the liberal tradition. Second, I seek to provide a framework to tracking the current traces of these notions of freedom and subjectivity: detention and deportability; the political prevalence of the camp and the theoretical allure of its figure; practices of border crossing and global hierarchies (religious, racial, economic); mass incarceration and citizenship, all are different contexts within which the ideas herein have incarnated.

The core of my argument is simple and is limited to a particular (even if quite wide) discursive moment in which we begin to see forming the idea that the citizen—to some extent a newly emerging political entity at the time—is a function of particular patterns of movement. I claim that in the seventeenth and eighteenth centuries, free movement was a quintessential element in the corpus of work that would become the foundation of liberal thought. This element was later suppressed, even denied in the more formal versions of later liberalism, but remains latently central. This historical demarcation does not aim at intervening in the much-disputed question regarding where and when to draw the line from which we can begin to talk about liberalism.[8] Since discourses form slowly and gradually and by an ongoing series of exclusions, demarcations, and reflections, marking an exact line here seems to me a futile task. Within the many definitions given to this school, my use of the term seeks to denote a political philosophy that relies on a particular ontology of the subject—an ontology deriving a certain understanding of governance, rule, and order. This ontology can be traced back to the seventeenth century, if not earlier, and this chapter examines some of the key texts from which it emerges. For this reason the core of the argument and the historical limits set upon it must be unraveled. Hence, this chapter proposes momentary glances to other, earlier or later moments, including nineteenth century suffragists or Plato. By allowing the argument to resonate with other historical moments I seek to define the focal point of a particular logic or structure, but also to identify its roots, to point to the traces it leaves after it seemingly dissipates, and to demonstrate that this structure is much more pervasive than what the narrower demarcation allows us to see.

I begin with Thomas Hobbes, who provides us with one of the clearest articulations of the symbiosis between physical movement and liberty. In addition, Hobbes roughly marks the chronological departure point for my argument. I then move to some shorter reflections on Immanuel Kant, Mary

Wollstonecraft, and John Locke—a somewhat associative assemblage that is brought together to show the links between movement and rationality and to demonstrate that movement remains a privileged form through which the subject appears as corporeal in the liberal political sphere even when freedom is conceived in more abstract terms (such as the reign of rationality in Kant). The preceding section provides a more systematic analysis of freedom and movement in Locke, which is followed by an endeavor, anchored in William Blackstone, to reveal some of the facets of movement that have rendered it so available and appealing for liberal thought. I end in the nineteenth century, with a campaign for dress reform lead by key American suffragists. As I shall argue, by this period freedom would largely be detached from the moving body and attached to the will, and yet I believe that the story of this campaign powerfully demonstrates my claims herein. Bringing gender—and with it the body—to the fore, the campaign for dress reform reveals how the body is primarily configured as a moving body when it surfaces in later liberal constellations. As I briefly argued in regard to Mill in the introduction, at the margins of liberal discourse, embodying those who still struggle to obtain the full status of the subject-citizen, movement is found as the primary manifestation of freedom, even in the nineteenth century.

Hobbes: Motion and Corporeal Liberty

The emergence of "that social and political structure of self-determination we recognize as liberalism," argues John Rogers in *The Matter of Revolution*, was bound with a revolution in the way science largely understood physical motion.[9] As the scientific models of motion shifted in the seventeenth century, with the theories of Kepler, Galileo, Harvey, and Newton, philosophy was riveted by debates concerning the nature of movement.[10] This fascination with motion was not just the concern of philosophy of nature. It was the concern of political philosophy as well (if the two could be separated).[11] Mid-seventeenth-century theorists, predominantly in England, configured the world of social and political hierarchies and that of physical motion (the circulation of blood, the falling of stones, or the collisions of atomic particles) not simply as analogues (as substance of metaphorical illustrations), but as ontologically interdependent. Hobbes, argues Rogers, is "perhaps the best example for this fascinating discursive interdependence."[12]

In a way, Hobbes is a philosopher of movement.[13] For him, everything is eventually reducible to motion. From his account of cognition, sensation, and imagination, to his understanding of desire and pleasure and to his conception of good and evil, "life," he argues, "is nothing but motion."[14] And since "motion produces nothing but motion,"[15] political reality cannot consist of anything else. Not only are motions political matters according to Hobbes, then; as the matter of everything, they are also the matter of politics. Yet this claim remains somewhat empty. Encompassing everything, it says almost nothing. While it indicates that one cannot fully understand Hobbes's political theory without understanding his natural mechanics of which movement is the foundation, it does not indicate the particular nature of *political* movement within the Hobbesian political thought.

Rogers, much like Thomas Spragens before him, situates the coproduction of motion and political relations primarily in Hobbes's state of nature and the political arrangement it dictates. Like the bodies of people in the state of nature, the bodies in Hobbes's natural philosophy collide violently. Their movement has no telos, and their motion is not a function of agency but the result of the physical force of one body against another. Therefore, this movement has to be controlled from *outside*. Rogers contends that this model "offered scientific proof for the necessity and inevitability of a political process of conquest and domination."[16] Accordingly, Hobbes is situated in *The Matters of Revolution* on an opposite pole to vitalist notions of self-motion that would give rise to the liberal configuration of anti-authoritative individual liberty. Without contradicting this claim, I propose that a more detailed account of the particular human movement in Hobbes's writings (rather than the violent, frenzied motion of physical particles) collapses this opposition. It ties Hobbes's movement to liberty rather than necessity (which is bound in these accounts to absolutism) and situates him on a continuum with liberal theories.

Liberty, Hobbes asserts, is merely a particular relation between the body's natural ability to move and the available possibilities to actualize it. In other words, liberty is "the absence of . . . *external impediments of motion*." It is primarily "freedom from chains, and prison,"[17] situated within a minimal matrix wherein the degree of one's freedom is a function of her available space for movement ("so that a man who is held in custody in a large prison has more liberty than in a cramped one").[18] Accordingly, liberty is an attribute of bodies alone. Applying the concept "to any thing but *Bodies*," is an "abuse" of the term according to Hobbes, "for that which is not the subject of Motion is not the subject of Impediment."[19]

This definition applies to the freedom of water going downstream, as well as a pen falling from the desk or a person moving her arm. Still, there are some modes of motion that are more particularly human and may thus have more political bearings. Within a political community human beings have a dual existence. As Quentin Skinner notes, "as soon as we leave the world of nature . . . and enter the artificial world of the commonwealth, we are no longer simply bodies in motion; we are also subjects of sovereign power." Hobbes upholds this duality not for its own sake but to counter republican notions of liberty by "[turning] every subject into the author of all the actions performed by the sovereign,"[20] yet this duality nonetheless means that he has to assume some bifurcation within the individual: in the commonwealth, humans are (a) bodies in motion as well as (b) artificial (juridical) creatures: subjects.[21] When running away from a king seeking to kill him, for example, the subject is divided: as an individual body he escapes punishment, yet—Hobbes insists—he escapes from *himself* in his capacity as part of the sovereign: after all, "he is the author of his own punishment, as being by the Institution, Author of all his Sovereign shall do."[22]

Undoubtedly, all this is crucial to Hobbes for one major purpose: to be able to argue that "to do injury to ones selfe, is Impossible";[23] to claim that the sovereign cannot be accused of injustice. Yet I am more interested in the ontological apparatus that must be at play for this argument to work. The question then arises: who, or what is this "author" whose body is the sovereign (or commonwealth; and Hobbes keeps moving between these two anatomies). As such an author, I will aim to show, the subject must be a juridical being, trading in rights and liberties.

Once we recognize this bifurcation we can probe the typology of freedom across these two strata of political subjectivity. On the first level, that of subjects as moving bodies (but eventually, as we shall see by the end of this section, on the second level as well), "life is but a motion of Limbs."[24] It is on this level that the liberty to move without external impediments is at play. That is to say, on this level, subjects remain free within political communities as natural men, that is, precisely in the domains in which they are not integrated into the sovereign's will/action. Put differently, here we face the corporeal liberty of the subjects *as individuals*. Freedom here is primarily what is often referred to as "negative" freedom: a freedom that "dependeth on the silence of the Law," which is indeed, "the Greatest Liberty of subjects."[25] This freedom is a function of the existence of natural enclaves within political existence, of some islands maintaining the logic and structure of the state of nature, even if they are now circumscribed by law. Some of these enclaves are created in the areas to which the law does not penetrate (when there is no law forbidding a specific action); some are produced because some natural rights can never be denied;[26] other enclaves are a function of the always-given possibility not to obey the law: the subject's abstract existence is limited by abstract, "Artificiall Chains"[27]—laws—which as such pose a weak limitation upon one's natural, corporeal capacity of movement and can always be broken. The first two enclaves point to the areas of life that were not—or not yet, or cannot be—subsumed by the sovereign. In these areas we do not have subjects in the full meaning of the word: those entities composing sovereignty itself, the authors of the sovereign action, the delegators of authority. We have a natural multitude which, as such, "in not *One*, but *Many*."[28] The last enclave points to the fact that even when she is integrated to the statist, legal order, like those small figures composing the commonwealth on the frontispiece of *Leviathan*, even when her movements are the function of the sovereign's will and the sovereign's movements are but a function of hers, the subject can always reassume her individual existence. She can always act in her capacity as an individual body, even if it means disobeying the law. Political existence and political limitations upon liberty are therefore but a thin shell, covering an ever-lingering natural (corporeal) existence. At the core, we remain bodies in motion.

It is worthwhile emphasizing that this understanding of law as chains and of a contract as something that binds, situates all modes of freedom within the paradigm of corporeal liberty. Hence, within these different variations, freedom remains but the lack of external impediments on motion.

Yet this notion of freedom does not fully satisfy Hobbes, who appears to be torn between two concepts of liberty. On the one hand, he maintains that "a free subject" is but "words . . . without meaning"[29] (significantly a claim he makes as an aside to provide an example of the meaning of absurdity). However, on the other hand, Hobbes endeavors to find a concept of freedom that would enable him to assert the individual's freedom also *as a subject*. This is the second level of human's political existence. Yet talking about freedom on this level (that is, as applying to subjects rather than "natural" men) is not straightforward. Let us examine it more closely.

Whereas at moments the law appears in *Leviathan* as a limitation upon freedom, as chains (even if abstract) impeding corporeal movement, at other moments Hobbes can argue that "the use of Lawes . . . is not to bind the People from all Voluntary actions; but to direct and keep them in such a motion, as not to hurt themselves by their own impetuous desires, rashnesse, or indiscrimination; as Hedges are set, not to stop Travellers, but to keep them in the way."[30] Here the law seems to be a fence indeed, yet rather than an impediment it is a means to facilitate (safe) movement. Nancy Hirschmann identifies this tension in Hobbes's conceptualization of the law and tries to solve it by reading Hobbes as proposing a positive concept of freedom alongside his negative one. The social contract, she argues, is a means "to create people to want the very order that the sovereign is to impose, to 'tame' natural man into civil man and substitute one set of desires for another."[31] The social contract, Hirschmann argues, forms not merely the sovereign as an artificial person, but a new person in each of us, who would learn to *will* the limits of the law.

This solution, however, seems to require a complete suspension, at least in certain moments, of Hobbes's negative concept of liberty: the hedge, after all, remains an external impediment of motion no matter how our will is formed. Unless, that is, we take seriously his understanding of the subject as a fragment of the sovereign. This returns us to my claim regarding the split within the subject: to avoid this externality of the hedge, Hobbes must assume alongside our individual will a will to which the law itself (as an impediment) is immanent. Only then the law no longer poses an external impediment of motion; it would rather be integrated to one's internal calculations and motivations. But it seems that if the law operates immanently, within a subject now configured within judicial language, its symbiosis cannot be with the body. The individual's "own impetuous desires, rashnesse, or indiscrimination" in the above quote, attest to the fact that as a corporeal being, the subject is at odds with the law (or the sovereign). The law appears here as operating against the natural inclinations of the body, which in turn shivers with fear. Both this fear—the primary doing of the sovereign—and the desire that should be restrained, suggest that unless we want to read the multifaceted Freudian subject into Hobbes,[32] the law remains external to the body. How can it thus be immanent?

The one element the individual gives to the common—thereby both creating the sovereign and becoming a subject—is his rights.[33] Therefore, it is as a contracting anchor of rights that he becomes free not only as a man (free *from* the intervention of the law) but also as a subject (free *in and through* the formation and operation of laws, "the Author" of the sovereign actions[34]). And here, I believe, we see emerging the model that will become so crucial to the liberal ontology of the subject: the subject as an empty, juridical, contracting artifact.

However, how can the subject be free (potentially or actually) if she is indeed a noncorporeal being? Any attempt to argue that she is free or not—any attempt to even pose the question of freedom—would be, in Hobbes's own words, "an abuse" of the concept. To cast it in Hirschmann's terms, it seems that if Hobbes indeed has both negative and positive concepts of freedom, they are in conflict with each other. I want to propose first, that Hobbes's concept of movement enables him to bypass this tension and think of the transference of rights as a corporeal process; and second, that this solution entails a conceptualization of the subject within the aforementioned logic of self-regulated movement.

Before moving to Hobbes's solution let me reiterate the argument. Since he sees movement as the lack of external impediments on motion, that is, as an attribute of bodies alone, Hobbes seems to be in a bind. This notion of freedom can be applied to people as individuals, in as much as they are given in a certain conflict with the sovereign: corporeal beings, driven by tendencies and desires,[35] whose freedom is *from* the law. On its side of this equation, the law is seen as an external impediment: chains. But Hobbes upholds a second notion of freedom, in which the subject and the sovereign are in harmony. Almost paradoxically, it is here, in his most absolutist moments, that Hobbes begins to conceive the model of subjectivity that Rawls would bring to perfection.

There are elements in Hobbes's thinking that have been identified as kernels of the liberal tradition: the radical individuation, the isolation of human beings, or the ontological and chronological primacy of the individual over the state. Here transpires an additional element: the division, even tension Hobbes has to assume between the political, judicial existence, and the material one. At this point we return to the problem in which we paused: such a divorce of formal subjectivity and material one seems to require a concept of freedom that is no longer the lack of external impediment of motion applying only to bodies. And yet Hobbes does not provide us with another such concept. Rather, he reconstructs the contracting, judicial being as a body in motion. I do not put forth this claim (that will be explicated momentarily) to advocate yet another reading of Hobbes as radically reductionist in his materialism. My purpose is rather to propose that through an amalgamation of consent with motion, the model of self-regulation crystalizes. Hobbes's account of servitude demonstrates this point most lucidly.

Differentiating servitude from slavery or captivity, Hobbes points to two intertwined elements that reveal the essential attributes of his concept of freedom. First, the servant, unlike the slave or the captive, is not bound with chains (or confined within the walls of the prison). To put it differently, he can move freely. And second, unlike the others, the servant has conveyed, "either in expressed words, or by other sufficient signes," a will.[36] The servant has agreed to his situation. The two, consent and movement, are what makes him free and they cannot be separated: consent can be inferred precisely from the lack of bondage. At the same time, since in the Hobbesian mechanics an action always entails the will to act,[37] will and movement conflate at the moment of action. Movement, will, consent, and freedom thus become inseparable. Since the servant functions as Hobbes's model for subjecthood in general,[38] the split between the two dimensions of the subject is thereby bridged. We can therefore see that also as an artificial, contracting being, the subject maintains at least a certain degree of corporeality (and thus of potential liberty). Even if as a scared, desiring creature his body is not integral to his political existence, *in its capacity as a moving entity, his body is an essential part of the political domain.*

Note that this notion of "corporeal liberty" is quite limited. The servant is the one who agreed "not to *run away*"[39] and was taken out of his chains only due to this agreement. His external chains are merely replaced by internal ones. The point here is not to rehearse the claim that a narrow concept of freedom allows Hobbes to maintain that subjects can be free even under the most absolutist regime. The point goes further also than showing that the assumption of internal chains allows Hobbes to coherently argue the servant is free, given his definition of freedom as the lack of *external* limitation on movement. The point, furthermore, is that *freedom becomes here self-restrained motion.* The servant who does not run is precisely the individual who regulates himself—restrains himself so not to be restrained by others. And significantly, it is movement that is (self) regulated here. Unlike the chaotic movement of ceaselessly colliding particles of the state of nature with which I opened this section, *the servant's movement is the rudimentary foundation for the ideal Schiller saw in the English dance (in the epigraph of this chapter): a movement that "is so ordered," it follows merely one's own inclinations yet without ever colliding with others.*

In Hobbes, this regulation still lacks the apparatuses that would cultivate it and integrate it with the identity of the subject (apparatuses ranging from education to national symbols). Hence, it rests on fear alone: fear is the only political technology in the Hobbesian world and therefore, much like in Greenblatt's proposition that the Hobbesian subject is but its own surface,[40] the mechanism we see with the servant remains shallow. Nevertheless, this is the idea—the ideal—liberalism is to develop, better, and refine and that would eventually frame the state as a mechanism for monopolization of the means of movement, to refer back to John Torpey.[41] This would be the ultimate and perfected meaning of the internalization of the hedge above.

Once the individual limits her own movement, an act of substitution allows a sphere of full freedom: Hobbes's idea that from the moment of consent (or covenant) the will of the master, as well as the master's actions, are also the servant's, implies that the scope of available movement of the latter is as wide as the former's.[42] With this displacement of liberty/movement to the master, the liberty of the subject maintains its full potency and is even boosted by being attached to the body of the sovereign.

Indeed, Hobbes's sovereign is itself an artifact and not a concrete master (or king), but Hobbes insists on the corporeality of this artificiality. At stake, as Steven Shapin and Simon Schaffer have shown, is not merely a consistency in Hobbes's philosophy of nature (or his political philosophy, as I argued here), but the very possibility of political order.[43] And unlike the individual subject, who may maintain some degree of corporeality even as a political being, the sovereign is a truly political body and hence the only political being that can genuinely be free. Hobbes's repeated emphasis that within a political community freedom is primarily an attribute of sovereigns should therefore be understood not only through the prism of war (through the idea that sovereigns maintain the absolute natural liberty for all things and are, therefore, in a state of nature vis-à-vis each other), but also through the prism of movement (and on some level the two are intimately connected[44]). Moreover, his insistence that the commonwealth is indeed a body suggests that at all political levels, Hobbes conceived freedom as the potential scope available for motion.

This last statement, however, remains somewhat perplexing unless we understand it as an allegory. After all, the state and the body do not move in the same way; the movement of the sovereign is not identical to the movement of nerves or bones. At this moment the argument collapses: understanding this statement as an allegory re-presents the paradox emerging from ascribing liberty to noncorporeal beings. Hobbes, then, does not solve the tension at the core of his notion of liberty. He rather hides it by relying on the flexible nature of the concept of movement, its ability to house ambivalence between the physical and the figurative we identified in the previous section. We may further propose that by enabling the concrete meaning to dwindle and become figurative without becoming a metaphor, the ambivalent nature of movement enables Hobbes to slide from the movement of the organic to the movement of the artificial and thereby disguise a gap between the organic and the artificial that is embedded to his concept of sovereignty.[45]

This ambiguity will continue to occupy the text (Hobbes's, as well as my own) and it might not be accidental. Much like Hobbes, I will keep sliding here between, on the one hand, motion-as-a-metaphor in political thought, as a metonym, an index, a symbol, or a figurative illustration (for something else); and on the other hand the role of concrete motion, both in political thought and in politics. This is since these two hands, as it were, cannot be distinguished quite easily as might often seem.[46] Movement is at once a *physical* phenomenon that becomes a *metaphor* (and we should ask: why? for what purpose? with what implications?); a metaphor that constitutes a *concrete reality*; and the *material* form through which other questions are negotiated (questions of freedom, citizenship, location, right) and that thereby becomes a *technology of rule*. The question should therefore not be how literal was Hobbes (or many others philosophers in the many pages to follow), but rather: what does this prism of movement allow him to do; how does it circumscribe the political frame he demarcates; and what is the relation—if the separation can at all be assumed—between these images, these figures of movement, and the physical movements of political realities?[47]

Rational Bodies, Mobile Subjects, Confined Movement

Whereas Hobbes is quite exceptional in the systematic and explicit account of movement in his political writings, many of the texts that would become part of the cannon of liberalism keep appealing to movement as articulating freedom. We may begin by taking Mary Wollstonecraft as another example.

The body plays a dual role in Wollstonecraft's *The Vindication of the Rights of Women*. On the one hand, it is a "prison," a "cage" for the mind. Encaged within a body, the mind might be spatialized as well—and one may read Wollstonecraft as calling to set it free to its own movement. (And hasn't rationality, whose cultivation Wollstonecraft advocates, been conceptualized as such a movement since Plato has perceived it in the image of a movement of the soul towards the ideas?[48]) At any rate, women are, "literally speaking, slaves to their bodies," and at times the *Vindication* seems to assume a zero-sum game between the body and a different entity (or entities) marked as the soul or the mind. It is a game in which "calling the attention continually to the body cramps the activity of the mind."[49]

Yet this body, in its capacity as woman's cage, is a very particular body. We find the typology of this body in the figure of the idle woman (an early incarnation of the figure of the hysteric woman Foucault has captured so well), which was the object of countless conduct manuals at the time.[50] It is the pampered body, the object of beauty, whose essence is genteelness and hence weakness. This obsession with pampering and its resultant fragility confine women to "sedentary employments:" "To preserve personal beauty," writes Wollstonecraft, "the limbs and faculties [of women] are cramped with worse than Chinese bands and the *sedentary* life which they are condemned to live, while boys frolic in the open air, weakens the muscles and relaxes the nerves." This, in turn, "naturally produces dependence of the mind." In short, sitting too much jeopardizes rationality. Indeed, "most of the women, in the circle of my observation, who have acted like rational creatures, or shown any vigour of intellect, have accidently been allowed to run wild."[51]

At this moment the role of the body is transformed. The body appears as conditioning the liberty of the mind rather than suppressing, or even endangering it. Yet it is a different body: an essentially moving (free?) body. If we follow this argument seriously, we can perhaps take my point regarding the role of motion in liberalism even further—although I'm not yet sure it is not taking it too far: Motion (and more accurately, the movements of limbs) was not simply the materialization of freedom, and not simply the privileged mode by which the liberal subject was corporealized, but the corporeal condition for rationality itself (and perhaps it was the first two because it was also the latter).

Barbara Arneil calls our attention to the connection made in Western political thought between rationality and ability. Arneil seems to be quite perplexed by what she sees as a recurring "conflation of physical and mental disabilities" and concludes that "there is *something* about *disability* itself and not simply the principle of 'irrationality' that leads some liberal theorists to exclude *all* disabled people from their principles of justice."[52] She traces this "something" to narratives of tragedy and loss (an account to which I shall promptly return). Yet I propose that there is a way to link rationality and presumably desirable modes of movement without recourse to notions of memory and narrative. These lines from Wollstonecraft enable us to either further refine, or somewhat revise, Arneil's conclusion: the inability to move is assumed to hold implications about a person's rationality.

If this reading seems somewhat speculative (and surely it is), Locke's notes from *Some Thoughts Concerning Education* provides us with some support. Locke's *Thoughts* is seemingly a nonpolitical conduct manual for parents or caregivers. Yet the text's objective is utterly political:[53] the goal of the book is securing the construction of, precisely, rational individuals who can become political actors on the playfield of the liberal state. Locke dedicates the first part of the book to the physical vigorousness and health of boys and girls. He argues that children should be allowed to run freely in the open air, wearing shoes with very thin—if not leaking—soles, or even better, barefoot. The shoes, much like any other item of clothing, should be tailored in a way that would not constrain the body and its movements, in order to "let nature have scope to fashion the body as she thinks best."[54] The resultant freedom of movement, which is perhaps inextricably linked to what Hirschmann described as Locke's "particular passion for the strengthening benefits of cold wet feet,"[55] is necessary, according to Locke, to the children's physical well-being. This, in turn, "set[s] [the] stage" for Locke's discussion of the development of reason by the means of education in philosophy, Greek, Latin, math, and more. The physical strength, or activity, is thus the substance upon which rationality can appear.[56] However, "ignorant nurses and other bodice-makers," who meddle "in matters they understand not,"[57] limit too often children's freedom of movement, thereby causing them permanent physical damages, and potentially—given the link above—also jeopardize their mental development. Like those "women of China" who tightly bind their daughter's feet and forever damage "the growth and health of the whole body," these ignorant English women hinder development of both body and mind.[58] The intersecting imperial and gendered dimensions of freedom as movement revealed through this appeal to the icon of the bound feet (an appeal we already met with Mill in the introduction) merits further analysis. For now I seek merely to point to the manner by which, with this image of hindered mobility and the context of its appearance in the text (other feet, and other more-or-less tight shoes, and clothes too), rationality is embodied.

This symbiosis of rationality and movement, whose reasons and full explanation still evade me, can probably best be made via Kant, the philosopher who demands we make reason the axis of everything knowable. In line with the brief temporal demarcation I sketched earlier and to which I shall return in more details later, Kant identifies freedom with autonomy, which for him, signifies first and foremost the freedom of reason. Yet when he introduces, in "What is Enlightenment," his notion of political freedom—the "freedom to make public use of one's reason"[59]—Kant appeals to a metaphor which, by now, can be taken as doing more than simply borrowing an image from one field to illustrate an altogether different one: "The man who casts off [dogmas and formulas that prevent him from 'using his own understanding'] would make an uncertain leap over the narrowest ditch, because he is not used to such free movement. That is why there are only a few men who walk firmly, and who have emerged from nonage by cultivating their own minds."[60] Emerging from nonage into the age of enlightenment is establishing a degree of free movement, which is thinking independently.[61]

If enlightenment is ultimately the moment when political freedom and rationality converge (via critique: a process through which reason learns to limit itself so to not enter into dark places of contradiction), reason can take upon itself the attribute of political liberty: movement. The conflation of free movement and free thinking here shows, once again, the leap from physical motion to something else: a physical metaphor for a nonphysical phenomenon; a disembodied thinking that might itself somehow move (not metaphorically, that is, even if abstractly—assuming we can understand movement not via spatial representations); or a metonym for rationality. It is a "critical" conflation, to use Arneil's observation, which "permeates contemporary political theory." "Critical," not merely because, as she goes on to argue, this conflation is part of a normalizing regime in which "the *physically* disabled are systematically excluded from political theories ostensibly rooted in *rational* agency";[62] not merely—moreover—because, as other scholars of disability studies have taught us, particular assumptions regarding the "normal" manners of carrying our bodies in space are translated to the construction of democratic spaces that thereby produce hierarchies, if not exclusions, by facilitating and impeding movement. This conflation is critical also because it divulges the corporeal thread of freedom (and subjectivity) in a tradition that identifies abstractness as a precondition to universalism and that presumes to pose both as its goal.

Locke: Fencing Freedom

If we return to Locke we see that the equation linking rationality and freedom is not reducible to the idea that confining the body is confining the mind. The movement that is interlaced with rationality is not each and every movement but rather restrained movement that should always be given within certain bounds—a structure we find also in Kant, and as I tried to show, is latent in Hobbes as well.

Indeed, these bounds are so significant, that at first look it might seem that in his more widely read political writings, Locke offers a version of freedom that is quite different from the concept of freedom as movement I delineated so far. Like Kant, Locke tied freedom primarily to reason (rather than the body); moreover, he emphasized stability (of the law) as a precondition for freedom; and (perhaps above all) he associated freedom with having a fence (a fence that secures one's property and limits movement, though significantly—it is the movement of others that it limits). In the *Second Treatise* Locke defines freedom under government as the a function of having "a standing rule to live by, common to every one of that society and made by the legislative power erected in it; a liberty . . . not to be subjected to the inconstant, uncertain, unknown, arbitrary will of another man."[63] Liberty thus relies on stability and regulation, and thus cannot be identified with boundless motion. Moreover, it may be limited not by physical impediments but by a will.[64] Indeed, freedom of movement—or movement in general—is not mentioned once in the *Treatise*.[65]

Almost opposite to movement, one might claim, the *Treatise* is inlaid with fences. As Wendy Brown observed, "fences, titles and enclosures are among Locke's most fecund and ubiquitous metaphors on the *Second Treatise*; they secure freedom, representation, and limits to the right of rebellion, as well as actual territory."[66] From a rather different perspective we can add that the law can function as simultaneously stabilizing and liberating—indeed, to function as liberating because of its stabilizing qualities—due to a restraint of another boundless movement: that of reason. Uday Mehta shows that Locke's free and rational individual is not a given. The rational individual has to be constructed by taming the mind from an early age to restrain its desire to cross boundaries. "Strangely," Mehta aptly notes, freedom is thus dependent upon some confinement of the individual, upon adhering to a "sedentary injunction to sit in quiet ignorance of those things beyond our reach."[67] Locke "ostensibly" uses "a language of limitations," in the words of Kirstie McClure. McClure, akin to the vast majority of literature on Locke, sees this language as one whose "primarily political concern was to delineate to proper boundaries of state power over the liberties and properties of its citizens and to discriminate between the due exercise of such power and its arbitrary excesses."[68] However, while McClure focuses on the need to limit the state, presumably to maximize the individual's (negative) freedom, Mehta enables us to see that not merely state power but the individual himself—and moreover, his liberty—may become excessive and should therefore be kept in check.

As I suggested, all this may be taken to demonstrate that Locke's definition of freedom is opposite to the one I outlined in the previous sections. However his anxiety of excess (to draw on Mehta's vocabulary) suggests that what is at stake in this enterprise of stabilization and regulation is not stopping movement but restraining it. Indeed, neither of the elements in the Lockean definitions is necessarily stationary. Take, as a first example, the law, which earlier I identified with the fixity of a fence. Contrary to such a reading—or more precisely complementary to it[69]—McClure proposes to see Locke's law (primarily his moral and/or natural law) as reflecting the countours of a divine edifice which, "amidst the flux and change of material appearances, ... directed the movement of things in a harmony analogous to the visibly regular motions of the heavens themselves."[70] Moreover, even as a fence, the law "ill deserves the name of confinement" since it "hedges us in only from bogs and precipices."[71] This fence then does not impede us, but allows us to move freely. It does not limit our movement (the movement we can rationally desire at least, if this combination makes any sense), but rather ensures that our movement is safe and secure.[72] Much like the fence that does not confine us to our home, but turns home into property, protecting the products of our toil, the bounds of freedom (as movement, but also as the rule of law or as the rule of reason, the limits of our desires, imagination, even needs) are not an impediment but a *security* measure. It is precisely the lack of such fences that prevented Locke from seeing the movement of the natives in the Americas as free. But this last claim will be suspended until the next chapter.

As a final example of the role movement has in Locke's concept of freedom in the *Second Treatise*, we can look to his notion of tacit consent. Locke presents the idea of tacit consent to argue that the generations who never explicitly gave their consent to the powers ruling them are nevertheless free. Locke claims that in this case we can infer consent, and hence freedom, from the absence of movement (the "sons," much like Hobbes's servant who agreed not to run away, do not move elsewhere), yet this inference is conditioned upon the concrete possibility of movement. The sons are free under a rule to which they have never actively consented, because they do not leave their country[73] even though they *can*: at least as Locke sees it, they can always leave and "plant in some inland, vacant places of America."[74] Furthermore, this form of staying put is itself a function of movement: the individuals concerned here do not have to be in possession of land forever. Locke argues it is sufficient they enjoy "lodging only for a week," but even "lodging" is not necessary for him: The fact that they are "barely traveling freely on the highway" is all it takes to infer their consent.[75]

Indeed, in the *Essay* Locke provides a definition of freedom that is much more in accord with the definitions of freedom as movement. It seems that Locke merely adds another component to the equation: freedom is not only the power to move but also the power to think. "All the actions, that we have any idea of, reducing themselves to these two, *viz*: thinking and motion. So far as a man has a power to think, or not to think; to move or not to move, according to the preference or direction of his own mind, so far is a man *free*."[76]

There are two main points concerning this definition that are crucial to what follows. First, one may maintain that the words "according to the preference or direction of his own mind" resituate the question of liberty within the will, thereby sidelining movement. Locke, however, provides us with an alternative way to think about liberty and to distinguish free from unfree movement without an appeal to volition. "Suppose a man be carried, whilst fast asleep, into a room where is a person he longs to see and speak with," he proposes a thought-experiment:

> and be there locked fast in, beyond his power to get out: he awakes, and is glad to find himself in so desirable company, which he stays willingly in, i.e., prefers his stay to going away. I ask, is not this stay voluntary? I think nobody will doubt it: and yet, being locked fast in, it is evident he is not at liberty not to stay, he has not freedom to be gone. So that liberty is not an idea belonging to volition, or preferring; but to the person having the power of doing, or forbearing to do, according as the mind shall choose or direct.[77]

Eventually, freedom is a function of the possibility to move otherwise or the possibility not to move. Freedom is thus a function of certain material conditions—an open door, a road to be traveled, or a land, a certain degree of rootedness.

This materiality notwithstanding, it is nonetheless important to stress that the "power to think, or not to think" was not just an addendum to physical movement or its equal pair in this definition. Ultimately, Locke's motion was an abstract principle and as such "could be ascribed to either body or mind." The impression of a moving object cannot teach us anything about this object's capacity for an action, he argues. The idea of "any *active power* to move . . . we have only from reflection on what passes in ourselves, where we find by experience, that barely by *willing* it, barely by *thought of the mind*, we can move the parts of our bodies, which were before at rest."[78] Moreover, the Lockean motion itself was "nothing but the change of distance between any two things." Put differently, motion was the trait of space rather than of bodies. Therefore, although he counts movement among the primary qualities of bodies—qualities that "are utterly inseparable from the body"—the primary site in which motion occurred was empty space.[79] And given that Locke (unlike Hobbes) thought of space in terms of void or vacuum, motion was somehow abstracted.[80] The bottom line is that this dialectic of materiality and abstraction was still not translated in Locke to the idea that the will is the bearer of liberty. In 1690 Locke could still argue that the question whether a will is free or not "is altogether improper":

> it is as insignificant to ask, whether man's *will* be free, as to ask, whether his sleep be swift, or his virtue square: *liberty* being as little applicable to the will, as swiftness of motion to sleep, or squareness to virtue.... *liberty*, which is but a power, belongs only to agents, and cannot be an attribute of modification of the *will*, which is also but a power.[81]

Almost exactly two hundred years later T. H. Green would provide a similar critique that rests on the exact opposite assumptions. It makes no sense to ask whether a will is free, he argues, because the will is free by definition: "willing constitutes freedom, and 'free will' is a pleonasm = 'free freedom.'" It is not simply that in Green's version, asking whether the will is free makes no sense since the answer is obviously yes, while in Locke the will *cannot* be free. The important difference is that in Green's view the answer can be yes because the will is no longer a power or faculty but a substance: "man's will is himself," according to Green.[82] In other words, will *is* man rather than *of* him. The subject became an abstract entity.[83]

Locomotion and the Liberal Body

This shift would become one of the most significant shifts in liberalism. It is perhaps this shift that, as Samantha Frost diagnoses in regard to Hobbes, has led us to read many earlier liberals through the prism of the Cartesian subject.[84] In other words, it is perhaps this shift, that has led us to thinking of liberal theory as posing a notion of subjectivity (and freedom) that is reducible to willing, if not reasoning. In *The Rise and Fall of Freedom of Contract*, P. S. Atiyah dates this shift to the last decades of the eighteenth century. Atiyah shows that late in the eighteenth century freedom of contract became the most essential form of freedom, as well as a paradigm for freedom in general. With it, liberty was largely detached from action and attached to intention and will. Accordingly (Atiyah nearly goes as far as to claim), with the rise of the legal paradigm of contract, a shift in the paradigm of "man" had to occur: man's *will* became the core of man's relations with his fellow men and consequently also the bearer of freedom (or oppression).[85]

As I argued (and will further demonstrate in the next section), the moving body continues to play a role even in theorists who see freedom as a function of autonomy, rationality, or law. Nevertheless, by the end of the eighteenth century, these appearances become interruptions; a mode through which the body emerges on a surface that is characterized by the very attempt to erase the body rather than the organizing principle of this surface.[86] One may argue that this shift enabled liberalism to form a more coherent, fully abstracted model of subjectivity. Indeed, Maurice Merleau-Ponty argues that the moving body poses a challenge to liberal thinking. Motion, he maintains, collapses the mind/body dichotomy by allowing us—almost forcing us—to become aware that our body is not an object like any other object but rather a threshold between objectivity and subjectivity that renders this very dichotomy impossible. Experiencing our moving body "reveals to us an ambiguous mode of existence" in which one does not "exist as a thing, or else . . . as a consciousness."[87] In so doing, our body's motions disrupt the Cartesian and then liberal model of subjectivity. Yet, the movement that transpires in many liberal texts seems to circumvent this typology, and while Merleau-Ponty's critique is undoubtedly indispensable, no less striking is the ability of liberalism to reconcile movement—more than any other facet of corporeality—with its model of subjectivity.

To examine this reconciliation (or perhaps more accurately this circumvention of the typology of motion identified by Merleau-Ponty) we can look at the concrete articulations of movement as freedom, primarily in legal writings. William Blackstone's *Commentaries on the Laws of England* thus provides an aperture to thinking of the particular configuration of movement in this context. It demonstrates how liberty can be entangled with movement without postulating a thick corporeality of the right-bearing subject. Blackstone holds to a clear bond between liberty and movement: liberty, he writes, "is the power of locomotion, of changing situation or removing one's person to whatsoever place one's own inclination may direct; without imprisonment or restraint, unless by due course of law."[88] Note that freedom is not defined here generally as freedom of motion but freedom of locomotion—it is the power to change one's position in space.[89] Since locomotion is but the power to change loci, the political question of liberty no longer focuses on the movement of limbs, as we saw with the previous authors. Although perhaps still an assumed means of movement, limbs are not mentioned at all in Blackstone's account of liberty and their role as a vehicle of locomotion remains latent. This could have been merely accidental, thus irrelevant, unless limbs would have been central to Blackstone's framework. Alongside liberty, Blackstone counts two more clusters of personal rights: property and security. Limbs repeatedly appear within the latter; they are a means of protecting the body.[90]

This centrality of limbs to security suggests that their absence from liberty might be significant.

"Liberty," "security," and "property" are all implicated in the body to some degree: security is the protection of bodies and limbs, among other things, and the primary property (both logically and temporally) is the body. Yet there is a crucial difference between these two clusters and the cluster of liberty. Security and property shape the body as a nonpolitical element, protected precisely because it belongs to the divine or natural realms. In the case of imprisonment, however, of denying liberty as the freedom of locomotion, the body becomes a political player: It is there that we find the right of habeas corpus: the right "to bring his body before the Court of King's Bench or Common Pleas."[91] So it is with motion as freedom that the body of the subject enters the law almost literally; it is here that the body is brought to the king's court, to stand, as it were, in front of the law.

But what is this body? And why is it around movement that the bodies of subjects could consolidate and draw political significance? If Merleau-Ponty keeps returning to the movement of limbs and their extensions as the manifestation and illustration (if not demonstration) for the collapse of the subject-object dichotomy, we may speculate that Blackstone's uncoupling of limbs and movement constitutes a different mode of corporeality, specifically, a much narrower body. At least as far as the question of liberty is concerned, the body is politically relevant only as a dot, changing its coordinates on a space/time matrix. We can see this change in the configuration of the body also by comparing Blackstone's account of life to Hobbes's, for whom, as we saw, movement was above all the motion of limbs. For both, life begins with the motion in the womb. In Hobbes it begins with the movement of limbs, as the embryo, "while it is in the womb, moveth its limbs with voluntary motion, for the avoiding of whatsoever troubleth it, or for the pursuing of what pleaseth it."[92] In Blackstone, however, life is the function of "stirring": of changing positions. There is life, he claims, as soon as an embryo is able to "stir in his mother's womb." The image of the full body in Hobbes's description, versus the thin image in Blackstone may be carried to their configuration of subjectivity more broadly.

This narrowness is not merely a matter of a diluted presence. With it, the body becomes objectified. It is no longer primarily a human body, or more accurately a *living* body (to refer to Merleau-Ponty) but an object that can be moved from one place to another and is not necessarily the agent of its own movement. Whereas, in an important way, the individual is still an agent of this movement—his inclination indicates its direction—it seems that something in the visual clarity (at the very least) of the moving body's agency is lost.[93] Finally, with this twofold process of thinning and objectification the body is deconcreticized and becomes a *universal* body.

These three aspects—the thin nature of a body that remains but a dot on a grid; the relative stability of the body as an object that also sets the mind apart; and the body's universality that enables us to think of an embodied subject who is nonetheless universal (or a universal subject who is nonetheless embodied)—render the body available for liberal thinking. These three aspects enable the body to enter the fore of liberal political thought, to capture the very question of liberty, without troubling too much the liberal frame.

As a Means of Conclusion: Stanton and the Chains of Fashion

I want to conclude with a story; an anecdote[94] that will manifest, first, the tie between freedom and movement; second, the fact that this tie, while repressed by the turn of the nineteenth century, is not completely effaced and resurfaces especially when other facets of the body (in my story, gender) presence it; third, the particularities of movement that render it so useable and available to the liberal universalistic framework; and finally, the meaning of movement in my analysis. History tells us that this is a true story whose protagonists should be quite familiar to anyone with some background in the history of feminism. Being a story, it has a clear point of a beginning. It was one day in 1852, when Elizabeth Miller appeared on the front lawn of her cousin, Elizabeth Cady Stanton, dressed in what would later become known as "the bloomer": wide trousers that narrow at the ankles, covered by a knee-length skirt and a corsetless top. Stanton, one of the leading suffragists of what is often termed "First Wave feminism," had a long, rich, and at times paradoxical philosophy concerning women's political status, and simply classifying her as a "liberal feminist" would be misleading. Nevertheless, it is more or less safe to argue that in the first half of the 1850s, during the time our story takes place, her arguments were primarily based on a universalistic logic, focused more on equality than on difference, sought primarily legal equality, and were translated into a form of activism that may best be described as a performance[95] of liberalism. As such, and even though the picture is more complex, we may see the Stanton of our story as a liberal feminist. But let us return to the lawn.

Stanton was enthralled by the new dress. "To see my cousin," she described it, "with a lamp in one hand and a baby in the other, walk upstairs with ease and grace, while, with flowing robes, I pulled myself up with difficulty, lamp and baby out of the question, readily convinced me that there was sore need of reform in woman's dress, and I promptly donned a similar attire."[96] Following Stanton, many other women's rights supporters began wearing the new dress[97] and a two year-long campaign for dress reform got under way.

The campaign made two main claims: First, it was argued that the tight, heavy dresses of the period caused severe damage to the bodies of women (lasting damage to their spine and many kinds of nerve diseases) and must therefore be replaced with a new, emancipatory form of dress. Second, and more significant for my purpose, it was argued that the new dress was indeed emancipatory because it enabled women to *move freely*. Stanton reported that the change of dress made her feel "like a captive set free from his ball and chain." She celebrated the new freedom the bloomer bestowed upon her body: "I was always ready for a brisk walk throughout sleet and snow and rain, to climb a mountain, jump over a fence, work in the garden . . . what a sense of liberty I felt with no skirt to hold or brush."[98]

This freedom of movement, however, was more than just a matter of leisure and enjoyment (climbing a mountain or working in the garden). It was a matter of life and death (or so it was portrayed). When her son, who stayed at a boys' boarding school, asked her not to come visiting him in her new costume (since it was the target of much scorn and was considered quite scandalous), Stanton pleaded with him to reconsider. She asked whether he would enjoy walking down the fields with her when she arrived, and how he expected her to do so with her former long and heavy dress. But even if she were able to take this walk with him, slowly and with much effort, what would happen, she queried, if a bull suddenly ran toward them; how would she be able to run, jump behind a fence, and preserve her life in that dress?[99] Since this argument is somewhat preposterous, one cannot avoid wondering whether it is not overargued in order to make another point.

When we consider the bloomer episode against the history and symbolism of Victorian dressing, this point may become apparent. What would become known as Victorian women's dress began to fashion in the eighteenth century together with the establishment of the separate spheres, as a mark, as well as a technology, of confining upper- and middle-class women to the domestic sphere.[100] Accordingly, the appeal for dress reform emphasized locomotion as a form and a symbol of transgressing the private sphere and occupying an equal position in the public, economic, as well as political spheres. Yet "symbol" may be too weak of a term here. At times it seemed that the dress and the freedom of movement it enabled became the essence of women's liberation. Gerrit Smith (Elizabeth Miller's father), a keen supporter of woman's suffrage as well as the bloomer, went as far as refusing to attend the 1856 Woman's Rights Convention because most suffragists abandoned the new dress:

> I believe that poverty is the great curse of woman, and that she is powerless to assert her rights, because she is poor. Woman must go to work and get rid of her poverty, but that she cannot do in her present disabling dress, and she seems determined not to cast it aside. She is unwilling to sacrifice grace and fashion, even to gain her right. . . . Were woman to adopt a rational dress, a dress that would not hinder her from any employment, how quickly would she rise from her present degrading dependence on man! How quickly would the marriage contract be modified and made to recognize the equal rights of the parties to it! And how quickly would she gain access to the ballot-box.[101]

Smith was not exceptional in these words. Similar arguments, in which various explanations of women's oppression are channeled through dress, recurred throughout the bloomer episode. For two years then, the old style of dress became the emblem, the cause and the foundation of all other types of women's subjection—from economic dependency to the lack of the vote—and a striking share of the debates concerning women's political status suddenly passed through the question of clothing and fashion, which was predominantly a question of physical mobility.

"Mobility" in this context has a double meaning: the physical movement of human bodies, as well as social mobility; simultaneously a transgression of a sphere and the crossing of a doorstep. Yet these meanings, which can perhaps be marked as literal and metaphorical, collapse here into one. The social mobility *is* a function of the physical ability to walk, climb upstairs, or run in a field, and these physical movements *are* the manifestation (the result, but also the meaning) of a social transgression. This duality of the concept was central to this chapter, and so is the context within which it appears. At a specific moment in the history of women's suffrage, movement emerges as "the most perfectly appropriate symbol of the assertion of one's own freedom," to use Schiller's words with which the chapter was opened. But the bloomer was more than a symbol for movement (which in its turn symbolized freedom); it was a schema to understanding how freedom is negotiated. Movement functioned here as the substance of claims for equality—and even more so, claims for women's inclusion within a universalistic frame—that nonetheless took the body into account. Finally, and most important in the context of my argument: through it, the moving body became a conduit through which other modes of oppression could be attached to the body, and essentially corporeal challenges (such as health) could appear as political.

This story can thus be seen as encapsulating the meaning I suggest movement has within the liberal frame. Within this story, motion emerges as a privileged mode of materialization of the liberal political subject, a key form through which the liberal subject could appear as both political and corporeal.

But this story makes visible another feature of the idea of movement as freedom that so far remained latent. Through Locke (but also Hobbes) we saw that to become the matter of freedom, movement must be given within bounds. In Stanton these bounds receive a denser normalizing texture. While she does mention climbing a mountain as a desired result of her new freedom of movement, most of the movements to which she points are modes of movements within quite traditional gendered prescriptions: moving with a baby (and a lamp) and working in the garden. Moving freely does not necessarily entail departing from existing roles and social expectations. It is given within an array of limits of many kinds and the notion of regulation situates it within a matrix of (self) control. Liberalism cannot imagine a freedom without this matrix, as I will try to show in the next chapter. When it is presumed to be absent or lacking, liberalism does not assume full emancipation but calls for much more pervasive control.[102]

4 / The Problem of "Excessive" Movement

> Among the supposed juridical distinctions between civilized and non-civilized peoples was an attitude toward land, almost a doxology about land which non-civilized people supposedly lacked. A civilized man, it was believed, could cultivate the land because it meant something to him; on it accordingly he bred useful arts and crafts, he created, he accomplished, he built. For an uncivilized people land was either farmed badly (i.e., inefficiently by Western standards) or it was left to rot. From this string of ideas, by which whole native societies who lived on American, African, and Asian territories for centuries were suddenly denied their right to live on that land, came the great dispossessing movements of modern European colonialism.... Land in Asia, Africa, and the Americas was there for European exploitation, because Europe understood the value of land in a way impossible for the natives. —EDWARD SAID, "Zionism from the Standpoint of Its Victims."

"The state," James Scott argues, "has always seemed to be the enemy of 'people who move around.'"[1] At the same time, movement—in its varied meanings, attached to various objects, circulating between the metaphoric and the concrete—has been celebrated as a manifestation of freedom. In the seventeenth century, with early modern formulations of the idea that the state can either be free or promote freedom, these two configurations of movement came into conflict. This chapter focuses on Hobbes and Locke to examine how this tension was negotiated, settled, and unleashed. More specifically, it seeks to trace a history of the ideas that articulate the desire to regulate and restrain movement—even before the state was able to systematically and pervasively do so, and potentially before it could even conceive of the possibility of such regulation.[2]

As the previous chapter argued, movement had to be regulated, and self-regulated, for it to appear as the principle and matter of freedom. It had to be tamed—domesticated as William Walters would have it—before it could materialize into a substance of liberal politics: a form, a symbol, and an articulation of individual freedom or a globalized regime of circulation of "resources, whether investment, goods, services, and . . . (the right kind of) people."[3] In this chapter I want to propound that land and property served as rudimentary mechanisms of the later technologies of self-regulation. They furnished movement with gravitas that stabilized it, restrained it, and allowed it to take shape *as* freedom. Land and property, however, were not the share of all, and therefore, neither was freedom. Whereas the previous chapter focused on the subject capable of freedom, this chapter shifts our gaze to those who presumably lacked such mechanisms of restraint, whose movement was deemed as excessive, and who were therefore conceived as always already unfree. Without a particular model of settled ownership, movement was not the "safe" movement directed by the law in its capacity as a hedge. It was rather erupting savagery. And ever since Plato, whose democratic city is terrifyingly a city in which animals roam freely in the street and citizens jump too much when engaged in legislation,[4] such unbound movement carried the danger of excess, and when marked as excessive was configured as a threat.

The division that transpires splits the regulated and ordered movement of able and masculine European bodies (a type of movement configured as freedom) from other movements. This is the division we encountered in the first chapter between the addressees of the imaginary and the white lines. The bifurcation is marked upon several, shifting lines (the most familiar on the list are racial, geographic, ethnic, class, or gender lines) and it is part of establishing and justifying a divided mode of governance within a presumably universal frame of liberalism. The circulation of images of transgressive movement, as well as concrete apparatuses that rendered movement transgressive, formed a strikingly shared network of justification upon which many modes of exclusion and hierarchization rested: colonialism as a mass project of land appropriation, the denial of women's equal political status and their confinement within the domestic sphere, and the usurpation of poor populations.

Here I focus on two of these dividing lines which, I will show, overlap in significant ways. The primary focus of this chapter is a split that can be marked—even if anachronistically—as "racial" but should more accurately be termed "geographical": a division between European and colonized subjects.[5] The second is a division between two newly emerging classes: landowners and those whose access to land was tenuous, who thus often became (or were assumed to be) vagrants, and who would later give rise to a more stable class: the poor.

Critiques of liberalism often accuse it of fabricating a fiction of universality by allocating corporeality to subjects at the margins of the discourse (women, poor, colonized, and so forth). This fiction of abstractness enables liberalism to present itself as a universalistic project while engaging in practices of exclusion.[6] In other words, difference was produced by constructing some subjects as "overwhelmingly corporeal,"[7] and others as essentially bodyless. Without undermining this critique, I propose that the fundamental difference between the subjects at the core of liberal discourse and those at its margins was rather a *difference within bodies*. Movement itself played a significant role in ingraining difference into the bodies of subjects. Some forms of movement functioned as a pivot around which the body was able to materialize and yet remain universal. Moreover, these forms of movement served to encapsulate the liberal notion of nonauthoritative order: self-regulated, contained, and anchored to the land. They thus enabled liberalism to imagine and point to the possibility of an ordered freedom. Other forms of movement served to construct an undisciplinable—an uncivilizable—corporeality, which was configured outside of normalizing regimes of subjectivity (and yet still within liberal governance).

I should clarify at this point that the notion of "surplus" movement should not be read as a claim regarding real patterns of movement of specific groups or people. Rather, it is a claim regarding what Serhat Karakayali and Enrica Rigo refer to as "figures of mobility," which represent "categories of governance" more than the concrete bodily experience of individuals (or groups).[8] I therefore seek to trace certain modes of mapping. I seek to examine how the assumed movements of different groups (movements that rest on images that may be real, imagined, or some combination of both) were mapped into schemas of governance. Yet the ideas of "assumption," "figures" or "images" should be posed more carefully, and within a more Foucauldian framework. The image of excessive movement of colonized, feminized, or classed subjects (and there is always an etcetera here) can never be limited to a subjective impression of some upper/middle-class European men. The excess of movement is a material effect of the assumption regarding its existence. Some movements are constantly produced as nonrestrainable, nondisciplinable, excessive. Often this production is tightly entangled with the depictions I shall survey herein, even if they are essentially mythical or imagined. In a way, this is a banal point: assumptions about someone or something often constitute its reality. As Edward Said observes in the epigraph above, the very postulation of "improper" movement facilitated—still facilitates—a process of breaking the tie between indigenous populations and the land (expropriation, occupation). It thereby often produces concrete instances of movement, whose excess distances it from an experience of freedom (expulsion, diaspora, an almost permanent refugee status).

After a short introduction, I turn to the portrayal of excessive movement in Hobbes. Writing still at the early stages of colonial expansion, Hobbes is situated on the threshold of the particular logic for which Locke will serve as a more iconic example. My argument will be in two parts. First, I will show that Hobbes sees some modes of movements—though still, significantly, not exclusively the movements of "othered" subjects—as excessive and thus dangerous. Second, I shall read Hobbes's civil society as a mode of taming movement—though still not completely. I propose that the main benefit of this taming is time: society decelerates, as it were, the hectic nature of life. Eventually time becomes for Hobbes the meeting point of security, rationality, and freedom. The ensuing section moves from Hobbes to Locke, and from time to space. I argue that Locke's rational, self-regulating, and free man was also a function of an enclosed, demarcated, even fenced space. I begin this chapter, however, with Plato in order to identify not the roots of, but perhaps more accurately, the pervasiveness of the framework that ties moderated movement to freedom, and presumably excessive movement to problems of security (a configuration of unbound movement as a threat). This is not to propose that we have here the same configuration of the relations between movement, security, and freedom, but rather to point to different incarnations of a similar logic. What remains to be unfurled, and what this book outlines only partially, are the particularities of the material formations of this logic in different spaces and times. We need, in other words, to unpack the manner in which particular configurations of rule articulate, materialize and give rise to the conjunction of security and movement, as well as the metamorphoses of freedom within these configurations.

As a Means of Introduction: Plato and the Problem of Movement

In his critique of the democratic *polis*, Plato marks a triangularity connecting liberty, movement, and danger. As he saw it, one of the main problems of the democratic polis—the form of political organization valuing liberty most of all—is that people are too free to move. Beyond democracy's failure to confine those who should be constrained, so that "people who have been commanded to death or exile" can be found "strolling around" the city's streets,[9] the democratic man himself engages in politics in a frantic manner, "leaping up from his seat and saying and doing whatever comes into his mind."[10] This duality of leaping and having things in mind (things that move in and of themselves—coming and going), foregrounds the tie between rationality and freedom we have already encountered. And I do not intend to propose that movement takes some primacy over the mind (or rather the soul) in this duo. It would be misleading to argue that Plato emphasized in his analysis of the illness of democracy a disordered, uncontrollable mobility over a disordered soul, a failure of rationality's leadership. My point, rather, is that Plato often conceives the proper organization of the soul (that should be reflected in the formation of a polis, and that is, moreover, a constitutive element within this formation), as well as the struggle through which this organization (of both the soul and the polis) may be obtained, in terms of movement.

More specifically, particular patterns of movement—or certain images thereof—are inextricably linked to thinking about rationality in Plato. While movement and rationality are not fully collapsible into each other, they often seem to be folded into each other, that is, each is thought of in terms of the other, imagined and demonstrated by appealing to the other. Adi Ophir contends that the movement of arguments is the main movement toward which the dialog gravitates. Opening with the movement of people (Socrates and Glaucon leaving Piraeus on their way back to Athens; Polemarchus orders his servant to run after them) and with a series of questions regarding this movement (who must stop and who may go on his way[11]), the *Republic*'s physical space becomes static. People stop ("wait"). They "sit down" (at Cephalus's home, where he is already "seated"[12]). This suspended movement allows arguments to move in the discursive space. As the dramatic setting slowly fades out and is forgotten,[13] reason occupies the space of movement: arguments have to bypass obstacles; conversations change direction; interlocutors "walk" arguments to their end (and ideally they "go" in "whatever direction the argument blows" them); finding truths and definitions is described as walking in the dark amid shadows, finding a proper track, or being clustered close together so the truth itself would not "slip through."[14]

Within this composition, different modes of movement also differentiate political constellations. As the rule of the *demos*, democracy is the mode of governance of those who are bound to move. While we have become accustomed to thinking of demos as the body of citizens or "the people," its original meaning was "country" (or land) and later the concept came to refer to the people of the countryside, and thus the poor.[15] The demos, therefore, was composed of those who did not live in the city but had to *walk* to participate in acts of legislation and governance. As Stuart Elden argues, beyond marking the entire populace and a segment within it, "the Greek *demos* had a third sense, that of the *deme*, a location."[16] Accordingly, the necessity to labor, which was contrasted to the freedom of the citizens of Athens (a freedom precisely from the necessity of work), was interwoven into another necessity and another contrast: the contrast between the privilege of stability, of the ability to stay put, or of having an estate on the one hand, and the curse of requisite movement on the other. This curse, it seems, has stained the demos's political organization (democracy) with some form of excess.

This emphasis on stability reflected a more general Greek paradigm (to the extent one can speak of such in the singular) within which the orderly movement of all things gravitated toward rest. Movement was seen as a temporary interruption, a process by which things find their proper *place*—which was the privileged category in the logic of movement prevalent at the time.[17] Accordingly, moving away from one's place, as necessarily occurs in the case of the demos (if they are to participate in matters of politics), was a problem, a disturbance in the order of things. This disruption is what Plato illustrates in his descriptions of the hectic nature of democracy.

Yet even if he privileged a logic of place, Plato was not a thinker of motionlessness. One must recall that while the possibility not to move is the privilege of the citizen, the impossibility to move characterizes the prisoners in Plato's parable of the cave (even if effectively we have here the same entities: the captives are the citizens in the allegory). Thus, some degree of movement was nonetheless desirable. As Claudia Baracchi perceptively noted, "our" problem (as this "us" is demarcated by Socrates) is "a stiffness, staticity." The people in the cave (but also in the polis) are characterized by "a certain inability to turn around, a powerlessness with respect to movement, to a dynamic connection with the surrounding."[18]

Interestingly enough, while all the people in the cave are bound, the desired movement of the many is not the ability to be released from their chains and climb up and out of the cave. This is the power—the privilege—of the few; one may speculate that a more widespread act of climbing would produce precisely the threatening excessive movement that characterizes democracy. The desired movement of the many (desired by Plato, that is) is the ability "to turn . . . their heads around."[19] It is a more metaphorical movement of heads (thinking?, souls?) toward knowledge.[20] Yet, we must bear in mind that as we saw in the previous chapter in regard to Hobbes, the distinction between the metaphorical and the literal cannot be kept. A movement toward knowledge is, quite literally, moving toward—turning toward (and returning to)—its objects: the ideas. Even this movement, however, had to be constrained and moderated: "a kind of resistance to flux is necessary for anything to come to be, according to its order, to its law and rhythm. Life does not flow in a broad, undifferentiated course. It flows through shapes, forms and configurations. As shapes, forms and configurations it flows."[21] Since according to Plato what is to be known is eventually eternal and stable, knowing—moving one's head, if not untying oneself and climbing out of a cave—necessitates lingering.

Movement is thus both politically and epistemologically desirable only against a backdrop of some stability. The problem begins when this stability, which is the privilege of the citizens-as-the-few, is interrupted by the movement of the demos-as-a-mob entering the city and subjecting the polis to its rule of excessive freedom.[22] With that movement, the city is contaminated with wildness and savagery that ultimately manifests itself in one of the most horrifying effects of democracy in Plato's satirical version of Athens: animals "roam freely and proudly along the streets, bumping into anyone who doesn't get out of their way."[23] As we see in Locke centuries later, it is eventually the animal (and the animal-like-savage), not the free citizen, whose freedom of movement is unlimited.

Plato thus sets here the stage for the idea that freedom is only politically valuable if it relies on some mechanism that regulates the movement that manifests it. The idea that such mechanisms can be internal to the subject (who can thereby achieve within himself[24] some equilibrium between movement and stability/security/order) would become more and more systematically theorized in writers from Locke to Kant, from Hobhouse to neoliberals. This idea would become concretely plausible with an array of disciplinary mechanisms that stand at the basis of Foucault's primary object of research. And yet, the movement of some groups of people would always be excluded from this frame. This chapter focuses on some of them.

Hobbes and the Excessive Movement of "Savages"

In the previous chapter I argued that Hobbes poses a basic model of a self-restraining subject. His servant (who is eventually the model for the subject within the commonwealth) embodies this idea: The servant is the one who agreed not to run away in order to not be constrained by chains or imprisoned; he is the one who agreed to limit himself so as not to be limited by others, and this is precisely the meaning of his freedom.[25] However, in Hobbes, this remains a somewhat abstract archetype—still without the concrete technologies and ideologies that would become so central to the formation of disciplined subjects, to use Foucault's terminology.[26] Indeed, once the notion of self-regulation became even slightly more developed, a distinction would be made between "real" freedom and "license." Later theories (as early as Locke) would insist on this differentiation, yet Hobbes still thinks of this state of unbound liberty as freedom, even if excessive. And since for Hobbes—"a man almost bemused by the wonder of motions"[27]—freedom was but "the absence of . . . *external impediments of motion*,"[28] the phenomenon he describes can be seen within his framework as that of excessive movement.

James Scott shows that movement had to be ordered, contained, and constrained because it posed a challenge for governance.[29] The appeal to Hobbes frames the question of movement as a problem of security (these may be merely different angles from which to approach a single question). And if one claim should be underscored from this section it is this: the state is a mechanism not merely for the monopolization of movement, as Torpey has it, or for the monopolization of violence in Weber's formulation; it is a mechanism for the monopolization of movement qua violence. By identifying Hobbes as one of the main architects of this process, the analogy between Torpey and Weber can become more than a playful parallelism. In Hobbes, too much freedom and too much violence are one and the same, and they both take shape via the notion of excessive movement. As a mechanism of security then, the function of the commonwealth is to slow movement down.

When we think of security today (particularly following the operations of the Bush and Obama administrations) we often think of a certain trade-off: one "must trade some liberty and autonomy for the sake of the protection [the state] offer[s]," as Iris Marion Young phrases the terms.[30] One may argue, moreover, that such a paradigm can be traced back to Hobbes: Within the Hobbesian social contract one relinquishes her absolute liberty (the natural right to do anything within one's own natural capacity to execute one's goals and desires) for security (minimizing the permanent threats to her life in the state of nature). Yet such a reading ignores the crucial distinction between natural and political rights. Hobbesian unbound natural liberty—a "Right to every thing"[31]—is indeed a security problem: it facilitates the war of every man against every man. Civil liberty, however, is the *very limitation of rights achieved with (if not through) security*: the civil state is a state that enables "each one [to] securely [enjoy] his limited right."[32] This reconciliation of security (order) and freedom is crucial for the modern concept of political freedom, yet in Hobbes it was not complete. He still could not quite imagine an ordered freedom.

Since it was primarily based on fear (and since it was conceived in the early seventeenth century, when state bureaucracy was largely inefficient and could barely "embrace" the body of ruled subjects[33]), the order provided by the commonwealth was quite fragile. The subject's freedom/movement could not be fully moderated and tamed, but only countered and suppressed. This in turn, meant that to the extent that he remained free within the commonwealth, the subject could always refuse to obey the terms of the social contract.[34] The edge of this refusal is a civil war and the disintegration of the commonwealth. In other words, the subject's freedom rendered the state a tenuous structure, and even the most absolute state could quickly disintegrate (indeed an absolute regime is an attempt—the success of which can never be guaranteed—to address this fragility). The point here is not merely that with this disintegration of the commonwealth, the unity between security and freedom achieved within civil liberty is broken, and the individual's natural, unlimited freedom once again manifests itself as a complete lack of security—as violence—with some "return" or "arrival" at an expolitical state of nature. More important, for Hobbes civil liberty itself *is* the ever-lingering possibility of violent death.[35]

Since in Hobbes freedom is violence, restraining violence is always also restraining freedom and vice versa; one cannot persist without the other. Later accounts of freedom tried to bypass this conundrum by interweaving restraints into freedom, but Hobbes's insight merits reflection: the notion that ultimately, what we want to maximize and what we want to minimize (even annul), the desirable and the condemned, are one and the same. We cannot simply claim that in the commonwealth this violence remains a potential (a horizon), while in nature, violence is constantly actualized. Such a claim would be inaccurate both because violence is actualized, time and again, within the commonwealth and because, as Foucault has beautifully shown, the war of every man against every man did not unleash actual violence, but was rather a game of simulations, wherein concrete battles are constantly suspended and "the nature of war consisteth not in actual fighting; but in the known disposition thereto."[36] Time introduces breaks between this disposition and its actualization as a concrete violence. Therefore, Hobbes tells us, "the notion of Time is to be considered in the nature of Warre."[37] Accordingly, both the state of nature and the social order are characterized by a potentiality of violence. The main difference becomes the degree of ease in the transition from the suspended to the present. What the commonwealth grants us is time: it decelerates the move between potential and actual violence.[38] It slows down the movement of violence itself.

This mode of slowing down—this check on the swiftness of the move from the potential to the actual—works in tandem with another mode: the subject, like the servant, needs to understand that sometimes, running away is not the best option. In the previous chapter I suggested, following Rogers and Spragens, that too much movement is one way of thinking about the Hobbesian state of nature. Accordingly, Hobbes's commonwealth can be considered as a mode of ordering movement: it mitigates our passions, which are but the "interior beginnings of voluntary Motion" toward objects, with our fear, which is a movement "fromward" a thing we think might hurt us.[39] The fear from sovereign power restrains subjects as it keeps pushing them backward ("fromward"), while their desires and appetites keep pushing them forward. Since these movements—these "endeavours"—are but the "small beginnings of Motion, within the body of Man, *before* they appear in walking, speaking, striking and other visible actions,"[40] it seems that these countermovements should render subjects less inclined to move at all. In other words, between desire and fear, an equilibrium of movements is formed within the body of the subject, before she has made any visible movement. If, indeed, "there really is no such thing as 'rest' for Hobbes; there are only motions and contrary motions,"[41] this mitigation of fear and desire may be as close as one gets to immobility. Such countermovements, then, temper the constant, frantic movement that we otherwise see in the state of nature.[42] Moreover, beyond the fear from the sovereign, the structure of sovereignty also curbs the subject's movement. The Hobbesian law—which Nancy Hirschmann saw as already entailing some rudimentary notions of social construction[43]—should teach the subject to restrain her movements. As we saw, the law protects people from their own "rashness." It keeps people "in such a motion, as not to hurt themselves by their own impetuous desires, rashness, or indiscretion, as Hedges are set, not to stop travelers, but to keep them in the way."[44] Political life directs and slows down the actualization of violence, reduces and narrows the subject's movements, and guides the subject so that he is protected from his own "rashness."

Each and every subject in the Hobbesian world suffers from a dangerous tendency for rashness, however it is much stronger without a sovereign power establishing fear. Hence, there is one place wherein the problem of excessive movement is most acute, given the complete lack of such hedges (laws); one place wherein "there can be no security to any man."[45] This place is America.[46]

America is only mentioned in passing in *Leviathan*;[47] but as Quentin Skinner shows, about a decade earlier, in *De Cive*, this location was presented quite vividly. The cover of the book, contrasting free life to secure life, is inlaid with iconography that was used in Hobbes's time to portray indigenous Americans.[48] In a barbarian—almost beastly—manner, they are free but "wholly lacking in that solace and beauty of life which *peace* and society are able to provide" and completely vulnerable to everything around them, be it other men or animals.[49]

According to Carl Schmitt, America and the Hobbesian state of nature were tightly connected.[50] Hobbes's state of nature, he argues, "is a *no man's land*, but it does not mean it exists *nowhere*. It can be located—and Hobbes locates it—among other places, in the New World."[51] According to Schmitt, Hobbes's America was clearly a place "beyond the line," wherein there were no more lines, no more demarcation (hedges, laws); it was overseas and took upon itself the logic of the sea: it lent itself to no delineations; it was a space on which movement left no trace. It is crucial to note that according to Schmitt, these were the characteristics of the space rather than attributes of its indigenous subjects: the violence of America (as a state of nature) was the violence of the European conquerors no less than the violence of unrestrained savages. This would change as the century proceeded, and by Locke's time we will see a different marking of the line separating America and Native Americans from Europe and Europeans.

This location brings to light two important points in Hobbes's political theory of movement. First, with it we begin to see the divide between restrained and unrestrained freedom of movement; a divide between relatively secure freedom and danger, which we see here only beginning to take a geographic meaning, not yet within a pattern of radical otherness but within that of degree,[52] and still in an ambivalent manner. The status of Hobbes's America is, after all, quite paradoxical: While it was undoubtedly linked to a concrete geographical location (hence "there"), it was also a place that has never existed. Hobbes could thus claim that "there had never been any time, wherein particular men were in condition of warre one against another," only a paragraph after previously stating that "the savage people in many places of *America*" "live so now."[53] Hence, the geographical split is quite unstable in Hobbes, whose work is still not imbued with colonial frames, even if, as Schmitt argued, it was clearly affected by them.

Second, Hobbes's appeal to America shows the degree to which the possibility of moderate movement was tied to questions of rationality and the universal status of "Man." To make this point we should step back and pose the question in a broader context. Uday Mehta's eloquent formulation is a good starting point:

> In its theoretical version, liberalism, from the seventeenth century to the present, has prided itself on its universality and its political inclusionary character. And yet, when viewed as a historical phenomenon, the period of liberal history is unmistakably marked by the systematic and sustained political exclusion of various groups and "types" of people. . . . Perhaps liberal theory and liberal history are ships passing in the night, spurred on by unrelated imperatives and destinations. Perhaps reality—and, as such, history—always betrays the pristine motives of theory. Putting aside such possibilities, something about the inclusionary pretensions of liberal theory and the exclusionary effects of liberal practices needs to be explained.[54]

How can one reconcile the tension between the universality of liberal theory and the exclusionary nature of liberal practices? Are theory and practice foreign to each other, as Mehta proposes and dismisses here? Or is the presumption of universality merely a lie? Is theory in this case essentially a mask fabricated to facilitate, precisely, the practice of exclusion? Rather than following these directions, Mehta's solution rests on showing that a "thick set of social instructions and signals" has always mediated a potentiality of universality. While universality is accomplished by (or understood as) an "anthropological minimum," which, as such, is shared by all people, this minimum is not only left "buried under" social layers that may hide it, but may also remain completely unactualized due to some lack or failure in these layers.[55] In other words, while there is some kernel of universal individuality shared by all people, this may be differently developed, and moreover, remain ever hidden or even undone by social differences.[56]

To a great degree, this universal kernel is rationality, or more accurately, a capacity of rationality.[57] This difference is precisely what bridges a universal minimum that remains ever theoretical, and a hierarchical exclusionary praxis. The assumption that as a potential, all humans have some basic rational capacity is perhaps what enabled Vanita Seth to argue in her important *Europe's Indians* that indigenous Americans function as the archetype for the free and rational individual that stands at the basis of social-contract theories. Yet Seth, I believe, mistakes here the kernel for the archetype. While inherently rational,[58] the intellectual capacities of Hobbes's savages are but "the *natural plant* of human reason."[59] Hobbes does not merely imply that these "plants" need to be developed in order to arrive at the highest degree of human rational capacities such as philosophy (the context of the paragraph from which the quote is taken is philosophy and its origins). Rather, Hobbes suggests that without cultivation, these "plants" remain useless: "For as there were Plants of Corn and Wine in small quantity dispersed in the Fields and Woods, before men knew their vertue, or made use of them for their nourishment, or planted them apart in Fields, and Vineyards; in which time they fed on Akorns, and drank Water: so also there have been diverse true, generall, and profitable Speculations from the beginning; as being the naturall plants of humane Reason."[60]

"From the beginning" there are "true, generall, and profitable Speculations"—rational elements that can be found even among the savages. These elements, however, are of no use (akin to wild corn and wine in times when men only ate acorns and drank water). Even if Hobbes's argument refers to a capacity of philosophizing, one cannot but wonder whether this claim regarding complete uselessness can be read as anything but positioning the "plants" of indigenous Americans' rationality as *generally* worthless. Moreover, within this embryonic form "there was no. . . . Planting of Knowledge by it self, apart from the Weeds, and common plants of Errour and Conjecture."[61] This mode of rationality is so undeveloped, it is conflated with irrationality.

We further learn from Hobbes's discussion of America that he assumes that time (or better, a certain degree of slowness, a deceleration, as it were, in the constant busyness of life) is among the social and material conditions necessary for rationality to be actualized and become useful. To cultivate their reason—thereby extracting it from the natural realm, in which the metaphor itself resides, and rendering it a full capacity—the savages need "*leasure*." Yet with the lack of a strong enough power to "keep them in awe" and force them to keep contracts, they are constantly busy in "procuring the necessities of life, and defending themselves against their neighbors. . . . *Leasure* is the mother of philosophy," Hobbes concludes, "and *Common-wealth* the mother of *Peace* and *Leasure*."[62] One of the two commonwealth's ultimate benefits appears here, once again, as time. The security it provides is time; it allows us to stop running, to pause the war of existence, to linger, and thus, as we saw already in Plato, to know.

Even if the Hobbesian civic subject is still not a subject who is fully (re)formed within the civic state so as to be able to regulate and order his or her own freedom; even if, in other words, we still cannot see with Hobbes a subject who is constituted so that his or her freedom would largely conform with order, Hobbes does see the commonwealth as providing some significant conditions—even if external to the subject—that can tame the subject's movement in such a way that it will not constantly undo order. Among these conditions we have: (i) a fear that counters, if not reshapes desire, thereby hindering movement; (ii) time to slow life/violence down, and (iii) hedges to confine movement. As important to the very postulation of these conditions, however, is the assumption that none of them can be found in America.

Hobbes, then, marks a split—albeit tenuous and bridgeable—between the (slightly) more secure liberty of "civilized" countries and the less secure liberty of "savages."[63] Key to this division was Hobbes's assumption that his too-free-savages *themselves* suffer from the insecurity produced by their lack of a stable political order (and the resultant excess of freedom/movement, as the two are one and the same for Hobbes). Later, this division would change position, or more accurately, would double itself. Notions of conquest/occupation/imperial rule would focus more on the threats posed to *others* by those whose movement is deemed excessive, yet without completely abandoning the mode of justification contending that colonial subjects cause too much damage to themselves when left alone to self-rule.[64] Accordingly, the divide would no longer be within the notion of liberty, as in the case of Hobbes (that is, a divide between a more or less secure civil liberty on the one hand, and a natural liberty that is a permanent threat to the integrity of one's body and life on the other). Rather, it would become a divide within movement: between freedom (of movement) and excess (now defined as license, as a security problem, as a threat, but at any rate not freedom).[65] The result, as we saw in the first chapter, is that some political endeavors and spaces are rarely thought of within, or under, the question of freedom. Throughout its different incarnations, however, this divide remains a split between populations: between those whose movement is a manifestation of liberty, and should therefore be maximized, and those whose freedom is a problem, and should therefore be tightly regulated. In our global and local travel, in patterns of migration and border crossing, in deployments of checkpoints—be it in poor neighborhoods or occupied lands—we can still witness this split.

Locke: Enclosing Movement

The fluidity and temporality of the Hobbesian split in liberty is stabilized with Locke, who thus also presents a much more radical and firm partition separating safe (and free) movement from unsafe (and unfree) movement. Unlike Hobbes, whose writing on America is scarce, Locke's America is central to his thinking and has occupied a great deal of scholarly interest in recent years.⁶⁶ My aim in engaging with this scholarship is to show that Locke's America is carved into (or perhaps essential to the carving of) a more developed, stable, and spatialized version of the Hobbesian split described above. America is the space wherein too much movement becomes a problem, which in Locke's case, means this movement can no longer be seen as a manifestation of freedom. Unlike much of the literature on Locke and the New World, however, I do not seek to demonstrate that this geographical context was the salient context for Locke's thinking on land and property. Almost to the contrary: if we look at land and property through the prism of movement, several different contexts that inform Locke's discussion of that matter meet. Viewed as mechanisms of stabilizing and restraining movement, land and goods become not merely things one may or may not possess, but also elements within processes of subject formation: they become the precondition and the medium through which free, rational subjects can emerge. Therefore, when they are absent (as in the case of the "savages" of America, but also in that of the poor), freedom is drained of its substance (moderated movement) and crumples. This section considers these contexts to show that whereas Locke configured freedom as a secure movement within a fence, that therefore "ill deserves the name of confinement," movement unconfined by fences (that is, unenclosed) was for him a mark of irrationality and (accordingly) unfreedom.

Spaces of Reason: Freedom and Settlement

"From the 1620s to the 1680s in Britain, and then in North America, Australia, and Africa well into the nineteenth century" (we can add: and the Middle East well into the twentieth century), "the argument from vacancy (*vacuum domicilium*) or absence of ownership (*terra nullius*) became a standard foundation for English, and later British dispossession of indigenous people," argues David Armitage.⁶⁷ Locke, he continues, provided "the most extensive presentation of this argument."⁶⁸ Similarly to Hobbes before him, but much more elaborately and explicitly, Locke points to America as the paradigm of the state of nature: it is a place wherein the lack of apparent sovereignty and the lack of land appropriation (by means of cultivation) allow free political agents to assemble and contract a new commonwealth. Carole Pateman thus argues that the social contract is essentially a settler contract.[69]

In her analysis of Locke's account of the natives in the Americas, Vanita Seth proposes that the picture is more complex than that. She argues that in addition to imagining European settlers as political agents unrestrained by the constraints of sovereignty and thus free to form their own social pact, Locke turns to the Native Americans themselves as the prototype of the rational individual who stands at the base of his social contract. The people who were "first encountered in the 'woods of America,'" were not merely an "evidential defense of the state of nature" for Locke. Locke's "preoccupation with the New World" was rooted in his portrayal of the Native American as the paradigm of "the free, equal, rational, individual." Put differently, "the individual [in the state of nature] was no other than the indigenous Indian himself."[70]

This posited a paradox at the heart of Locke's theory (as well as of the theories of other seventeenth- and eighteenth-century social contract thinkers): indigenous Americans were, at one and the same time, "in contradictory fashion, . . . both the model of universal reason, freedom, equality, and property-accumulating individuality and a deviation from these same universal norms."[71] As the model, they were a certain archetype for men without any governing rule but that of reason. As a deviation, they were the almost transparent underpinning upon which the social contract took the form of a settler contract.

The question regarding the status of Locke's Indians is crucial to understanding his particular justification of land appropriation in the New World. The best venue for answering this question is probably reframing it via the question of rationality—the principal index of the subject-citizen.[72] The paradox is thus phrased (once again, in Seth's words): "the apparent inconsistency in Locke's representation of the Indians" lies in the fact that they are represented in his theory as "at once irrational and at other times constitute still-life portraits of pre-political, rational, individuals."[73] This tension will serve here as a platform from which to trace how movement and freedom converge and part, showing that the paradox ultimately dissolves via the paradigm of excessive (unrestrained) movement.

As we saw in the previous chapter, when considered from the perspective of movement, Locke's freedom had two main facets: the freedom "to think, or not to think; to move or not to move, according to the preference or direction of his own mind";[74] and freedom from arbitrariness that depended on the existence of some "standing" law (even when it was merely the law of reason or "nature"). Freedom thus relied upon some negotiation of movement and stability that was eventually a function of landedness, which in turn was a function of a certain model of property ownership. It was precisely this model of ownership indigenous Americans presumably failed to inhabit.

Locke's discussion of land appropriation is perhaps the most direct evidence of his judgment as to this "failure" and its repercussion. In recent years, many have argued that Locke's discussion in chapter 5 of the *Second Treatise* should not be read as an argument within an intra-European debate concerning the limits of property rights, and specifically the legitimation of enclosures, but as given within a colonial context.[75] "This context," James Tully proposes, "is the legitimation of the dispossession of Amerindians, the destruction of their way of life, and the imposition of European agriculture and industry." This legitimation rests on "a contrast between European techniques of land improvement and Amerindian culture"[76]—it rests on the assumption that there is one privileged mode of relating to the ground, and that this mode is that of dwelling. And while I do not aim to question the claim that the hinge of Locke's political and ethical edifice here is *property*, I do want to propose that property cannot be understood here without *settlement*.[77] "The chief matter of property," Locke states, is "now not the fruits of the earth, and the beasts that subsist on it, but the earth itself; as that which takes in, and carried with it all the rest."[78] And earth is more valuable *enclosed*. Locke estimates that "an acre of land" in America produces "not one thousandth" of an acre of cultivated, enclosed land "here."[79] These lands, therefore, could have been claimed to be laying "wasted." Settlement, and more particularly, enclosure, thereby become a precondition for freedom.

All this leads us back to Seth's paradox: the position of indigenous Americans as both the paradigm of the model (in her case a certain universal rationality) and the deviation from this model; both the standard and its abnormality. But if we closely examine Locke's claim about the individual's rationality, we see two different logics of property. According to the first, "He that nourished by the acorns he picked up under an oak or the apples he gathered from the tree in the wood, has certainly appropriated them to himself. . . . I ask then, when did they begin to be his? When he digested? Or when he ate? Or when he boiled? Or when he brought them home? Or when he picked them up? And it is plain, if the first gathering made them not his, nothing else could."[80]

Yet this was not the mode of operation of property for Locke's Indian: "the fruit, or venison, which nourishes the wild Indian, who knows no enclosure, and is still a tenant in common," he tells us only a few paragraphs earlier, "must be his, or so his, i.e. a part of him, that another can no longer have any right to it, before it can do him any good for the support of his life."[81] The hunted deer, the gathered fruits function as property ("his") only upon consumption—only after they become "a part of him." In the material and spatial condition in which the Indian lives, consumption, rather than mere labor, is necessary to produce right—a right that at this stage becomes fully redundant. Locke's Indian does not really enjoy a system of natural rights.

William Bassett argues that the "Myth of Nomadism"—that is, the assumption according to which the Native American was "a pagan nomad, a wandering gatherer and hunter, who roamed vacant and unoccupied lands as an alien to civilization and culture"[82]—was more than an assumption regarding patterns of mobility and stability. In a way, he argues, it was an assumption regarding rationality. Bassett declares that "this 'tragic myth,' according to which the Indian . . . knew neither stability nor possession of land, . . . stripped the Indian almost entirely of human and civil rights."[83] (As Nancy Hirschmann noted in a different context, "Locke linked industry and rationality very closely such that industry—the use of property in your person (labor) to acquire property in the form of land or goods—was taken as evidence of rationality, and the lack of property was evidence of a lack of rationality."[84] More accurate here, perhaps, would be to talk not about industry as such, but about a mode of acquisition.) In Locke, this entanglement of nomadism and irrationality operates on at least three related levels.

First, given the radical divergence in land productivity assumed by Locke, the assumed failure of the indigenous Americans to enclose the land is economically irrational. And we can begin to see here how we cannot fully separate the two requisites for stability to which I pointed earlier: a sedentary agriculture and a subjection to a stable law.

Second, this failure is a violation of a moral duty toward humanity. Since "he who appropriates land to himself" by enclosing ten acres produces "a greater plenty of the conveniences of life . . . than he could have from an hundred left to nature," he actually *gives* "ninety acres to mankind."[85] In a brilliant move of overturning the doings of private property, Locke can then see those who "know no enclosure"[86] as denying land to the rest of humanity; indeed, this was the main justification for framing the land-grab in the Americas within the frame of just wars. But more important for our purpose, the failure to enclose land tacitly attested to another failure: a failure to organize society according to and within the limit of laws. Parallel to the man who overaccumulates goods that therefore "perished, in his possession, without their due use; . . . the fruits are rotted, or the venison putrefied"—those who fail to appropriate the land, to settle and own it, can be seen as acting "against the common law of nature."[87] And while Locke only alludes to the position of indigenous Americans within the "bounds of the law of nature,"[88] here he is quite explicit. Furthermore, while the aforementioned, overconsuming man was an isolated individual, violating natural law out of greed, Locke's Indians represent not a secluded sin, but a systematic social order that cannot cross the threshold of natural law (even if it may reside in it). Since the law itself, as well as its circumventing apparatuses (the legislative and the judging bodies), is often referred to by Locke as a fence,[89] this failure is inherent to his Indian's way of life.

Thus, even if Locke cannot conceptualize his Indians as anything but rational,[90] a certain degree of stability is necessary for this rationality—this "anthropological minimum," in Mehta's words—to be actualized. Without executing this rationality within a property-accumulation model that rests on settlement and enclosures, they are neither rational nor free. Hobbes's argument regarding time is anchored here in space—a space that has, simultaneously, a local configuration (enclosure), and a geopolitical identification (the schism between England and America). In so doing, even one of the most iconic among liberal writers still holds to the understanding that Schmitt argues we have already lost in Plato: namely, that nomos "is a fence word"; that the organization of political order, legitimacy, and law is always also an organization of space—an enclosure.[91] Accordingly, the "Indian" way of life is incommensurable with the very structure of the Lockean law.

Indeed, the spatialization of time becomes clear in Locke's discussion of maturity, which again demonstrates that rationality requires time.[92] Children need to grow up to become rational; yet alongside them Locke counts others, who can never enjoy maturity/rationality: people with "mental defects," madmen, and the savages of America.[93] In the case of those, maturity, it seems, is not a function of time but rather of space. In the previous chapter I presented this claim vis-à-vis the first two categories, first, via Arneil's claim that the first category (the person with "natural" mental "defects") is tied to physical immobility; and second, via Mehta's claim that a mind of "overexcited frenzy," which has "no conceivable limits" and is not "tied down" or "kept in 'checks'" and thus sets meanings free from the "stabilizing support they ordinarily get from things," is the mind of a madman.[94] Locke's amalgamation of rationality and enclosure marks the savage as the third figure in the list whose rationality can never cross the threshold into maturity because of some "problem" in this rationality's relation to space: his location completely determines his position, so to speak, in time.[95] Indeed Barbara Arneil shows that, strikingly, the solution for all three groups is some form of territorial separation within different kinds of closed spaces: alongside the poor who were "voluntarily" idle (and to whom I will come shortly), these groups should be enclosed in domestic or external *colonies*.[96]

We therefore have a multilayered justification apparatus, in which first, the presumed lack of a particular model of agriculture[97] is taken as an indication of both the lack of civilization and the lack of appropriation, thereby rendering the framework of "vacant lands" possible.[98] Second, the tie between movement and rationality or the lack thereof, marks the presumably nomadic indigenous people as irrational, thereby justifying occupation and subjection to a foreign rule (as they are incapable of sustaining a stable political organization). And finally, the articulation and conceptualization of law as a "fence word" configures the political order itself as superimposed on a system of enclosures that the "savages" seem unwilling or incapable of forming. The cooperation of these three strata has contemporary resonances, and it repeatedly transpires as a justification mechanism for colonial and imperial projects. To a great degree it is the underlying apparatus for what we saw with the imaginary line in chapter 1 and its geopolitical context: a seemingly "vacant land"[99] (whose inhabitants are declared as nomads to break the tie between them and the land) that can thus be settled; indigenous people insisting upon being there despite the myth that insists they were not; the assumption of irrationality, and, moreover, the production of irrationality to justify occupation, expulsion, and violence. Both in the case of the Palestinians and that of the Americas, this production of irrationality is achieved via a legal framework that instead of being a visible, solid, systematic mechanism of stabilization beyond which there is an abyss (to refer to Locke's metaphor)[100] is rather an obstacle over which the indigenous are set to stumble.[101]

The Object of Enclosure

There is a debate in the literature concerning the context in which Locke's justification of land appropriation should be read: is it part of an intra–English quarrel regarding enclosures, or as Tully, Armitage, Arneil and others suggested, part of the effort to justify the land-grab project in the New World?

If we see the degree to which the movement of immigration to America was connected with the inability to move within England (or perhaps more accurately, the inability to settle in England); and if moreover, we see the degree to which this movement of immigration was entangled with the resultant movement (both assumed and produced) of indigenous populations in the Americas, we see that the two contexts eventually meet (even if Locke may have had only one in mind).[102] After all, the main justification of the colonial project in England rested on the need to remove "the 'swarms of idle persons' in England [by] setting them to work in Virginia," and later in other colonies.[103] "Swarms" of dispossessed people; dispossession that is created by the new system of enclosures;[104] hence confinement and involuntary movement; and then new confinements and new movements since "when the English took possession of the land overseas, they did so by building fences and hedges" and these new enclosures became crucial technologies in the system of indigenous Americans' dispossession.[105] So far, we have considered the story from the perspective of the context of land appropriation in the New World; I now want to briefly shift our gaze to the perspective of the intra-English debate.

The sixteenth and seventeenth centuries were a time of massive reorganization of lands and models of land ownership in England. It was only in the first few decades of the seventeenth century that the idea of absolute property became established in both legislation and practice. This radically changed the models of space and dwelling, primarily via a vast project of land enclosures.[106] The project of enclosures created a dual course for movement. On the one hand, it limited legitimate movement as it limited the commons; and on the other, it created a new class of vagrants—people who lost access to the land and were thus doomed to constant mobility and (so it was assumed) criminality.[107] It was not just the savage, then, whose excessive movement interrupted a desired order achieved via new modes of settlements and was connected with some moral deficiency; within England, the movement of another demographic threatened to destabilize the logic and legitimacy of this order: that of the poor.[108]

As a distinctive class, the poor emerged in early modern England precisely as a result of changes in patterns of movement and its regulations. No longer slaves, domestic servants, or serfs, whose "legal capacity to move lay in the hands of their landlords [or masters], the new class of free, impoverished workers was the class of those" who were bound to move.[109] Following Giovanna Procacci, we can further state that "pauperism"—which is "poverty intensified to the level of *social danger*" (in other words, at those moments when an economic trait is configured as a threat)—"is *mobility*." More than an economic category, she argues, pauperism is a "residue" that cannot be constrained: "Against the need of territorial sedentarization, for fixed concentrations of populations, [pauperism] personifies the residue of a more fluid, elusive sociality, impossible either to control or to utilize: vagabondage, order's itinerant nightmare, becomes the archetype of disorder."[110]

Unlike the "pauper" or the "savage"—so was the claim—a "Civilized man constantly restrains himself."[111] From the late sixteenth century the poor became the primary target of growing efforts to regulate movement within and across the borders of the state. The Poor Law of 1601, for example, conditioned relief on strict limitation of movement (limitations Locke strongly endorsed).[112] Previous anti-vagabondage laws and later public housing projects aimed at achieving the same goal.[113] Ultimately, the poor's "gradual transformation into a class of free laborers was the combined result of the fierce persecution of vagrancy and the fostering of domestic industry."[114]

Indeed, Foucault suggests that in the seventeenth century confinement was essentially an attempt to address some assumed failure in productivity. It was precisely this failure that subtended the logic of the "age of confinement":[115] a mass project of confining what for us may seem as a mixture of bodies (poor, insane, criminal). Therefore, one cannot think about the limitation of movement in the seventeenth century without thinking, not so much about class, but about labor.

The problem of the "growth of the poor" is rooted in "nothing else but the relaxation of discipline and corruption of manners," argues Locke in his own take on disciplining the poor into labor.[116] To facilitate the desired change of habits it was crucial that those who do not work (or do not work enough) be registered and *kept within* the boundaries of their parish,[117] and be further confined to poorhouses (in the case of adults) or working school (in the case of children). Ultimately, this confinement should create new habits—themselves motions—that would render the poor somewhat more virtuous by the capacity of industry. In the *Essay* Locke provides the theory for his assumption that repetitive motions—in our case, those of labor—can become "second nature," molding the subject's character into more desirable patterns: "Custom settles habits of thinking in the understanding, as well as of determining in the will, and of motions in the body; all which seems to be but Trains of Motion in the Animal Spirits, which once set a going continue on in the same steps they have been used to, which by often trading are worn into a smooth path, and the motion in it becomes easy as it were natural."[118]

The motion of labor—repetitive, confined, productive—should thus take over the motion of vagrancy and begging: unpredicted, unbounded, futile.

Yet significantly, these new corporeal habits were not followed by a rehabituation of the mind (another "train of motion in the animal spirits"), and poor children were not to be educated in those professions necessary for the development of rationality (such as philosophy, Greek, and Latin).[119] This was not because of some natural differences between men, but because of practical and material ones. While theoretically capable of being rational, Locke's poor, much like Hobbes's Indians, lacked the time to actualize rationality.[120] Hence, unlike the enclosed land, which was the mark, the product, the condition, but even more so, the meaning of rationality, the modes of the poor's confinement (which significantly did not assume the logic of property but of subsistence, labor, and charity) presupposed and marked irrationality.

With the lack of time, and therefore exercise, the minds of the poor seem to have a very similar fate to their bodies: oscillating between radical confinement and ungrounded movement: "Try in men of holy and mean education, who have never elevated their thoughts above the spade and the plough nor looked beyond the ordinary drudgery of a day-laborer," says Locke. "The thoughts of such an one," he maintains, cannot be taken "out of that narrow compass he has been all his life confined to." Should this (arguably undesirable) confinement be violated, he will be "perfectly at a loss."[121] It is almost as if in both body and mind, Locke's poor were doomed to fail in accomplishing the desired equilibrium between mobility and stability. Without this balance the pairing of rationality and freedom simply did not work:

> Without Liberty, the Understanding would be to no purpose: And without Understanding, Liberty (if it could be) would signify nothing. If a man sees what would do him good or harm, what would make him happy or miserable, without being able to move himself one step towards or from it, what is he the better for seeing? And he that is at liberty to ramble in perfect darkness, what is his liberty better, than if he were driven up and down as a bubble by the force of the wind? . . . the principal exercise of freedom is to stand still, open the eyes, look about, and take a view of the consequence of what we are going to do, as much as the weight of the matter requires.[122]

Being poor (and thus both idle and irrational—and it is not altogether clear whether for Locke, these are one or two attributes) is thus part of a condition in which one is simultaneously too mobile (with no anchor via land appropriation) and *therefore* confined (since her movement would ipso facto violate order).[123] Within this framework freedom resembles the motion of the people set free in Plato's cave: they remain still, yet can "open the eyes" and "look about." And when they fail to do either—due to social and material conditions or moral defects—confinement is the only possibility.

Concluding Notes

It has often been argued that race and class are two "axes" of identity that "intersect" or "are superimposed" on each other. Often, we see this intersection as the product of a long history of colonial and postcolonial patterns of global migration that have created a statistical correlation of poor and nonwhite. Yet here, in the seventeenth century, before the long history of colonialism could indeed produce such a correlation, we already see the same superimposition: the poor and the indigenous American, despite many differences in their sporadic appearances on the pages of the texts considered herein, share one attribute that is central to their portrayal as a political problem: they move too much. Their movement presumably becomes surplus and, therefore, can no longer encapsulate freedom; it has become a threat to order.

Indeed, the technologies that were developed to regulate the movement of the poor would, in the nineteenth century and onward, become the organizing principle of, and form the technological infrastructure for the regulation of the movement of foreigners (often colonized, and then previously colonized).[124] But already in Locke, in a different way, the solution to the excessive movement of the poor/vagrants is entangled with a colonial project.[125] The issue of the unwanted movement of vagrancy can easily be solved, Locke reassures us, if we "let" those who have been dispossessed through the structure of private property "plant in some inland, vacant places of America."[126]

This solution recasts the movement of the poor as the movement of immigrants, rather than forced laborers[127]—entrepreneurs who not only move, but also settle (plant).[128] Free or coerced, this movement—this solution—created another problem (that is, dispossession of indigenous populations). Moreover, this solution was conditioned upon the *configuration of a certain way of life—that of indigenous Americans—as a problem* (as an excess). In other words, we have here a constant production of "excessive" movement that derives from a dual movement-related project with which Locke was involved: (i) erecting of fences (enclosures), which limited legitimate movement (within and to the commons) and produced illegitimate movement (of newly landless vagrants); and (ii) transatlantic movement (immigration) that served to regulate and diminish the aforementioned illegitimate movement, but was conditioned upon the assumption of another mode of excessive movement (of indigenous Americans) as a justificatory mechanism for land appropriation without natives' consent. This transatlantic movement was itself more often than not the outcome of expulsion, and facilitated the movement of expropriation. Expropriation, in turn, not only *assumed*, but also *produced* the excessive (landless) movement of indigenous Americans, and was at least to some extent (and definitely according to Locke's view, or more tellingly his practices) conditioned upon another mode of expropriation and involuntary movement: the slave trade. The definition of movement as freedom that stood at the heart of the previous chapter should, therefore, be situated in a global context of land appropriation and global migration, of states and their colonies, as well as within other matrixes of subjugation.

5 | The "Substance and Meaning of All Things Political"

On Other Bodies

I argued that the classic liberal subject was a subject who learned to narrow her spatial presence, decelerate the motions of her body, restrain and contain liberty itself thereby allowing the notion of an ordered freedom. She was a subject whose movement was contained by a certain background of stability—property, estate or state. There is a dual movement here, in both the argument (my argument) and the technique (the political technology, the regulation of movement). On one level, there is a disciplining of the subject's movement, her body and her mind—if the two can still be thought of separately; a taming of freedom as Mehta would have it.[1] On the other level, a global distribution of movements that simultaneously connected and separated the metropolis and colony,[2] the city and rural areas, the home and public domains, and networks that constitute them.[3]

Between these two levels—the body of the subject on the one hand and larger bodies on the other (bodies of states, populations, aggregated masses, and other collectivities)—there was (still is) a constant diffusion. The structures and logics of one level keep taking shape within and reinform the other. The political technologies developed in one are then imported—or deported—to the other. The image of one is mapped to the other.

In previous chapters I focused on one aspect of this diffusion: a certain amalgamation of images and material mechanisms anchored in the individual body that served to carve different subject-positions which then coalesced into movements *en masse*: waves of immigration, imperial expansion, expulsion of indigenous and/or poor populations. To this diffusion we should add another layer: movement en masse often constitutes large, collective bodies, which are also considered, or conceive themselves as bodies in motion.[4] This chapter shifts its attention to these collective bodies. It is important to emphasize, once again, that my argument here will not be about the phenomena (I do not wish to argue that the social indeed moves, or that the state is formed via a collective movement), but about the ways in which they are thought of and described in political theory, sociology, or anthropology. And yet, beyond a history of ideas, I would like to ask what these claims and understandings do to the political field, to the organization of social relations and the conceptualizations of power relations. What, in other words, are the political implications of a political paradigm pivoting around the movement of collectivities?

Navigating between these movements, this chapter points toward possible directions, questions, and alternative modes of inquiry from which to approach the analysis of movement as a collective undertaking. Most remain gestures, initial provocations that envelope the analysis of this book, and are not fully developed here. Nevertheless, several themes will resurface throughout the chapter, consolidating into more substantial "moves."

First, through and between this chapter's sections an analogy will emerge between political and individual bodies in motion. The moving individual body often serves as a metaphor, a symbol, and a substitute for the body politic. A bound foot of a Chinese girl serves to symbolize China's immobility;[5] a man walking confidently marks European enlightenments;[6] an unconfined movement with no clear direction is taken to indicate barbarism;[7] a disabled figure works "as a critique of the social body."[8] Hence, at times, both sides of this equation, both "bodies" (individual and political) intermingle to the extent that it is unclear which is referred to. This relation of substitution underlies some of this chapter's arguments.

The second thread underlying this chapter is directly derived from the above concept. The question of substitution is frequently also a question of representation. Accordingly, the organic image of these bodies sometimes rests upon an individual body—or several bodies—whose role is to carry the personality of the collective body. For Hobbes the singularity of the sovereign was necessary in order to generate "a reall Unitie of them all in one and the same Person," a "Unity," he argued, that "cannot otherwise be understood in a multitude."[9] But in later theories of social movements collectivities emerge as bodies that cannot be represented by a one or a few: crowds,[10] multitudes,[11] groups of excluded and dispossessed.[12] The questions then, are: how can the collective body be represented, what are the relations between plurality and unity, how does a unity form out of a plurality of people? And to what extent is this unity desirable? I will try to show that at least in political thought, movement is a key to answering these questions.

Third, moving from (the individual) body to (a collective) space, this chapter also reflects on the relation between the two, or more precisely, between space and movement. If, as I argue here, collective bodies such as states or colonies are conceived as bodies/spaces in motion, then space can no longer be seen as a "container" in which movements occur or, in Doreen Massey's formulation, as a "surface on which we are placed."[13] I further propose that space becomes political[14] via the movements it allows and prevents, and the relations that are formed or prevented via these im/mobilities: events in which people suddenly come together, form a community (tentative[15] or permanent[16]), act together; or events in which they are moved apart, fracturing an existing community or disturbing it. Moreover, movement is one of the attributes of political spaces: political spaces are often moving spaces. Movement thereby becomes primary within the anatomy of political spheres.

Finally, this chapter completes an argument that was interlaced throughout this book, namely, that movement, in and of these various bodies, is the *material substance* of both freedom and violence. This concurrence appears in different ways in the different bodies herein considered, and calls us to rethink some of the agreed ethical divisions in accounts of violence, resistance, and political freedom. One of the concrete manifestations of this linkage of freedom and violence is the open sea, which is, accordingly, a recurring theme of this chapter. The sea is a "site" through which state violence was accelerated from the sixteenth to the twenty-first century, through which commerce—itself uniting violence and freedom—became effectively global, through which mass immigration to ever-growing distances became possible (again: a process in which freedom and violence are often entangled as choice, possibilities, and new horizons meet expropriation, deportation, sometimes forced labor, impoverishment and death).

This chapter, then, looks at different collective bodies and shows how movement becomes their principle: the principle of these bodies' unity (their very status as bodies) and then the principle of their action (movement as a condition for action; movement as a form of action; but also, a unity whose mode is movement in one direction). Two bodies with different principles of movement will be the main hinges of this chapter: states and social movements. Nevertheless, other bodies will surface: colonies as moving spaces, empires as the logical outcome of the state's mobile aspirations, or the many-headed hydra as symbolizing a body of resistance.

I begin with Hobbes and the concept of the state, probably the most prominent political body. My reading of Hobbes is a reading into a certain fantasy of the state. It is a reading that remains on a conceptual level, and yet the concept expresses a logic. While unattainable, this logic nevertheless functions as a regulative idea. It is "at once a fact and a task,"[17] even if the fact—by virtue of it being also a task—can never fully materialize; a failed fact, as it were; a political desire.[18] The concept thus shapes political realities, even if never fully and completely so. Taking as its point of departure one of the first conceptions of the modern, sovereign state as a unified, integrated, organic single entity (indeed a body), the first section shows that from its outset, this conceptualization of the state saw movement as knitted into it. Since this movement was primarily outbound, expansion (war, imperialism) emerges as essential to the very conceptual form of the state.

The state, with its dual movement—inward toward consolidation and outward toward imperial expansion—is a technology of relocating violence. By monopolizing movements[19] the state can slowly realize (again, never completely) the Hobbesian fantasy and become a unified entity, preserving a certain degree of bodily integrity by controlling and protecting its borders. The figure of the Leviathan—a giant organism swimming in the ocean without any impediments—conveys the idea that at this point of consolidation, the state has violence under its control: the organic unity is identified with annulling internal violence, and the unbound movement that can erupt in all possible directions demonstrates the state's ability to master violence, embody it, and inflict it. The second section of this chapter reflects on the different modes of violence's movement and the intersections of state violence with other collectivities (other states, political movements, and modes of resistance). It examines what happens to space amid these movements, and how the movement of space becomes a form of violence.

In the last section I move to examine the movements (violent or nonviolent) of transient bodies, coming together to resist the state or other oppressive powers from within or without. Some of these bodies (such as social and political movements) are political bodies par excellence, emphasizing plurality, collective action, and the importance of common spaces. We can follow here Virilio's insight that "revolution is movement but movement is not a revolution"[20] and to further argue that all modes of social change, resistance, and conflict are movements (and there is a double question here, regarding the nature and meanings of both the "are" and "movement" in this sentence). The task would therefore be to map these different movements and to untangle—to the degree that it is possible—the desirable effects, meanings, and facets of different types of movements from the undesirable ones.

Hobbes: The Body of the Leviathan

If one is to consider movements of entire political bodies, Hobbes is once again a key starting point. Hinging his philosophy on movement, and providing one of the most celebrated images of the political space as a body-politic, Hobbes's commonwealth is a body in motion. But to what degree should we take this concept literally? In chapter 3 I argued that Hobbes slips between the figurative and the literal in order to cover another slip, between the organic and the artificial in his concept of sovereignty. I also proposed that this slip is the patch that holds his argument together. Once we come to understand the body-politic as a metaphor, the Hobbesian argument collapses. Here I would like to play with a different reading—one that considers the possibility that neither of the above moves is a "slip." Furthermore, they may not be "moves" at all: the organic and the artificial may be one and the same in a cosmos in which nature can be imitated by "the Art of man," in which the heart is "but a Spring," and in which, accordingly, automata can be seen as having "artificiall life." When "life is but the motion of limbs" and God itself operates like a clockmaker, the separation between the organic and the artificial does not hold.[21]

In her history of the image of the body-politic, Aderana Cavarero argues that Hobbes's body-politic marks a shift in the conceptualization of the notion—both vis-à-vis Greek and medieval formulations (which emphasized the head) and vis-à-vis Harvey's model of the body (which centered on the heart and which greatly influenced Hobbes's notions of motion). Rather than privileging either the head or the heart, Hobbes's profoundly corporeal and mechanistic commonwealth surprisingly pivots around the soul.[22] The soul of the body-politic, the sovereign, is what gives "life and motion to the whole body."[23] Yet the body not only "receives its motion from [the soul]"; it also obtains its unity through it, thereby becoming subjected to the soul:[24] "The subjects are no longer a mere multitude in which each man moves according to his own will, clashing with every other man in a violent and murderous mechanism. They are now incorporated into a people, a union that moves with one will." The commonwealth can thus be seen as "a giant body politic that moves in one direction."[25] The leviathan is a huge machine—or perhaps a technology—of unifying movements.

The social pact vanquishes the plurality of wills, which is, according to Hobbes, the source of (civil) war. Unity and peace thus amalgamate in a cohesive movement of the body-politic. In a few sentences that may bring Plato to mind, Adriana Cavarero claims that "sovereignty is, in fact, the important cohesive power behind the logic of the one. This power embodies everything in a single form, since sovereignty itself is not an element, role, or part of that form, but the form itself, insofar as it is a unity."[26] We can tentatively summarize: *sovereignty as a form; as a unity; as a principle of movement.* Akin to Plato's forms, this unity is what draws the plurality of elements (wills, people, parts, phenomena—a certain multitude) into a single entity. It is what enables movement to become the principle of order rather than of chaos.

Without this unity, the political body gets sick, or disintegrates altogether. A body-politic cannot bear the chaos that is the natural (pre- or nonpolitical) order of things.[27] Thus, it cannot be sustained if a plurality endures. It seems that rather than the essence and substance of politics, as Arendt would have it,[28] plurality appears here as a perpetual cause of politics' disintegration. Yet a more precise account of Hobbes should refuse this very structure of negation. If we follow the direction proposed in the previous chapter—the claim that movement is a medium tying together freedom and violence—we can argue that war is politics and politics, with its necessary plurality, is war, even when war is (temporarily) suspended. Or resituated. The famous aphorism by Clausewitz might receive here another (in)version: politics is the continuation of war within a different spatial order;[29] politics is an order in which an integration of the many into one (a state, a body-politic, a leviathan) allows an externalization of violence.

Indeed, the peace this unity facilitates according to Hobbes (or perhaps the peace that *is* this unity within his framework), and the outlet from a state of nature it provides, is more accurately described as a spatial organization—a redistribution—of violence. In chapter 4 I argued that movements of individual subjects are tamed in the commonwealth by balancing movements "towards" and "fromwards" objects of desire.[30] This taming annuls private, conflicting movements whose collisions may impede the movement of the commonwealth as a whole. In other words, this taming guarantees that the commonwealth's movement would not be limited even from within. No longer torn or pulled in different directions by internal powers, the commonwealth is completely free to move. Accordingly, at the level of the Leviathan, this taming of individual subjects unleashes a beastly movement, which is the freedom of the commonwealth. Freedom remains the lack of impediments on motion: The "Libertie of the Common-wealth . . . is the same with that, which every man then should have, if there were no Civil Laws, nor Common-wealth at all." Moreover, "the effects of it also be the same," namely "a perpetual war."[31] War is the motion of the political body. It is the manner by which commonwealths "stretch out their arms."[32]

The point goes beyond rehearsing the well-known claim that for Hobbes the state of nature (and natural, unlimited liberty) is preserved at the level of the relations between sovereigns. It also goes beyond showing how this claim can be folded back to the definition of freedom as movement (sovereigns are in a state of nature vis-à-vis one another → this means—or this is because—only sovereigns enjoy natural right → freedom is movement → their freedom is war, which is movement → war is the condition of the state of nature, and the circle is completed).[33] The point also adds, even if in tension to the tentative summary above, these principles: *unity as war, as unbound movement, as a principle of violence*. Akin to Plato—for whom motion is totalized as war via "an unproblematic treatment of war as coextensive with motion, indeed, as the moving of bodies"[34]—the Hobbesian totalization of movement is a means of organizing violence. Baracchi's reading of Plato sheds further light on this function of war as necessary to protect, precisely, the cohesiveness of this unity: "There seems to be a deep unity, between a readiness for war outside . . . and the harmony, peace, and self-sameness of the inside. . . . Thus, it is to the extent that the πόλις [polis] is defined or founded (defines itself or arises) as unitary, self-same, and self-enclosed that it is fundamentally at war with others."[35]

A version of this argument is quite familiar in a cynical perception of politics. When factions threaten the integrity of the political community (or more often when there is a need to produce, or imagine, such an integrity), when the current government is threatened, war may provide a solution. Against an outside enemy communities can consolidate. Carl Schmitt organizes the very concept of sovereignty—its very possibility—around this principle.[36]

But if war is a principle of unity, then unity can no longer be imagined as closing or enclosed. It is a unity that has to keep moving. Hannah Arendt identified the extreme form of this link between a politics based on a unitary, organic movement and the refusal of territoriality in her work on totalitarianism. The paradigmatic incarnation of this model is the totalitarian movements of the twentieth century (to which she significantly refers simply as "movements") that seek to completely undo the figure of a state confined within borders: "One should not forget that only a building can have a structure, but that a movement—if the word is to be taken as seriously and as literally as the Nazis meant it—can have only a direction." Therefore, Arendt concludes, if these movements "find themselves physically limited to a specific territory," they "must try to destroy all structure."[37] "The movement" cannot bear the confinement imposed by territory. And note that this merely amplifies (rather than defies) the logic of the state we find in the Hobbesian concept. In both cases the fusion of the many into a single body does not enclose them in defined contours (of the body-politic, of the state's territory), but necessitates an openness to an externality-to-be-conquered.

There is a tension here, between a fantasy of closure and enclosure (of a clearly demarcated territory, sealed within a border, which is a container of the people, the body of the sovereign, or some other formulation[38]), and a movement outward, beyond the state's border, to other territories. Whereas the fantasy of closure cannot be fully realized, it is nonetheless constitutive within the normative conceptualization of borders, as well as within that of sovereignty.[39] Through this tension something is either undone or revealed, and it is unclear to me which or what. Many have argued that sovereignty can be conceived of as absolute only because it is prima facie limited and contained within a territory.[40] If so, then this tension may show that sovereignty's absolutism cannot endure its own conditions. But perhaps these conditions are themselves part of a different fantasy: a fantasy of (internal) peace without (external) violence, of sovereign states without imperial drives. It is a fantasy of international law, of the European notion of the balance of power in which one aspiration for expansion cancels the other, of an international system that is a self-regulating system that keeps moderating the violence of its counterparts. And if, indeed, these conditions are merely a fantasy, expansion appears as embedded in the very concept of the state.[41] Let us add, then: *expansion as a unity that keeps undoing itself by keeping its boundaries mobile, and thus fragile, or even open.*

But Hobbes's argument does not end here. If war is one of the primary movements of the giant, commonwealth-man, conquest is its outcome. And both war and conquest are indispensable for the Hobbesian Leviathan. They are neither accidental nor optional, but are tied to the vital motions of the political persona: the circulation of its blood.[42] Blood and war, blood and conquest, are in Hobbes two complementary movements, and they are both tied together via the movement of commerce. Let us look at this point more slowly.

If so far I have focused on movement as war, the equation can also be reversed. War itself is movement, the mobilization of bodies into motion.[43] This movement out (a manner of "stretching arms," and the double meaning of the word here is significant) is intimately tied to the inner movement of the political body; the movement that keeps every living body animate, that is, the circulation of blood. Whereas war is the concrete articulation of the former outbound movement, commerce is the concrete articulation of the latter.[44] First, the "reduction" of commodities into "Gold, and Silver and Mony" makes them portable enough "as not to hinder the motion of men from place to place"; almost as if a circulation of full-scale commodities would create clogs in the veins of the commonwealth. Commerce, which is thereby enabled, provides the necessary nourishment to the entire body-politic: it "goes round about, Nourishing (as it pathes) every part thereof."[45]

Yet, unlike the blood of mortal men, this blood does not flow in a closed system. On the contrary, the reduction of commodities into blood/money is necessary in order to allow its flow beyond and outside of the boundaries of the commonwealth: "For Gold and Silver, being (as it happens) almost in all Countries of the world highly valued, is a commodious measure of the value of all things else between nations. . . . By the means of which measures, all commodities, Movable, and Immoveable, are made to accompany a man, to all places of his resort, *within and without the place of his ordinary residence.*"[46]

The distinction between internal and external movements thus begins to give way to a single system of movements: commerce and war, blood and arms: "Silver and Gold . . . have the privilege to make Common-wealths move, and stretch out their arms, when need is, into foreign Countries; and supply, not only private Subjects that travel, but also whole Armies with Provision."[47]

The need to sustain the circulation of blood/money sets in motion other parts of the body politics, which has to reach out, beyond its borders, to obtain more of this vital power. Hobbesian war is thus situated not merely between the mutually constitutive duality of enmity and unity that arches from Plato to Schmitt, but calls us to bring Marx into the picture, and with him the movements of capital and its relation to colonial wars and imperial expansions.

This also means that the image of the organic moving Leviathan and the resonance with totalitarian regimes to which I pointed above should not be taken as foregrounding a facet in Hobbes's thinking that works counter to liberal frames.[48] The circulation of commerce within and beyond the contours of the body of the Leviathan is, after all, an early image of the liberal (British) empire: a body politic motivated by trade, almost compelled to reach arms out by the requirement of trade. (As a consequence, the location of the moving soul may require a more nuanced analysis that takes into account economic powers alongside the sovereign. As a seventeenth-century observer describes the emergence of the "empire of the seas": "What is terrifying is that all these powerful nautical organizations were not the doings of States, but almost a spontaneous product of nations' mercantile engineers, the State having played no further role other than to sanction them, to claim them for its own."[49] Trade and sovereignty—or market and state—circled through a shifting hierarchy, one subjected to the other and then the other way around until often, distinguishing between them became impossible.[50])

Trade as movement as freedom—the movement of ships, goods, and money—*was* the freedom of the sea[51] and the pair, "navigation and trade," was hardly parted in arguments justifying the idea of *Mare Liberum*.[52] Trade, that is the "Increase of Ships at Sea," was contrasted to "Arms at Land" and provided a new principle upon which the British Empire could perceive itself as an empire based upon liberty.[53] The crucial point for me is that the sea, *as a principle of movement*, enabled England to reconcile liberty and empire "both theoretically and historically."[54] And yet this trade as movement, as the freedom the sea both symbolized and promised, was also a principle of violence: "originally, before the birth of the great sea powers, the axiom 'freedom of the sea' meant something very simple: that the sea was a zone free for booty."[55] And even much later, freedom of the sea still meant that it was "an area where force could be used freely and ruthlessly."[56] The sea was thus the new normative notion of an accelerated movement of both trade and violence.[57] An unbound, wide-open field, in which ethic itself could set no limits and in which goods, capital, slaves and workers could be moved more and more rapidly, effectively, en masse. All these were tied, as Ian Baucom so powerfully shows: the Atlantic slave trade stood at the basis of creating the systems of financial capitalism, and unraveled the boundaries between state, empire, and trade. It constituted the "capitals of a long Atlantic twentieth century" as "spaces of flows" wherein "an endless variety" of human and nonhuman lives drifted into monetary value that could thus circulate almost unimpeded[58]—a movement that relied on violence to generate and secure it, which provoked violence to usurp it or resist to it, and which was a mode of violence.

The combination of trade and empire via the logic of the sea ultimately serves to tie violence (conquest, war, and new technologies of violence that the sea both enabled and necessitated[59]) and freedom (here, of trade, but this is not to deny other forms of liberal freedom) via movement. The organic image of the state is therefore given within a logic of imperial expansion: the political body, like any living body, must endure in its motion or else it will die; for this purpose it must venture out to feed itself, or else its internal, vital movement will come to an end. Another set of principles then, to complete the summary: *Unity as a certain openness; as the lack of sealed boundaries; as a principle of expansion.*[60] Gilles Deleuze and Félix Guattari identify this structure when they point to the "aptitude" of states "to constitute themselves as a war machine, following other models, another dynamism, a nomadic ambition, over against the state." Thus, despite what might seem, at first, an "opposition" and then a "tension limit"[61] between the interiority of the state's logic and the nomadic structure of "the war machine" (always external and defying borders), the state ultimately "'captures' the 'nomadic' power of war."[62]

To recapitulate: From its very theoretical origins the state is given within a logic of imperial expansion. As we see in Hobbes, sovereignty, thought of as a corporeal political unity, is a principle of movement. And whereas an objection can be put forward, arguing that this movement can be the inward movement of consolidation, David Armitage demonstrates the strong ideological, administrative, and military links between the creation and consolidation of composite states in Europe, and the formation and acquisition of empires overseas.[63] This movement, through which both states and empires come into being and through which they subsist—this movement as the unity of political life—is war: a principle of boundless, expanding violence that keeps the body-politic open, never abiding within its own contours.[64] And if, in some geopolitical context, there were strong powers stabilizing, moderating, and limiting movement, they "only fully [fix] it to the ground within the European continent," Carlo Galli observes, adding that "elsewhere, at sea or outside Europe, [the state] cannot or will not employ war which is completely 'in form.'"[65] In the colonies—"the Procreation, or Children of a Common-wealth" according to Hobbes,[66] the product of its reproductive motion—the state remains fully unbound, unlimited even by the form of its own movement, a point to which we shall return from different directions in the next section.

The State's War and Other Bodies Too

For Hobbes the movement of the body-politic is, at least potentially, unimpeded. Paul Virilio reflects a similar sense when he argues that war is a developing political field (perhaps the main field of politics) that is in constant acceleration. What changes war—and politics—is the boosting speed of its tools and technologies: bullets that can outrun a man; tanks that put entrenchments into motion; airplanes that can bomb a faraway city on short notice; drones that can constantly monitor every movement; ballistic missiles that can kill a distant target in a second; or telecommunications that convey information at an unheard of speed.[67] War, also under this account, is the unleashed movement of the Leviathan. Again, the maritime metaphor is telling: "Popular war is already no longer in a given territory. . . . Like the naval battle, popular war operates on the clash of dynamic bodies. It has to do with the 'excesses sanctioned by the very practices of the sea,' with absolute violence," Virilio argues and adds: "the new soldier will be 'like a fish in water,' and this allusion to the liquid element is hardly coincidental."[68] Modern wars ultimately render land into a sea of violence.

But whereas Virilio's or Hobbes's warring commonwealths move without any limitation, there are other modalities of state violence, with different temporalities or speed. Eyal Weizman articulates a different principle: liberal political technologies are technologies of *moderating* violence. Moderation, it is important to emphasize, is not a stage toward the end of violence, but rather the form violence takes within democratic regimes. It allows violence to persist with less critique and should therefore be seen as one of the conditions to perpetuating it. In short, "the moderation of violence is part of the very logic of violence."[69] This is not to say that liberal democracies are less violent than other regimes. It is merely to say that once it becomes visible, if it is to endure in time, their violence has to anchor itself in justification mechanisms. The mechanism of moderation, which is built into the logic of the lesser evil, is one such mechanism. We have encountered the conceptual infrastructure of this argument in different ways throughout this book: the structure of moderated movement as an essential liberal structure.

We can therefore add another component to the genealogy of moderated movement that has unfolded herein: a concept of individual freedom; a model of subjectivity; a model of the state; a desirable (self-balancing) international system; a technology of power; and now also the structure of violence. Across these different strata we see, first, the reoccurrence of the same structure, and second, its role within colonial rule. If so far (and more specifically, in chapters 1 and 4) moderated movement (of individual bodies) served to set apart a whole sphere of presumably excessive movements that became an anchor for violence, here another moderated movement—that of violence—operates in this space once set apart.

There are two contrary trajectories here: eruptions of unimpeded violence and the movement of its moderation. Both are not just a function of a language of justification that combines a judicial discourse and a particular self-perception of democratic crowds. They are also a function of material and spatial economies of violence. Take Palestinian refugee camps for example. Their narrow streets and dense construction set strict limitations upon the movement of military units. Brigadier general (Reserves) and philosopher Shimon Naveh explains in an interview to Yotam Feldman: "In urban warfare the military can no longer move within classic military structures [such as] the arrow or the tree." The force of unitary violence disintegrates, dissipates, and is dissolved by and in the narrow streets.[70] To put it in more Hobbesian terms, the Leviathan cannot move freely in the "Casbah" (which thus appears as a mode of resistance to military violence in and of itself[71]). If state violence seeks to continue in its full speed, it needs to either alter urban terrain or bypass it, relying on weapons that are not subject to the spatial limitations of narrow streets (such as missiles, airplanes, or drones that can move at greater distances to bomb urban areas).[72] From the redesign of Paris in the nineteenth century by von Haussmann (an urban architecture that would then be exported throughout the world) to the cycles of destruction and rebuilding of Gaza in the twentieth and twenty-first centuries (from the construction of refugee camps, to their destruction and reconstruction), urban design is also a function of the many points of encounter—potential and actual—between state violence and resistance. Wide boulevards are built to prevent the barricading of streets;[73] "long, straight, broad streets" are "tailor-made" to allow the free flow of military units and give full effect to new military moving objects—from cannons to tanks;[74] huge D9 bulldozers strip the land at the city's outskirt to demarcate clear and visible boundaries whose transgression is a visible violation;[75] cities and entire political communities are walled to prevent their potential violence from flowing out.[76] At the same time state's fences are met with insurgents' tunnels,[77] demolition with reconstruction,[78] and expropriation with t'sumud (persistence, in Arabic): a refusal to leave despite all difficulties; a footing in the ground.

Alongside changing space, military violence changes the form of its own movement. Naveh explains how in response to the new intensity of urban warfare during the Second Intifada, the Israeli army adopted new modes of movement: diffused, nonunitary movement whose shape is inspired by fractal geometry.[79] "Interpreting" (as Naveh put it to Weizman in a different interview) alleys as forbidden passageways and walls as sites of motion, this movement turns physical barriers into passageways. The military thus becomes "a worm that eats its way forward, emerging at points and then disappearing,"[80] as space becomes boundless.

In either case, military violence is revealed to be a form of architecture, a "design undertaken by destruction," as Weizman terms it, whose ideal pattern unsurprisingly takes the form of the sea. Naveh reveals in his interviews to both Feldman and Weizman "a military fantasy-world of boundless fluidity, in which the city's space becomes as navigable as an ocean."[81] In colonial urban warfare, the fantasy of unbound naval-like movement of violence and conquest, which we saw in the previous section, pervades every space.[82]

This fantasy—and its concrete realizations—amplify a wider strategy of rendering the space unstable. Imaginary lines keep changing their place as we saw in chapter 1, "flying checkpoints" move around,[83] "closed military zones" and restricted areas are opened and then closed again,[84] all maps become history even before they are published,[85] the laws of movement in the space, into and out of it, are unstable and unpredictable—the result is a space that becomes fluid.

In 2009 *Le Monde Diplomatique* published a map of the West Bank as an archipelago; islands surrounded by sea (figure 5.1).

The map is a critique demonstrating the isolation of the Palestinian enclaves, yet it also represents the fantasy of unlimited Israeli violence. The sea serves as a principle of boundless motion in which both settlers and the Israeli army can move uninterrupted. Accurately conveying the immobility of land versus sea (thereby, as an aside, completely naturalizing, if not dematerializing Israeli forces), the map misses an essential element of the regime of movement. Akin to the attributes Stoler identifies as part of what defines colonies in general,[86] these "islands" or land cells, are not "fixed designated space[s]" but spaces in movement.[87]

The oPt (perhaps other colonies too, or even "the colony," as Stoler argues), thus becomes another collective political entity in motion. Yet unlike the state, it is not a collective *body* in motion, but rather a "complex border zone";[88] an entire space that is composed of "fluctuating, yet omnipresent, border zones for permanent residence";[89] a political entity that is a moving border.[90] (And this permeation of the logic of the border—a site of closure and transit simultaneously—through the entire space of the colony[91] may explain how the *fluidity* of space produces the *immobility* of the colonized.[92]) As Handel shows, this "spatial uncertainty" is an effective technology of control.[93]

A structural perspective could conclude here by delineating the collec-

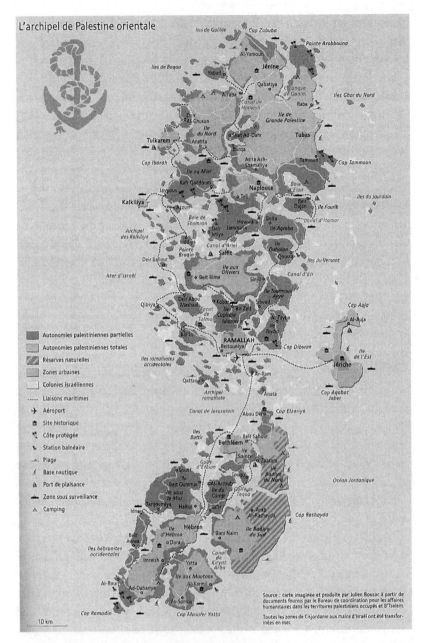

5.1 The West Bank as an archipelago. ©Julien Bousac. Courtesy Julien Bousac.

tive body of the colony in contrast to the state's body: an autonomous body presumably sealed by borders, versus a "body" that is a border, and yet completely breached to the movement of the colonizer (while pervasively limiting the movement of the colonized);[94] a body whose movement is determined by its own principle versus a body whose "legitimate means of movement" are not its own but are given to (or taken by) others; a body whose movement is moderated or free (without impediments) versus states of instability or immobility. This contrast, this analogy, is another element within a series of correlations and differentiations that can be drawn between a plurality of collective bodies in motion: states (and empires), multitudes of different types, (social) movements, and colonies. Another set of correlations can be drawn between political bodies and the individual bodies that they assume and constitute: the liberal subject and the liberal state,[95] the colony and the colonized subject,[96] and other duos, such as the activist and the social movement.

However, even though I find the possibility of drawing such a map fascinating, perhaps instead of such a structural analysis asking about the concept of "the" colony or "the" state, it would be more valuable to look at what people (some would say here "from below") "do" with movement: how they move; where they go; in what ways differential movements (prescribed, incited, or transgressive) dictate differential use of space; what strategies people develop when they are stopped; what obstacles do they find to block the violent movement of the state itself (building barricades, burning tires, sitting tight on a road). What movements become trivialized, naturalized, transparent in their routine actualization, and what movements appear—consequently or not—as transgressive, heroic, exceptional? What happens when people are too scared to move (and who is scared; and when and where—which streets are safe, and for whom; and how do people nonetheless find ways to move in threatening spaces)? What happens when people insist on moving despite this fear, or when they stay put despite powerful powers seeking to displace them? When, how, and why separate people come together, and what drives them apart? What happens in the temporary points of encounter that, even momentarily, render people a community? Such a mode of inquiry would have to go beyond the movements of people themselves and incorporate the movements of things and different forms of assemblages forming between them.

Let us take the analysis of colonial movements as a brief example for such a shift in the mode of analysis. From this perspective it is not sufficient to delineate the drawing of borders or the borders' own movements; the movements of armies and territories. A much more complex map of movements would be called for, charting different movements—of soldiers and citizens; of cars on roads, drones in the sky, or pedestrians on hills;[97] of insurgents and smugglers; of goods—permitted or not—and resources; of sewage;[98] of water—shrinking means of existence or overflowing threats, sites of leisure and a powerful mode of control; of factories (and other sites of employment, as well as pollution); humidity and malaria that determine and are determined by the circulations and settlements within the colonies. It would have to list the conditions of movement, the limitations set upon them, as well as strategies of bypassing them,[99] the destinations that remain open and those that are foreclosed (fully, partially, or potentially[100]). Moreover, such an analysis would have to take into account also affective movements that are tightly controlled but always defying the attempts to fully regulate them. Being moved by a place and its people has always been central to colonial administrations—the need to maintain separation between populations always threatens ideologies of separation, and questions of feeling foreign or at home are essential to establish the hierarchy between colonies and metropoles. Stoler's attentive reading in colonial archives has shown how this meaning of being moved is central to the calculation of the physical movements of both colonized and colonizers within and across the colonial map: governors, merchants, local populations, concubines, "mixed" children, or caregivers, had to be attached to certain localities and not to others, to certain people and not others.[101] The fear of attachments or the need to foster "proper" attachments—"proper" modes of being moved—thus further increased the circulation into, out of, and between the colonies and the motherland. Affective movements, then, have to be tamed too, alongside—and as a part of—the movements of populations throughout Earth and the local movements of individual bodies.

Political and Social Movements

This duality of the verb ("to move") is significant. What moves people affectively is crucial not only to moving them physically across empires, or to foster instead their rootedness (feeling at home; staying put). As Deborah Gould argues, emotions are also necessary for political action, and—if we are to stay with this chapter's focus on collective bodies—to the formation of social movements. To mobilize people, to move them out of their homes and into the streets, certain emotions must be at play (anger, rage, hope, affection and solidarity, perhaps even love).[102] Moving people (to the streets) by moving them (producing emotions) ultimately creates *a* movement, now in a third meaning. "The *movement* in 'social movements' gestures towards the realm of affect; bodily intensities; emotions, feelings, and passions; and towards uprising," argues Gould.[103]

The term, however, should be further unpacked. Within this context, "movement" denotes also the desire for change ("movement" as a goal: transformation, reform, or revolution) as well as some of the means of promoting it (techniques and modes of simultaneous movements that should bring about this change; the physical condition for assembly, and then the manners by which assemblies act). Put differently, the social movement is a platform for mobilizing people into action in order to stir the movement of the body-politic elsewhere, or in a different language altogether: to demonstrate that the world can be "set . . . into motion" in (or by) political action.[104] Being both the goal and the means of obtaining it, movement becomes almost equivalent with political work, if not with the political sphere.

Michael Hardt's analysis of the contemporary anti-globalization movement might serve as an example for this somewhat elastic use of the concept. Hardt thinks of a network of movements, itself in motion, that is being transformed via a movement between different localities. Furthermore, the network of movements, unlike the structure of parties or states, facilitates a different kind of politics, according to him: it operates "a sea-change, the flow of the movements transforming the traditional fixed positions; networks imposing their force through a kind of irresistible undertow." Accordingly, "the multitude in the movements is always overflowing."[105] A politics of change whose structure is change itself (a flow rather than an oppositional struggle; a sea—once again—that cannot be fixed).

But the term—"movement"—has another significant function in this context. If, as I propose, movement is essential in consolidating different political bodies, the term "movement" may also point to another desire: a desire that the dispersed many will become a plural body—"a" movement. And yet this unity, which Tilly identified as one of the main attributes defining social movements,[106] is quite ambivalent. It is sufficient to think of the feminist movement, the Zionist movement, the labor movement, or the Civil Rights movement (to name just a few), to see that most social movements are quite dispersed. People attach themselves to these movements sporadically and temporarily; flow in and out; join some activities and not others; identify with some goals and not others. Most do not have agreed-upon shared symbols or marks of identifications distinguishing their members (and if there are some, they are voluntary: adopted by some and not others, adorned on some occasions and not others, and hence never serve to unequivocally identify). Most do not have a single locus of power, nor agreed-upon leaders, sometimes not even a face to represent them (in the occupy and anti-globalization movement this has become essential and explicit, and the face that is often taken to represent these movements is the mask of Guy Fawkes, conveying simultaneously anonymity and iconized resistance). How, then, is a unity achieved? "When everyone raises their hands in the same time, and . . . makes the same call, [they] become one body, [they] become a community," Dana Yahalomi, the leader of the artist/research group Public Movement provides a possible reply.[107] "That is a very simple thing, but it functions on [a very] basic level."[108]

Episodes of orchestrated physical, individual motions take many forms, but most iconographic and most common among these are the protest march and the demonstration. When the many march—in the streets, on the roads, on the bridges—it is, in Elias Canetti's words, "as though the movement of some of them transmits itself to the others," to the extent that at some moments it feels as if everything is "happening in one and the same body."[109] Canetti points to the striking fact that it is almost only on such occasions that we no longer fear the touch of strangers.[110] The equality obtained in the crowd,[111] as well as a feeling that develops in it that we are part of a *single* collective body, permits this openness to others. And with this equality, this touch, this space "in which each man *moves* among his peers,"[112] power, in the political meaning on which Arendt insisted, appears. In this sense, the movement of the marching many is not merely the "manifestation," but the actual "materialization" of political power,[113] as well as the social movement's structure: like a march, a social movement endeavors to amass people on its way, to tread new paths, and reroute the body-politic into a new direction.

The unity of the social movement is thus a flexible unity that keeps unraveling and reforming. It is not the unity of the Hobbesian commonwealth (or the Platonic republic) that must be represented by a certain singularity (be it a "mon-archy," that is, a "one-man-rule," a single sovereign, or a democracy in which "the people 'is many in one'" in Arendt's formula,[114] or any other rule through which "'the many become one in every respect' except bodily appearance"[115]). Rather, it is a unity that must sustain the plurality and differences of the many.[116] Not just Arendt's plurality, but also the figure of the many-headed hydra, skillfully described by Peter Linebaugh and Marcus Rediker, can provide here the structure. Perhaps the body against which the Leviathan was formed,[117] the hydra is a body that defied all unity: a body not only represented by or composed of many, but a body that takes the form of a plurality.[118] Accordingly, if Hobbes argued that "Unity cannot . . . be understood in multitude" unless it is represented "by one man, or one Person,"[119] these political bodies are often represented by "an iconography of nonsovereignty and anonymity" or simply "the assembled masses."[120]

As an essential aside we should note that not all movements take this form, and it is important to be cautious when celebrating and romanticizing a politics of movement—of flux and change. After all, even though the term "social movement" was introduced in 1848 by Lorenz von Stein (a German sociologist),[121] it was first defined by Schmitt.[122] The fascist and pan-European movements offered a radically different unity of the political body. Presumably stable, natural, and cohesive, this unity too, was seen as a function of the movement itself. As the "dynamic engine" of the political body, only "the movement" could mediate between the state (which is seen as a static, juridical structure) and the party (as a faction representing not the whole but the part).[123] The movement then, was the only political power that coalesced the different elements composing a political entity (state, people, and movement, in the Schmittian formulation).[124]

Be they progressive or reactionary, egalitarian or not, all are "movements" not merely by definition (social movements, political movements, the movements of decolonization, of labor, of change), but also by their modes of action. Some social movements use sites of motion (streets) and assemblies (squares) according to the patterns originally ascribed to them (hence, even if a march changes the objects moving in the street—bodies rather than cars—it still follows a certain intended pattern). Others seek to break existing technologies and sites of motion: to block the street, to create walls with bodies, to interrupt or suspend the routine movements of daily life, to work against the liberal logic of flow (a sit-in would take place in the middle of a construction site; a tent would be built in the middle of the city; a hike would take place in a closed military zone).

Finally, both in terms of modes of action and in terms of representation, space is often what is at stake in civic resistance:[125] we learn to become civic—perhaps even democratic—via a movement in the public space, walking among friends and strangers ("our peers," as Arendt puts it). The call of many movements of resistance is thus not just for free movement (assembly, marching) but for a designated common place: streets, agoras, squares, cities—as places of encounter, dialog, even residence, rather than merely spaces of transit.

Therefore, the movement/s of revolution or social change are not given within a sharp dichotomy wherein movement is tied to freedom, politics, and action, whereas confinement is a technology of limitation and control. The examples of Zuccotti Park, Tahrir Square, or Taksim Square can be taken to emphasize what is already present in the very term of the *occupy* movement:[126] a demand to *take place*.[127] "Occupation is," in W. J. T. Mitchell's words, "the paradoxical synthesis of social movement and mobilization with immobility, the refusal to move. It is a movement whose central declaration is, as the classic protest song puts it, 'We shall not be moved.'"[128] We can return to Arendt to argue that the political space, as a space of movement, can sustain its political meaning only when it is confined.[129]

Concluding Notes

Shifting the attention to collective motions, this chapter opened the meaning of the concept ("movement") to uses and contexts that have been sidelined in my analysis so far. Adding to the physical movements that have stood at the heart of this book so far also emotions, social movements, and many uses that might seem quite metaphorical, it further developed the problem that subtended many of the discussions in the preceding chapters concerning the meaning of the term. Movement—perhaps merely as an example to any concept, at the very least any political concept[130]—cannot be stabilized within a series of differentiated meanings and linguistic functions. When a concept serves to symbolize or represent something else (when it functions as a metonym, a metaphor, a figurative manner of speech); when it is also a condition for that something (emotions to mobilization, or collective orchestrated motions to the consolidating of a movement); when it manifests and demonstrates that this something exists or can exist (like a march—or an occupation of a city square—to a social movement), can we distinguish between completely different meanings? Doesn't this simultaneously put under question our ability to distinguish, for example, metaphorical from literal meanings, or direct from derivative ones?

The list of matters at hand is thereby mounting: the patterns of motion the state tries to impose, or that are the state's movement, and the motion of the plurality of those who are ruled by the state (as citizens or colonized, and the many who show how these categories themselves are too simplistic: poor, women, migrants, travelers, deported, incarcerated); the motion of violence (of states, individuals, and other political actors, of slave trade, riots, disposition, and decolonization); the motion of labor (of immigration and work, itself often violent), and the motion of a lack of labor (hunger, pauperism, homelessness); the motion of power and revolutions, the motion of those who assemble and those (such as police forces) who break assemblies; e-motions, drives, and aversions: we can follow Hobbes's insight to argue that in all these motions violence and freedom are entangled.

In its most concretely political articulation, this bind demands us to recognize that the violence of resistance is part of a struggle for freedom as well as an expression of freedom—something we often tend to forget when violence is securitized and cast as "terror," and in different contexts as "anarchism."[131] Differently put, the bind of violence and freedom to which I point is not marked here to demonstrate that freedom is somehow already corrupted. It seeks to point our attention to the liberating endeavors at the foundation of what may sometimes appear to us as mere violence (and again, coming from the Israeli context this seems crucial). At the same time however, it is important to also bear in mind the other side of this equation, namely that freedom often rests on heavy security apparatuses, and at times also violence.

Since my argument here relies on a structural point—violence and freedom ultimately take the same form, and this form is movement—and since this may appear to be in tension with what I argued in previous chapters, a few words of clarifications are called for. My argument so far has drawn on movement primarily as a liberal apparatus *distinguishing* freedom and violence (order from chaos, civic liberty from license). Moderated movement represented and was the material articulation of liberal freedom, whereas modes of excess were taken to both articulate and further justify violence.[132] The crux of the matter is the urge to keep asserting differentiations in order to maintain an ethical claim; to untangle matters—movements—so to be able to distinguish the sphere of freedom from spheres of violence. This principle of differentiation, however, is completely artificial. "Moderation" can only be determined vis-à-vis an assumed excess, which is at times produced in order to configure some constellations (which we deemed to be normative, just, or good) as moderate. In this way moderation, which is but a fear of excesses, operates not only by taming movement but also by *producing excesses as external*. Since this production can change according to context, culture, history, or geography,[133] eventually movement remains the material medium through which both freedom and violence take form.

This last claim calls our attention to the radical difference between mechanisms of justification—which were at the focus of this book—and the reality on which they operate (and which they constantly alter, enable, shape, and re-imagine). If the mechanism of justification seeks to mark a radical difference between two modes of movement that also part freedom and violence, in reality the two collapse. As I proposed, too often, the freedom of one is a form of violence toward the other.[134] The question of justice cannot do away with this predicament, and I believe that any effort to promote more just political organizations must recognize the violence that is embedded within freedom. This is not to relinquish the struggle for freedom and justice, but rather to broaden the perspectives from which we consider those, to develop sensitivities, and to be attuned to the various apparatuses that are at play when we maximize some liberties.

To conclude, let me approach this task from a direction different from the one taken so far: from the point of view of the colonizer, which in my particular example, is also the point of view of settlement (which, if I was not mistaken in my arguments in the previous chapter, functions within this framework as a precondition for movement as freedom, and is therefore interwoven into it). Ann Stoler, who has defined the colony as "a principle of managed mobilities,"[135] argued that colonies are "rendered un-homely for those on whom [they are] imposed, as well as for those to whom [they are] offered as a stolen gift. There is no being 'at home,' [in a colony] only unsettled waiting for something else, for release from those unfulfilled promises and that anxious unfilled labor," she proposed.[137] Is this a statement seeking to point to a certain order of things? If so, we have here yet another version of the impulse of differentiation to which I pointed above. Reading Stoler's claim in this way reveals once again a desire for a more-or-less simply-achievable postcolonial justice: if the settlers are not "at home" in the colony, decolonization can be a struggle for freedom without a price; it would merely (as we indeed often hear) send the colonizers "back home." Decolonization would thus generate a home for all. But if this were the case, how could we explain projects such as Zionism (or American patriotism, which is not less based on a colonial history), the attachment to settlement, the assertions of homeliness, and a sense of deep belonging of so many colonizers (French in Algiers, or whites in South Africa)? Even more so, can colonial projects be sustained for prolonged periods without this sense of home that secures the presence of the colonizers in the colony (why else would so many of them settle, with the desert or swamps, the mosquitos and diseases, and above all, with the natives who insisted that this is actually their home)? Rather than reading Stoler's claim as denying this complexity, I therefore prefer to read it as an imperative set upon us, to remember the price that is paid by some so others can, precisely, be at home; to recognize that too often the home of one is a destruction of the other's. Only if we can sustain the two edges of this duality (the price and the home; the violence and the freedom) can we begin to develop and imagine new models of home, as well as "principles of mobilities," that form a radically different matrix of movement.

CONCLUSION

Let us begin anew, if only to unfold the argument one last time. "It is through the prevention of motion that space enters history," argues Reviel Netz in the opening to *Barbed Wire*.

> Define, on the two-dimensional surface of the earth, lines across which motion is to be prevented, and you have one of the key themes of history. With a closed line (i.e., a curve enclosing a figure), and the prevention of motion from outside the line to its inside, you derive the idea of property. With the same line, and the prevention of motion from inside to outside, you derive the idea of prison. With an open line (i.e., a curve that does not enclose a figure), and the prevention of motion in either direction, you derive the idea of border. Properties, prisons, borders: it is through the prevention of motion that space enters history.[1]

Motion, Netz further argues, can be prevented along three main technological lines: absolute material barriers, obstacles that make movement difficult and thus undesirable, or "purely symbolic definitions of limits" such as "a yellow line painted on the pavement." All, he claims, rely "on the potential presence of force (where there is a yellow line, there are usually also police nearby)."[2] While Netz is undoubtedly right in claiming that force is often involved in the regulation of movement, he might be too hasty in this sweeping attachment of police to yellow lines (that is, of violence to symbolic systems of regulating movement). Sometimes crossing a yellow line on the floor results in reprimanding looks (say, by the clerk at the post office, or by the person standing before you in line); sometimes you would simply be considered rude. The particular object of Netz's critique—barbed wires—surely provides a case of visceral force operating against the bodies of both animals and humans, but power is not reducible to force or violence and moreover, it is often internalized, rendering external enforcement mechanisms less and less necessary (mentioning Foucault here seems almost redundant).

There are three layers to peel away from this mechanism, if we are to understand it in its full complexity: (i) the modes by which the apparatuses and ideologies of self-regulation take form and the manners by which these apparatuses render the deployment of (external) violence less necessary; (ii) the apparatuses that are there to enforce (i) (the police next to the yellow line, in Netz's example); and (iii) the spaces that are excluded from (i) in which violence operates in a different manner than the violence of (ii). These are the spaces of imaginary lines. These are the spaces that stood at the focus of chapters 1, 2, and 4: the spaces in which the symbolic systems (or other material conditions) that often regulate movement are broken. In the gaps that are opened subjects emerge that cannot abide by the law that keeps constituting itself as foreign.[3]

In different ways, each of this book's chapters tried to touch upon these three layers. Akin to Netz's, my primary test case was one of a tight regulation of movement as a form of oppressive power: a regime of movement that constantly recruits violent means to secure the movement—regulations it enforces, and that is a form of violence in and of itself. In chapters 1, 2, and segments of chapter 5, I tried to show that we cannot understand this system of movement restrictions without also understanding the third layer: this system finds its very rationale and justification by its seemingly paradoxical and illogical modes of self-undoing. I also argued that this justification relies on a schism that dissects one mode of movement (I called it here "moderated" but the term itself can be questioned) from another mode: the former is cast as freedom, while the latter as a threat (we can call it, in the context in question, "terror"). Chapter 3, and to a lesser degree also chapter 4, sought to trace back this model of "moderation" (on the backdrop of which "excess" or "self-undoing" emerge as such) via a reading in canonic political theory (thereby providing a segment of layer (i). At least partially, my aim was to show that the model of regulated freedom has historically served, and still serves today, within a matrix of differentiations and hierarchizations that is classed, gendered, and colonial.

Time and again we find the idea that stability, and with it the possibility of moderated movement, is based on a particular relation to the ground (appropriation, ownership, settlement, if not a particular geographical location). On the one hand, those who have land—those whose land is their own (be it property owners or full citizens of the state)—are not merely entitled to move in it freely (the movement of others has been blocked by a fence or a wall); their movement is free movement and must therefore be protected. On the other hand, the movement of others may be restricted because this restriction is not conceived as an infringement upon freedom, but primarily, as the containment of a security problem.

This model, then, goes way beyond Locke or Mill. It forms an ideology of governance that runs as a thread through a long political tradition that is by no means cohesive, coherent or unitary, but that nonetheless can be seen developed from Hobbes to Bentham and to Kant and within which we still live.

Ultimately, the configuration—but also the production—of movement cannot be understood separately from schemas of race, gender, ethnicity, or class, in which bodies are produced and organized. However, we cannot fully understand the cases above if we try to trace them in bodies already racialized (or gendered, classed, made foreign or disabled) or—as seen in chapter 3—even universalized. Understanding the processes and frameworks I described in this book as operating on *already* categorized bodies, molding them into particular patterns of identity and then imagining them as moving in ways that are somehow "improper" in order to provide an excuse—a justification—for their exclusion from the liberal frame of subject/citizen would miss the point. Such an attempt would endeavor to remove a certain mask, yet in so doing might miss what the mask (the myth) does and how it becomes part of the reality of bodies and their governance. The movement of subjects—which is always given in this dialectic of myth and reality, of possibilities and actualizations—partakes in the formation of bodies. Put differently, schemas of identity are formed in tandem with schemas of mobility.

Taking form via im/mobility, identity categories can function in several ways. Identity itself can become (or be revealed as) fluid, and movement can thus function as a critique of stable and static images of subjectivity (as Manning proposes, and in different ways also Harraway, Grosz, or Butler[4]). This book, however, focused on how this configuration of identity circulates rather within a network of violences. State violence always seeks a justification; it is as if states cannot bear their own violence for too long unless it is anchored in some ethical schema. Assumptions of difference—economic, gendered, racial—have long provided such a justification for exclusionary practice and violence. Yet the more a regime perceives itself as egalitarian, the more reluctant it is to draw on identity categories in order to justify different principles of governance. One cannot be arrested simply because he is black;[5] one cannot be denied suffrage simply because she is a woman;[6] one's village cannot be demolished simply because she does not belong to the Jewish majority in Israel.[7] Patterns of mobility have functioned, and still do, to convert these identities into punishable (criminal, as well as pathological) practices. That is, they serve to frame marginalized subject-positions in a seemingly universal language (presumably merely the modes of changing one's position in space), and, moreover, as actions. Discrimination can thus take the form of a sanction (punishment or other forms of either retribution or disciplining). It thereby becomes more transparent somehow, more acceptable.

To work, however, mechanisms that justify state violence or other structural modes of discrimination must be embraced and "bought into" by significant segments of the public. I believe that the justification mechanism this book identified is so prevalent also because for some, a different principle of movement might carry a substantial price. If movement indeed—as I tried to show in different ways throughout the book—mediates freedom and violence to the degree that in some contexts they can barely be distinguished, then the liberal fantasy of separating the peaceful existence of some from the violence inflicted upon others is disturbed. Several years ago I moved to Morningside Heights in New York City (next to Columbia University, bordering with Harlem). Different friends who saw the location of my assigned apartment and who used to live in the vicinity of the neighborhood had similar versions of the same reaction: "Don't worry," they said (I never worried . . .) "it is very safe now." Indeed, it seemed safe enough, or at least safe enough *for me*. Police officers deployed around the block kept safety, and I was never afraid to walk around, day or night. But making the streets safe for some—and the feminist campaign of taking back the night should resonate here—entailed rendering them unsafe, and less accessible, for others (who were residents of the neighborhood before me, and who stayed there after I left). In the accounts of my friends, my safety and the violence inflicted upon other residents of the neighborhood seemed to be both necessarily entangled and constantly denied. Coming from Israel, this conundrum was not unfamiliar.

It was Israel—rather than racial profiling in NYC streets or many other possible points of departure—that served as the primary geopolitical hinge for this book, not because it is exceptional, but because it presents a lucid representation of a rather pervasive and widespread principle of movement. Whether here, there, or in so many other contexts, the amalgamation of freedom and violence within the phenomenon of movement proposes that there are important reasons to have doubts about the possibility of a simple postcolonial or racial justice (a version of which ended the last chapter) in which everyone is more free (or more accurately, some maintain their freedoms while others can become equally free). This is not to suggest one should abandon the struggle for justice. Rather, it is to claim that mapping and recognizing the prices some of us would have to pay in this struggle is crucial in forming real coalitions (indeed, movements), that might, ultimately, construct more just systems of movement and residence—ones in which the above conundrum would be sidelined, if not dissolved. In some rare spaces, such coalitions already work toward these goals.

NOTES

Preface

1. The technical data in this preface is based on a series of interviews with a CEO of a security surveillance company, who until recently worked as a senior developer of algorithms for a leading international provider of security systems.
2. Michel Foucault had already identified this meaning of norm in his 1977–78 lectures at the Collège de France.
3. Suicides are one of the main causes for delays in train schedule in the Western world and preventing them is a high priority for public-transport companies.
4. Seeing movement requires very primitive calculation abilities, requiring virtually no memory. It relies merely on the ability to compare images taken over short intervals, annul similarities, and indicating change.
5. The surveilled movement in the description above, for example, is the "thing" that differs (the substance that is either protected or is sought to be prevented), the anchor for identifying differences (between passengers and thieves or travelers and terrorists), the prism through which differences are articulated (that is, normality as a pattern of movement). As a consequence of all these, difference is also *concretely produced* by the production or restriction of distinct modes of movement. Since movement enables differentiation between subjects on seemingly universal grounds (the mode of shifting positions in space), it is summoned to justify discrimination, exclusion, domination, and the use of force in liberal regimes.
6. We conducted a second interview shortly after the 2013 Boston Marathon, in which

two bags exploded, killing three and wounding 170 people. The CEO noted that the previous security algorithms could have probably identified the bags, yet that they would have probably prevented the marathon from taking place, triggering many alerts every time an object is forgotten or disposed of. "This is why no one uses such systems anymore," he remarked.

7 Michel Foucault, *Security, Territory, Population: Lectures at the Collège De France, 1977–78* (New York: Palgrave Macmillan, 2007).

Introduction

Epigraph: Liisa Malkki, "National Geographic: The Rooting of Peoples and the Territorialization of National Identity among Scholars and Refugees," *Cultural Anthropology*, 7, no. 1 (1992): 24.

1 Hannah Arendt, *Men in Dark Times* (London: Cape, 1970), 9. Arendt does not merely provide here a report concerning the history of an idea, but shares crucial elements concerning the sense of its importance. Yet, her perception of both freedom and movement is radically different from—and is to a great extent written as a *critique of*—the idea of freedom as movement at the focus of the book: a liberal notion that anchors freedom/movement to an *individual* body. Her own way of thinking about and through movement then calls for a separate analysis.

2 Hanna Arendt, "Introduction into Politics," in *The Promise of Politics* (New York: Schocken Books, 2005), 129.

3 Michel Foucault, *Madness and Civilization: A History of Insanity in the Age of Reason* (New York: Vintage Books, 1973).

4 Michel Foucault, *Discipline and Punish: The Birth of the Prison* (New York: Vintage Books, 1979); and *Society Must Be Defended: Lectures at the Collège De France, 1975–76*, 1st ed. (New York: Picador, 2003).

5 Foucault, *Security, Territory, Population: Lectures at the Collège De France, 1977–78* (New York: Palgrave Macmillan, 2007).

6 William Walters, "Deportation, Expulsion, and the International Police of Aliens," *Citizenship Studies* 6, no. 3 (2002): 267.

7 Nicholas De Genova and Nathalie Mae Peutz, *The Deportation Regime: Sovereignty, Space, and the Freedom of Movement* (Durham, NC: Duke University Press, 2010); and Liisa Malkki, "National Geographic: The Rooting of Peoples and the Territorialization of National Identity among Scholars and Refugees," *Cultural Anthropology* 7, no. 1 (1992): 24–44.

8 It is important to stress here that it is highly problematic to call Israel "liberal" or "democratic," given that roughly a third of the people under its rule are not citizens and are denied of basic rights and liberties. Nevertheless, if we look at the practice, rather than the mere ideal of democracies, this is their rule, rather than exception. Ever since the emergence of democracy in Greece, the institutional slavery in

America, or the lack of voting rights for women in most liberal democracies until the middle of the twentieth century, democratic regimes include (and some would say are based upon) an exclusion of large groups of people from their egalitarian principles. To a lesser degree this is the case with most—if not all—of democracies still today. It is therefore possible to say that Israel shares the logic of liberal democracies that were—many still are—colonial and imperial in nature.

9 See John C. Torpey's *The Invention of the Passport: Surveillance, Citizenship, and the State* (Cambridge: Cambridge University Press, 2000).

10 James C. Scott, *Seeing Like a State: How Certain Schemes to Improve the Human Condition Have Failed* (New Haven, CT: Yale University Press, 1998); Tim Cresswell, *On the Move: Mobility in the Modern Western World* (New York: Routledge, 2006).

11 Adi Ophir, "State," *Mafteakh: Lexical Journal for Political Thought* 3 (2011). Thus, even if we think of liberalism as an ideology of openness—of laissez-faire—we must take into account the array of potential closures that is at play for this free circulation to work in tandem with the logic of sovereignty. Foucault's lectures from 1977–78 can be read as working on this distinction between the nonintervention and the raison d'état (*Security, Territory, Population*). The logic of the state necessitates it to adhere also to considerations of security, that—even though they begin to be conceived of in the eighteenth century precisely under the terms of free circulation—also necessitate the potential of governability. If, for example, we are to open the food market to importation, the state must ensure it knows what is being imported and from where, in order to be able to halt the imports should a plague be detected at the country of origin, or should this country be sanctioned.

12 "The idea of the 'nation-state' as a prospectively homogeneous ethnocultural unit ... necessarily entailed efforts to regulate people's movements" into, outside of, and within the state's borders. Therefore, "in the course of the past few centuries, states have successfully usurped from rival claimants such as churches and private enterprises the 'monopoly of the legitimate means of movement'—that is, their development as states has depended on effectively distinguishing between citizen/subject and possible interlopers, and regulating the movements of each" (*The Invention of the Passport*, 1–2, my italics). See also Wendy Brown, *Walled States, Waning Sovereignty* (New York: Zone Books, 2010), chapter 2, "Sovereignty and Enclosure."

13 John Stuart Mill, *On Liberty, and other Writings* (Cambridge: Cambridge University Press, 1989), 72 (my italics).

14 Mill, *On Liberty*, 70, 72.

15 Uday Singh Mehta, *Liberalism and Empire: A Study in Nineteenth-Century British Liberal Thought* (Chicago: University of Chicago Press, 1999), 81–82, 94.

16 Mill—and many others—appealed to the image of the bound feet of Chinese girls to illustrate a lack of freedom through an image of disabled mobility. This lack of freedom was not merely the fate of the Chinese female; it came to encapsulate

China itself. The bound feet served as a metonym for a law that became too tight, and for a society whose addiction to idle fashion made stagnant.
17 Mill, *On Liberty*, 72.
18 Thus, Europe may "tend to" become China, but will never become *quite* China. Indeed, he reassures us, "if a similar change should befall the nations of Europe, it will not be in exactly the same shape: the despotism of custom with which these [European] nations are threatened is *not precisely* stationariness" (Mill, *On Liberty*, 71, my italics).
19 Claudia Baracchi suggests that in the *Republic*, it is not only war that "emerges as a mode of motion. Discourse itself, opening up in its temporality, belongs to motion." "In fact," she claims, "the whole dialogue can be seen as a movement from one battle to the next, as a *moving through* the several stages of war," *Of Myth, Life, and War in Plato's Republic* (Bloomington; Chesham: Indiana University Press, Combined Academic, 2002), 153.
20 For Thomas Hobbes "Common-wealths move" by "[stretching] out their arms, when need is, into foreign Countries." *Leviathan* (Cambridge: Cambridge University Press, 1996), 175.
21 Ann Stoler, "Colony." in *Political Concepts: A Critical Lexicon*. Accessed June 2012. www.politicalconcepts.org.
22 Étienne Balibar, "Cosmopolitanism and Secularism: Controversial Legacies and Prospective Interrogations," *Grey Room* 44 (2011): 12.
23 Hobbes, *Leviathan*, 141.
24 Andrew Hewitt, *Social Choreography: Ideology as Performance in Dance and Everyday Movement* (Durham, NC: Duke University Press, 2005), 80, 81.
25 In this way, the appeal to the term "liberalism" here is largely anachronistic. The term itself emerged "as a self-conscious tradition" only in the nineteenth century, and many would argue that the tradition coalesced, even if not yet explicitly referring to itself by the name, only in the eighteenth century. Yet, as Jennifer Pitts puts it "while it is impossible and probably counterproductive to attempt anything like a definitive or narrow definition of the term, liberalism has been usefully evoked to describe overlapping strands of thought long prior to the term's invention at the turn of the nineteenth century." *A Turn to Empire: The Rise of Imperial Liberalism in Britain and France* (Princeton, NJ: Princeton Unversity Press, 2005), 3.
26 Scott, *Seeing Like a State*; Torpey, *The Invention of the Passport*; Foucault, *Madness and Civilization*.
27 Cresswell, *On the Move: Mobility in the Modern Western World*, 161.
28 In one of the largest demonstrations of the Occupy Wall Street (OWS) movement, the police arrested more than seven hundred demonstrators on the Brooklyn Bridge. Changing and contradictory reports on the *New York Times* online edition from that day (October 1, 2011) suggested that the police steered the demonstrators to the

road, only to arrest them en masse, http://www.huffingtonpost.com/2011/09/30/occupy-wall-street-protests-new-york_n_989221.html.
29 Cresswell, *On the Move*; Malkki, "National Geographic." Cresswell argues that theories of citizenship or immigration rely on "a notion borrowed directly from physical science": that "things (including people) don't move if they can help it." Hence, "place, in its ideal form, is seen a moral world, as an insurer of authentic existence, and as a center of meaning for people," whereas "mobility is portrayed as a threat and dysfunction" (29, 30).
30 Brown, *Walled States, Waning Sovereignty*, 7–8.
31 See also Sandro Mezzadra, "Citizen and Subject: A Postcolonial Constitution for the European Union?," *Situations: Project of the Radical Imagination* 1, no. 2 (2006): 39.
32 Serhat Karakayali and Enrica Rigo, *The Deportation Regime*, eds. Nicholas De Genova and Nathalie Peutz (Durham, NC: Duke University Press, 2010), 127; see also Saskia Sassen, *Territory, Authority, Rights: From Medieval to Global Assemblages* (Princeton, NJ: Princeton University Press, 2006).
33 As William Walters puts it: we witness a conjunction of logics and schemas of governance which produces "a particular politics of mobility whose dream is not to arrest mobility but to tame it; not to build walls, but systems capable of utilizing mobilities, tapping their energies and in certain cases deploying them against the sedentary and ossified elements within society; not a generalized immobilization, but a strategic application of immobility to specific cases coupled with the production of (certain kinds of) mobility" ("Secure Borders, Safe Haven, Domopolitics," *Citizenship Studies* 8, no. 3 (2004): 248.
34 Didier Bigo, "Detention of Foreigners, States of Exception, and the Social Practices of Control of the Banopticon," in *Borderscapes: Hidden Geographies and Politics at Territory's Edge*, eds. Carl Grundy-Warr and Prem Kumar Rajaram (Minneapolis: University of Minnesota Press, 2007), 9–10.
35 Shamir, "Without Borders? Notes on Globalization as a Mobility Regime," *Sociological Theory* 23, no. 2 (2005): 197–217. Mobility gaps between different social groups are the outcome from the dual work that is embedded into globalization: developing new forms of closure and containment, while facilitating the increased "hypermobility" of a selected minority.
36 Walters, "Deportation, Expulsion, and the International Police of Aliens," 282. See also Barry Hindess, "The Liberal Government of Unfreedom," *Alternatives: Global, Local, Political* 26, no. 2 (2001).
37 Israel can thus serve as an example or case study within the examination of liberal democracies not because it fits the egalitarian fantasy of a democracy wherein all those who are ruled partake in the rule governing them. Israel fits this model in so far as it shares the rhetoric of this fantasy, while practicing, like most major liberal democracies, its constant undoing.
38 As suggested by Malkki or Creswell above.

39 Karakayali and Rigo, "Mapping the European Space of Circulation."
40 Saskia Sassen, *Guests and Aliens* (New York: New Press, 1999).
41 Council of Europe, Report by the Committee on Migration, Refugees and Demography (2000), "Arrival of Asylum Seekers at European Airports," Doc. 8761, June 8. These are zones that are defined as exterritorial, and in which asylum seekers or immigrants to Europe may find themselves detained.
42 Rebecca Stein diagnoses that too often, this celebration of flux takes the form of "laundry lists," which has an "equivalence effect, whereby differences among different histories and experiences... are smoothed over or ignored." "'First Contact' and Other Israeli Fictions: Tourism, Globalization, and the Middle East Peace Process," *Public Culture* 14, no. 3 (2002): 519.
43 L. T. Hobhouse, *Liberalism and Other Writings* (Cambridge: Cambridge University Press, 1994), 8. Once again, we see that the centrality of movement to liberal thought also entails a spatialization of time as something through which one moves.
44 These are restraints upon government (Hobhouse, *Liberalism and Other Writings*, 10–12); individuals (13–15), and at times even upon industry (17–18).
45 Michael Freeden, *Liberal Languages: Ideological Imaginations and 20th Century Progressive Thought* (Princeton, NJ; Oxford: Princeton University Press, 2005), 11, 3.
46 Freeden, *Liberal Languages*, 21–22.
47 Carl Schmitt, *State, Movement, People: The Triadic Structure of the Political Unity; The Question of Legality* (Corvallis, OR: Plutarch Press, 2001), 11–12.
48 Schmitt, *State, Movement, People*, 18.
49 Schmitt, *State, Movement, People*, 13.
50 Giorgio Agamben, "Movement," 2005. Accessed June 2014. Lecture transcription at http://www.generation-online.org/p/fpagamben3.htm.
51 Paul Virilio, *Speed and Politics: An Essay on Dromology* (Los Angeles: Semiotext(e), 2006), 53–54.
52 Virilio, *Speed and Politics*, 62.
53 Karl Marx and Friedrich Engels, "Manifesto of the Communist Party," in *The Marx-Engels Reader*, ed. Robert Tucker (New York: Norton, 1978).
54 Karl Marx, *Capital: A Critique of Political Economy*, vol. 1 (London; New York: Penguin Books in association with New Left Review, 1981).
55 Perhaps above all Gilles Deleuze and Félix Guattari, *A Thousand Plateaus: Capitalism and Schizophrenia* (London: Athlone Press, 1988).
56 Saskia Sassen, *The De-Facto Transnationalizing of Immigration Policy* (Florence: Robert Schuman Centre at the European University Institute, 1996); Manuel Castells, *The Rise of the Network Society* (Oxford; Malden, MA: Blackwell, 2000); Alejandro Portes and Rubén G. Rumbaut, *Immigrant America: A Portrait* (Berkeley: University of California Press, 2006).
57 Jacques Rancière, *Disagreement: Politics and Philosophy* (Minneapolis: University of Minnesota Press, 1999).

58 See, for example, Judith Butler, *Gender Trouble: Feminism and the Subversion of Identity* (New York: Routledge, 1990).
59 Hannah Arendt, *The Human Condition* 2nd edition (Chicago: University of Chicago Press, 1998).
60 The work of Barbara Arneil is a noteworthy account of this obsession, "Disability, Self Image, and Modern Political Theory," *Political Theory* 37, no. 2 (2009): 218–42.
61 Hewitt, *Social Choreography*, 81.
62 Caren Kaplan, "Transporting the Subject: Technologies of Mobility and Location in an Era of Globalization," PMLA 117, no. 1 (2002): 32.
63 Erin Manning, *Politics of Touch: Sense, Movement, Sovereignty* (Minneapolis: University of Minnesota Press, 2007), xv.
64 Cresswell, *On the Move*, 54.
65 Manning, *Politics of Touch*, xviii.
66 Hannah Arendt, *The Promise of Politics* (New York: Schocken Books, 2005), 117.
67 Herman Melville, *Moby Dick* (Oxford; New York: Oxford University Press, 1988), 287. Or, in Arendt's words, "no human life, not even the life of the hermit in nature's wildness, is possible without a world which directly or indirectly testifies to the process of other human beings," *The Human Condition*, 22.
68 Thomas Hill Green, *Lectures on the Principles of Political Obligation, and Other Writings* (Cambridge: Cambridge University Press, 1986), 37.
69 Even in the third chapter of *On Liberty*, when Mill moves—so he declares—to consider *actions* (rather than opinions or thoughts that were at the focus of chapter 2 of that book), the object of Mill's account is *preferences* and ways of life. Eventually, Mill situates the problem of freedom primarily in the process of judgment and decision making, and less in one's ability to execute an action once chosen (movement); what is important here is not the act itself but the "inward forces" of man, his mind and soul, rather than body (*On Liberty*, 60).
70 Jürgen Habermas, *The Structural Transformation of the Public Sphere: An Inquiry into a Category of Bourgeois Society* (Cambridge, MA: MIT Press, 1991). While this movement might seem to be abstract, it relies on material circulations: from the voice that carries speeches to print that allowed circulation of pamphlets, books, and newspapers, and to the radio, television, or the Internet. "Opinion" and "ideas" are assembled from things collected, dispersed, and rotated: words, images, data—all are the mediums through which ideas could circulate on growing speed and distribution. The modern public realm and such phenomena as "public opinion" formed via these material developments of circulating words.
71 Mill, *On Liberty*, 70, 71. And these movements are tightly related: the free circulation of ideas is the only guaranty against social stagnation, which is the result of "despotism of Custom" once it becomes "complete."
72 John Rawls, *Political Liberalism*, expanded ed. (New York: Columbia University Press, 2005), 161.

73 In the ten major books written by Dworkin, freedom of movement is not mentioned even once. While Dworkin is primarily a thinker of the law and not of freedom per se, in his discussion of rights, this absence is significant.
74 Freeden, *Liberal Languages*, 25.
75 Rawls, *Political Liberalism*, 72. Rawls counts three qualities that make citizens free and allow them to perceive themselves as free: (a) "having a moral power to have a conception of the good"; (b) being "self-authenticating sources of valid claims"; and (c) being "capable of taking responsibility for their ends," which in turn, "affects how their various claims are asserted" (30–33).
76 Rawls, *Political Liberalism*, 18n20. To a certain degree, *Political Liberalism* refines and distances itself from the model unfolded in *Theory of Justice* according to which as political players, subjects should be thought of as abstracted from all concrete traits. The "veil of ignorance," Rawls clarifies in *Political Liberalism*, does not "[presuppose] a particular metaphysical conception of the person" and "has no specific metaphysical implications concerning the nature of the self" (27). Yet, whereas Rawls perhaps avoids metaphysics, he does assume a particular political ontology wherein subjects, precisely as political players, remain abstract.
77 David Hume, *An Inquiry Concerning Human Understanding* (Indianapolis: Hackett, 1993), 63.
78 Rawls, *Political Liberalism*, 228–29. The status of freedom of movement is further weakened with Rawls's assertion that in these matters of distributive justice we are less likely to agree and hence these matters take us further away from his desired consensus.
79 Rawls, *Political Liberalism*, 181 (my italics).
80 Loren Lomasky, "Liberalism Beyond Borders," in *Liberalism: Old and New*, eds. Ellen Frankel Paul, Fred Miller Jr., and Jeffrey Paul (Cambridge: Cambridge University Press, 2007), 226.
81 Lomasky, "Liberalism Beyond Borders," 226.
82 Shamir, "Without Borders?"; Didier Bigo, "Security and Immigration: Toward a Critique of the Governmentality of Unease," *Alternatives: Global, Local, Political* 27 (2002): 63–92; William Walters, "Border/Control," *European Journal of Social Theory* 9, no. 2 (2006): 187–203; David Newman, "Boundaries, Borders, and Barriers: Changing Geographic Perspectives on Territorial Line," in *Identities, Borders, Orders: Rethinking International Relations Theory*, eds. Mathias Albert, David Jacobson, and Yosef Lapid (Minneapolis: University of Minnesota Press, 2001), 137–52.
83 Adriana Cavarero, *Horrorism: Naming Contemporary Violence* (New York: Columbia University Press, 2009), 4, 5.
84 De Genova and Peutz, *The Deportation Regime*, 4. "In this nervous state of affairs . . . 'governmentality of unease' (Bigo's term) has transformed global anxieties about migration into a mode of ruling." Peter Nyers, "Abject Cosmopolitanism: The Politics of Protection in the Anti-Deportation Movement," *Third World Quarterly* 24, no. 6 (2003), 1069–70. See also Didier Bigo, "Security and Immigration."

85 Brown, *Walled States, Waning Sovereignty*, 116. As Junaid Rana shows, we can witness at play a "faulty syllogistic logic . . . in which the words 'illegal immigrants *may have* terrorist intentions' changed to an imagined 'Middle Eastern illegal immigrants *have* terrorist intentions.'" Rana analyzes a case from 2002 in which false information on five men who allegedly crossed the border illegally led to an FBI goose chase of illegal-immigrant phantasms who soon became terrorist phantasms, to show how all presumably "illegal" movement of particularly racialized bodies ("Muslim," "Middle Eastern") is completely conflated with terror, see "The Language of Terror," in *State of White Supremacy: Racism, Governance, and the United States*, eds. Moon-Kie Jung, João H. Costa Vargas, and Eduardo Bonilla-Silva (Stanford, CA: Stanford University Press, 2011), 215. I would like to thank Cindy Gao for this reference.

86 The two main modes of political operation against or under the occupation are configured by Israel as apolitical. On the one hand, violent resistance is detached from its political context, and instead of being perceived as part of a struggle for freedom against a power whose use of force is far more deadly, is seen by Israel and the United States, as well as many European countries, as part of an irrational, fundamental evil contrasted to the democratic, secular good of the West. On the other hand, nonviolent political activity is securitized. First, from the early weeks of the occupation, any political gathering and organizing of Palestinians and any demonstration or distribution of pamphlets were declared as a threat of Israel's security and were forbidden. Simultaneously, Israel's retaliations following Palestinian (successful, attempted, or presumed) military operations included punishing (often by killing) also the political leadership. Finally, alternative political leaderships (such as the Village Leagues in the 1980s) were established by Israel and were trained and armed, expected to be "subcontractors of the Israeli military whose role was to police the population and forcefully suppress all forms of opposition," Neve Gordon, *Israel's Occupation* (Berkeley: University of California Press, 2008), 113. This conflation of politics and security became a full reduction of politics to security after the Oslo Accord, which is seen by Israel first and foremost as a provider of security for Israelis. It is precisely due to this configuration that Hamas's winning in the Palestinian election in January 2006 was perceived by Israel and the United States as a failure of the democraticization process, even if it was the first time in which "an Arab polity passed to the opposition in a democratic election," Yezid Sayigh, "Inducing a Failed State in Palestine," *Survival: Global Politics and Strategy* 49, no. 3 (2007), 13. If democracy in Palestine is defined as a function of Israel's security, then with the rise of an organization that upholds the right to continue an armed resistance against the occupation, democracy has come to its end. See also Ariella Azoulay and Adi Ophir, *This Regime Which Is Not One: Occupation and Democracy between the Sea and the River (1967—)* (Tel Aviv: Resling, 2008), 74–77, 138–40, 194–95; Samera Esmeir, paper presented at "Crisis in Gaza and Prospects

for Peace," University of California, Berkeley, March 2009; and Yezid Sayigh, "The Palestinian Paradox: Statehood, Security and Institutional Reform," *Conflict, Security & Development* 1 (April 2001): 101–8.

87 Amira Hass, "The Natives' Time Is Cheap," *Ha'aretz*, February 23, 2005.

88 Ariel Handel, "Where, Where to and When in the Occupied Palestinian Territories: An Introduction to a Geography of Disaster," in *The Power of Inclusive Exclusion*, eds. Adi Ophir et al. (New York: Zone Books, 2009), 179–222.

89 Jeff Halper, "The 94 Percent Solution: The Matrix of Control," *Middle East Report* 216i (2000). Accessed June 2014. http://www.merip.org/mer/mer216/94-percent-solution.

90 Yoav Peled and Gershon Shafir, *Being Israeli: The Dynamics of Multiple Citizenship* (Cambridge: Cambridge University Press, 2002).

91 Yehezkel Lein and Najib Abu-Rokaya, "Builders of Zion: Human Rights Violations of Palestinians from the Occupied Territories Working in Israel and the Settlements." B'Tselem (1999). Accessed March 2014. http://www.btselem.org/English/Publications/Index.asp?TF=1&image.x=10&image.y=10: B'tselem; Rebeca Raijman, and Adriana Kemp, "Labor Migration, Managing the Ethno–National Conflict, and Client Politics in Israel," in *Transnational Migration to Israel in Global Comparative Context*, ed. Sarah S. Willen (Lanham, MD: Rowman & Littlefield, 2007), 31–50.

92 Gordon, *Israel's Occupation*.

93 Ariella Azoulay and Adi Ophir, *The One-State Condition: Occupation and Democracy in Israel/Palestine* (Stanford, CA: Stanford University Press, 2012).

94 Gordon, *Israel's Occupation*.

95 Foucault, *Security, Territory, Population*.

96 Tal Arbel, "Mobility Regimes and the King's Head: A History of Techniques for the Control of Movement in the Occupied West Bank," in paper presented at "Commemorative Occupations: Chechnya, Iraq, Palestine, Governing Zones of Emergency," Harvard University, 2006.

97 For example, Gordon, *Israel's Occupation*; Amira Hass, "Israel's Closure Policy: An Ineffective Strategy of Containment and Repression," *Journal of Palestine Studies* 31, no. 3 (2002): 5–20; Azoulay and Ophir, *This Regime Which Is Not One*; Eyal Weizman, *Hollow Land: Israel's Architecture of Occupation* (New York: Verso, 2007).

98 Walters, "Deportation, Expulsion, and the International Police of Aliens," 95.

99 B'Tselem, "Ground to a Halt: Denial of Palestinian's Freedom of Movement in the West Bank," 2007, 7–8.

100 In the particular case of this chapter, the *regime of movement* is analyzed as the function of two such frames. The first is the prolonged Israeli-Palestinian peace process (the control over movement became a primary technology of control in the period following the Oslo Accords—the formal launching of the peace process). The second frame is that of regulatory power (disciplinary and biopower), which in the Foucauldian framework presumably sidelines the violent form that sovereign power takes.

101 Derek Gregory, *The Colonial Present: Afghanistan, Palestine, and Iraq* (Malden, MA: Blackwell, 2004), 4. See also Neve Gordon, "Democracy and Colonialism," *Theory & Event* 13, no. 2 (2010).

Chapter 1. Between Imaginary Lines

The first chapter was previously published in *Theory Culture and Society* (*TCS* 28.1, January 2011). I thank the editors for the wonderful experience of working on that paper, for their ongoing productive feedback and generosity.

1 For a more systematic history of the regime of movement see Neve Gordon, *Israel's Occupation* (Berkeley: University of California Press, 2008); Ariel Handel, "Where, Where to and When in the Occupied Palestinian Territories: An Introduction to a Geography of Disaster" in *The Power of Inclusive Exclusion*, edited by Adi Ophir et al. (New York: Zone Books, 2009); and Ariella Azoulay and Adi Ophir, *This Regime Which Is Not One: Occupation and Democracy between the Sea and the River (1967—)* (Tel Aviv: Resling, 2008).

2 I use here the "I" voice, but this chapter, previously published in *Theory Culture and Society*, was written in a "we"—including me and Merav Amir, my coauthor for this text. The "I" was eventually chosen for the sake of continuity with the rest of the book, but the words here—as well as the ideas and arguments—are not only my own.

3 This type of rationale can be found in semiofficial proclamations; see for instance, E. Lavi, "The Palestinians and Israel: Between Agreement and Crisis—the Next Round," *Adkan Astrategi* [in Hebrew] 12, no. 4 (2010): 67–80; Institute for Policy and Strategy, "National Strength and Security Balance," in *Third Annual Conference on "The New Strategic Landscape: Trends, Challenges, Responses"* (Edmond Benjamin De Rothschild Herzliya Conferences Series 2002).

4 Yehuda Shenhav and Ya'el Berda, "The Colonial Foundations of the Racialized Theological Bureaucracy: Juxtaposing the Israeli Occupation of Palestinian Territories with Colonial History," in *The Power of Inclusive Exclusion: Anatomy of Israeli Rule in the Occupied Palestinian Territories*, eds. Michal Givoni, Adi Ophir, and Sari Hanafi (New York: Zone Books, 2009), 337–74.

5 As I argue in this chapter, the structures and technologies of Israel's occupation are characterized by flux and rapid changes. In the time passed since this chapter was first published in 2011, much has changed in the deployment and operation of the checkpoints. Many of the checkpoints inside the West Bank were removed; some operate only occasionally and enable free access most of the time, others operate according to new regulations, permitting crossing only by car. Thus, while not completely eliminated, many of the burdensome aspects of some of the checkpoints have been reduced; or more accurately they fluctuate. Sometimes they are in force, and at other times they exist only as a potentiality. At the same time, an-

other system of separation was perfected—apartheid roads, a vertical separation between the (caged, underground) movement of Palestinians and that of Jewish settlers; see Eyal Weizman, *Hollow Land: Israel's Architecture of Occupation* (New York: Verso, 2007). Nevertheless, the procedures described in this chapter can still be found at all functioning checkpoints. Moreover, these processes can be found at sites that were less central at the time Amir and I wrote this essay, such as the many gates around the seam line. But almost all checkpoints, even those which were officially "removed," remain an ever-lingering potential since the removal of the checkpoints was done in such a way that they can be reinstalled in moments. What this chapter describes remains relevant also in this potentiality, serving as a reminder—and a possible future punishment—for Palestinians.

6 Azmi Bishara, *Yearning in the Land of Checkpoints* (Tel Aviv: Babel Press, 2006), 48–49, my translation.

7 Shlomo Gazit, the first Israeli administrative governor over the oPt, describes these rituals of punishment with shocking honesty:

When the need to punish someone [a Palestinian] who was the leader of inciters [sic], and not wanting to persecute him for incitement . . . measures were taken which were intended to harm his pocket or the property of his family. They usually owned a property or a business, and there was always a way to shut down and close their business and to target their private property. Under the pretense of searching for terrorists the area of the orchards was closed off precisely during the irrigation season or in the midst of the urgent fruit picking time. Under the pretense of public safety a pharmacy was shut down, under the pretense of sanitation—a restaurant. The person himself and the people around him understood the "hint" very well, but stood helpless and could not file a complaint against the administration . . . sometimes these same measures were on a larger scale, against the residents of a city or an entire district. Because of "local security problems" checkpoints were placed and checks were conducted. The residents of Hebron were prevented from marketing their grapes during the high season and severe limitations were posed on the residents of Nablus in September of '67 to break the school strike.

The Carrot and the Stick: Israel's Policy in the Administered Territories, 1967–1968 (Tel-Aviv: Zmora–Bitan; Washington, DC: B'nai B'rith Books 1985), 281. The same type of reasoning can be found in numerous responses of Israeli politicians to acts of Palestinian resistance. See, for example, the expressions coined by Moshe Ya'alon, who was the commanding officer over the oPt when the second intifada started and the Israeli chief of staff between 2002 and 2005: "imprinting into the [Palestinian] consciousness" and "putting a price tag" on Palestinian acts of resistance. "The Strategic Environment and the Principles of Responses," the Third Herzliya Conference, Herzliya, Israel: Interdisciplinary Center (IDC), 2002; *Walla! News*,

"Ya'alon: Not Willing to Pay Any Price for Shalit," December 4, 2008. Accessed August 2010. http://news.walla.co.il.

8 Gordon, *Israel's Occupation*, 5. Gordon marks a reversed Foucauldian shift from a politics of life—characterized by Israel's endeavors to normalize the occupation by concealing violence and by deploying power in order to manage life—to a politics of death, culminating in the second intifada. In other words, while Israel deployed primarily disciplinary and biopolitical technologies during the first two decades of the occupation (ranging from surveillance of potentially subversive individuals to intervening in school curricula, from monitoring livestock to improving the variety of seeds planted, from establishing vocational schools to model plots for training farmers), in the current decade Israel relies primarily on the deployment of sovereign power, which is characterized by prohibitions and violence.

9 Ariella Azoulay and Adi Ophir, "The Monster's Tail," in *Against the Wall: Israel's Barrier to Peace*, ed. Michael Sorkin (New York: New Press, 2005), 7.

10 Pradeep Jeganathan, "Checkpoints: Anthropology, Identity and the State," in *Anthropology at the Margins of the State*, eds. Veena Das and Deborah Poole (Santa Fe: School of American Research Press, 2004), 67–80.

11 Accordingly, some aspect concerning the existence of imaginary lines at the checkpoints may be found in almost any account of the operation of the checkpoints. For example, see Bishara, *Yearning in the Land of Checkpoints*; Eyal Ben-Ari, *From Checkpoints to Flow-Points: Sites of Friction between the Israel Defense Forces and Palestinians*, Gitelson Peace Publication (Jerusalem: Harry S. Truman Research Institute for the Advancement of Peace, Hebrew University of Jerusalem, 2005).

12 Rema Hammami, "On the Importance of Thugs: The Moral Economy of a Checkpoint," *Middle East Report* 231 (2004).

13 It is important to emphasize that this is not always, and not necessarily, a cynical operation, in which the soldiers knowingly cast an innocent person as "terrorist." Soldiers are often scared at the checkpoint, feeling exposed and vulnerable to attacks. Educated within a historical and political framework of radical enmity, and indeed, being an occupied power that is at times the target of violent resistance, many of them feel genuinely threatened.

14 Frantz Fanon had already identified the centrality of such failing symbolic systems—of such matrixes of imaginary lines—to colonialism: "The colonized subject is constantly on his guard: Confused by the myriad signs of the colonial world he never knows whether he is out of line." Here I show that such systems set the grounds for the violence of the colonizers; for Fanon, it links rather to the violence of decolonization: this eventually produces "a constant muscular tonus [of the colonized]." He argues, "It is a known fact that under certain emotional circumstances an obstacle actually escalates action." I shall return to this point in the last chapter of this book. *The Wretched of the Earth* (New York: Grove Press, 2004), 16–17. Edward W. Said would adopt this term to characterize colonialism albeit in

a different way: as the imaginary line dividing East and West in *Orientalism* (New York: Pantheon Books, 1978).

15 These depictions go back as far as Hobbes's depictions of the inhabitants of America; see Hobbes, *Leviathan*, 89; Quentin Skinner, *Hobbes and Republican Liberty* (Cambridge: Cambridge University Press, 2008), 98–102.

16 Lindsay Bremner, "Border/Skin," in *Against the Wall: Israel's Barrier to Peace*, in ed. Michael Sorkin (New York: New Press, 2005), 131. See also Hilla Dayan, "Regimes of Separation: Israel/Palestine," in *The Power of Inclusive Exclusion: Anatomy of Israeli Rule in the Occupied Palestinian Territories*, eds. Adi Ophir, Michal Givoni, and Sari Hanafi (New York: Zone Books, 2009).

17 Balibar, "Cosmopolitanism and Secularism"; Neferti Xina M. Tadiar, *Things Fall Away: Philippine Historical Experience and the Makings of Globalization* (Durham, NC: Duke University Press, 2009).

18 Arbel, "Mobility Regimes and the King's Head."

19 Hagar Kotef and Merav Amir, "(En)Gendering Checkpoints: Checkpoint Watch and the Repercussions of Intervention," *Signs: Journal of Women in Culture and Society* 32, no. 4 (2007). This is no surprise if we consider the unintended contribution of CPW's presence to the pretense by the Israeli army to be "the most moral army in the world," as is so often claimed. This presence is configured as part of the army's "effort" to make sure no "severe" violations of human rights occur at the checkpoints, and hence takes part in the widely shared assumption that the occupation can be maintained as a just form of rule as long as some basic humanitarian rule, presumably secured also by CPW presence, is safeguarded.

20 Shenhav and Berda, "The Colonial Foundations of the Racialized Theological Bureaucracy."

21 CPW report from Za'atara, Hawwara & Beth Furik, CPW website. August 8, 2005. machsomwatch.org.

22 Kotef and Amir, "(En)Gendering Checkpoints."

23 Kotef and Amir, "(En)Gendering Checkpoints."

24 Eilat Maoz, "The Privatization of the Checkpoints and the Late Occupation." Accessed May 2014. www.whoprofits.org. This mask of civilian border crossing is further achieved by the means of another process that started in 2005 when the Israeli government began to outsource the management of the checkpoints to private security companies. The formal rationale for this outsourcing, like that of the very formation of the terminals, is that by excluding the army from these sites of daily "friction" and having (Israeli) civilians "providing this service" to other (Palestinian) civilians, violence will be radically reduced. In fact, this idea has proven to be questionable.

25 Weizman, *Hollow Land*, 151.

26 Tal Arbel has discovered that an explicit demand was made by the Israeli army to construct the turnstiles with shorter metal arms (55 cm instead of the standard

75–90 cm). The tighter arms were designed to press against the Palestinian passing through them, thereby revealing whether he or she has something (read: a bomb) under their clothes. The newer turnstiles are often slightly wider but still tighter than the Israeli standard ("Mobility Regimes and the King's Head"). Tamar Fleishman from CPW found current turnstiles to be 60.5 cm.

27 Weizman, *Hollow Land: Israel's Architecture of Occupation*, 150–51.

28 See the CPW report from Qalandia, March 29, 2006; www.machsomwatch.org. This is far from being exceptional. See, for instance, the CPW report from Qalandia, May 9, 2010.

29 This distinction can also be understood as that between suspended and structural violence. For this distinction and the manner in which it pertains both to the occupation and to the logic of liberal democracies see Azoulay and Ophir, "The Monster's Tail."

30 Sari Hanafi, "Spacio-Cide and Bio-Politics: The Israeli Colonial Conflict from 1947 to the Wall," in *Against the Wall: Israel's Barrier to Peace*, ed. M. Sorkin (New York: New Press, 2005), 251–61.

31 Meron Benvenisti, *Intimate Enemies: Jews and Arabs in a Shared Land* (Berkeley: University of California Press, 1995).

32 Ariella Azoulay and Adi Ophir, *Bad Days: Between Disaster and Utopia* (Tel Aviv: Resling Publishing, 2002). Published in Hebrew.

Chapter 2. An Interlude

1 The Tunnels Road was built in 1996, to bypass Bethlehem before the Palestinian Authority gained control over the city. During the second intifada Palestinians attacked parts of the road. In response, the Israeli army built walls to protect sections of the road (such as the wall on the bridge seen in figure 2.1).

2 The definition here is wide and telling: the access to the "apartheid roads," as they are infamously called by critics, is limited to "Israelis." Yet "Israelis" are defined in this context as "any resident who is a citizen of Israel or allowed to immigrate to Israel according to the law of return (1950) [meaning a Jew], or anyone who has a valid visa [meaning a tourist]." While no official prohibition exists in writing from which we can learn the nature of the restrictions on Palestinian movement along the different roads in the West Bank, this formulation can be found on signs and in military decrees declaring closed military zones in the West Bank, and serves as a guideline also for the restriction of movement. Yael Barda's claim that the administration in the West Bank is based on racial, rather than any other category, situates this definition within a wider context. See *The Bureaucracy of the Occupation: The Regime of Movement Permits 2000–2006* (Tel Aviv: Hakibbutz Hameuchad, The Van Leer Jerusalem Institute 2012).

3 B'Tselem, "Forbidden Roads: Israel's Discriminatory Road Regime in the West

Bank." August 2004. Accessed May 2014. http://www.btselem.org/download/200408_forbidden_roads_eng.pdf. The separated road system gradually developed between the fall of 2000 (the beginning of the second intifada) and May 2002 (the end of the extensive Operation Defensive Shield in the West Bank and Gaza). Access to forbidden roads is denied by patrols and by means of manned checkpoints, roadblocks, and locked gates that obstruct entrance to these roads from Palestinian villages and towns. Some roads, like Road 60, are "sterile roads," on which Palestinian travel is forbidden without exception (on some Palestinians are not allowed to travel; others they are not even allowed to cross); other roads are restricted, but Palestinians may travel on them if they hold a permit titled "Special Movement Permit at Internal Checkpoints in Judea and Samaria" issued by Israel.

4 A series of separations defines this mode of governance: separations between two different geographical zones; between citizens and noncitizens see Ariella Azoulay and Adi Ophir, *The One-State Condition: Occupation and Democracy in Israel/Palestine* (Stanford, CA: Stanford University Press, 2012); between people and territories see Neve Gordon, *Israel's Occupation* (Berkeley: University of California Press, 2008); between two (and actually more) legal systems see Orna Ben-Naftali, Aeyal M. Gross, and Keren Michaeli, "Illegal Occupation: Framing the Occupied Palestinian Territory," *Berkeley Journal of Int'l Law* 23, no. 3 (2005); and between different vertical layers of the same land area see Eyal Weizman, *Hollow Land: Israel's Architecture of Occupation* (New York: Verso, 2007).

5 Azoulay and Ophir, *The One-State Condition*. Which must nonetheless be viewed as a *single* regime.

6 These two divisions are not synonyms: there are non-Jews within the Israeli citizenry, including Palestinians. There are, however no non-Palestinians who are noncitizens in the oPt (that is, all regular inhabitants of the oPt who are not Palestinians, meaning settler Jews, are citizens). The area zone between these two divisions can be taken to mark the areas where citizenship becomes fragile and precarious in Israel.

7 "As it leaves Jerusalem it cuts a straight line through mountains and valleys much like the nineteenth-century colonial routes designed by the engineers of France's School of Highways and Bridges (to tame an arbitrary nature and express the 'Cartesian logic' of the empire and the goals of Reason)." Weizman, *Hollow Land*, 179.

8 Ariel Handel, "Where, Where to and When in the Occupied Palestinian Territories: An Introduction to a Geography of Disaster," in *The Power of Inclusive Exclusion*, ed. Adi Ophir et al. (New York: Zone Books, 2009). Handel brilliantly shows how the measurement of movement must take into account not merely the distance between two points but also the use-value of the space between them. Distance thus becomes also a function of time. By undermining the use-value of the space available for Palestinian movement, distance is stretched while the actual territory available for Palestinians is ever shrinking.

9. As Amira Hass describes it: "A person can drive all over the West Bank without knowing not only the names of the villages and towns whose lands were taken for the building of Jewish settlements and neighborhoods, but also the very fact of their existence." "To Drive and Not to See Arabs," *Ha'retz*. January 22, 2003, translation in Handel, "Where, Where to and When in the Occupied Palestinian Territories," 206. Indeed, Danny Tirza, who was involved in designing the separation wall, and beforehand in outlining the borders of the three types of Palestinian enclaves in the West Bank (areas A, B and C) explained that, "Israelis should be able to travel through the upper highways 'without even noticing the Palestinian traffic underneath.'" Weizman, *Hollow Land*, 181.

10. This, in turn, is part of a mode of "territorialization by means of movement control," molding of space into "a continuous, rapid, tightly knit Jewish space and a fragmented, slow, uncertain Palestinian space gated by its Jewish counterpart." This system ultimately means that "Israeli stability is the cause of Palestinian instability; *Israeli acceleration generates Palestinian deceleration*; the coming closer of Israeli points to each other have the effect of pulling apart the Palestinian points from one another; certainty for Israelis spells uncertainty for Palestinians." Ariel Handel, "Gated/Gating Community: The Settlements Complex in the West Bank," *Transactions of the Institute of British Geographers*, forthcoming 4, 2, 21 of essay, respectively (my italics). Indeed, "mobility for some creates immobility for others" also in other, very different contexts, from the interaction of cars and public transport, to the ramifications of the feminist logic of taking back the night. See Malene Freudendal-Pedersen, *Mobility in Daily Life: Between Freedom and Unfreedom (Transport and Society)* (Burlington, VT: Ashgate, 2009), 6.

11. Handel, "Where, Where to and When in the Occupied Palestinian Territories."

12. During the Boer War the British, confronted by new guerrilla war, faced a problem: how to bring the territory under their control. Netz describes the process that led to a solution: the railroads were protected by barbed wire, which was a common practice designed to protect the rails from cattle and other animals. Unlike cows, however, the Boer soldiers could cut the wire, and so outposts were put up to protect the wire itself. "At this point the British realized they had obtained something unexpected." While they installed this system to protect the rails, and thus to connect points, the lines of the rails could also serve to divide areas. "Suddenly" the British had more than a system to protect the rails. They had "a pure space-controlling mechanism." Reviel Netz, *Barbed Wire: An Ecology of Modernity* (Middletown, CT: Wesleyan University Press, 2004), 66.

13. The actual purpose behind the construction of the roads is insignificant. The roads were built to connect settlements; they may have also been built as part of a land-grab project, yet many roads in the oPt are constructed at the edge of existing Palestinian populated areas blocking potential expansion. "Contrary to the customary purpose of roads, which are a means to connect people with places, the routes of

the roads that Israel builds in the West Bank are at times intended to achieve the opposite purpose. Some of the new roads in the West Bank were planned to place a physical barrier to stifle Palestinian urban development. These roads prevent the natural joining of communities and creation of a contiguous Palestinian built-up area in areas in which Israel wants to maintain control, either for military reasons or for settlement purposes." B'Tselem, "Forbidden Roads."

14 Handel, "Where, Where to and When in the Occupied Palestinian Territories," 196.

15 Eyal Weizman further explains the general framework within which such structures find their logics: "Chaos has its particular structural advantages. It supports one of Israel's foremost strategies of obfuscation: the promotion of complexity—geographical, legal or linguistic. Sometimes . . . this strategy is openly referred to as 'constructive blurring'" (Hollow Land, 8).

16 A report from CPW, "Nablus and Surrounding." December 9, 2008. Accessed June 2014 http://www.machsomwatch.org/en (my translation; emphasis in original).

17 This mechanism works not just in relation to the occupied Palestinians, but also, even if less invasively, in relation to Palestinians who are citizens of Israel. Sagi Elbaz writes that the Palestinian minority in Israel receives media representation only as *criminal deviations*: Palestinian citizens of Israel are covered in Israeli media almost exclusively by reporters specializing in law and order, whose main sources are the security agencies in Israel, Sagi Elbaz, Minority Opinion in Israeli Media (Tel Aviv: Dionun, 2013). Published in Hebrew. To illustrate this form of representation Yitzhak Laor told once how his son was surprised to meet a Palestinian poet in a festival. According to the son the poet "did not at all looked like an Arab." In response to Laor's question—how should an Arab look—the son replied: "like a person after a car accident." Yitzhak Laor, "How the Media Defines the Arabs as a Criminal 'Deviation,'" Ha'aretz, May 9, 2013 (my translation).

18 CPW, "Nablus and Surrounding."

19 This rhetoric, which is essential to Israel's foreign policy and to its international relations is itself changing and is slowly replaced with an explicit and declared project of sustaining control over the entire territory between the Mediterranean and the Jordan River (including, in other words, the West Bank). A 2012 committee, chaired by the retired supreme court judge Edmund Levy, issued a report arguing that the West Bank is not an occupied territory (since it never belonged to a sovereign state before). See the full report at: www.pmo.gov.il under the title "Report on the Status of Building in Judea and Samaria" ("דו"ח על מעמד הבניה ביהודה ושומרון") Accessed June 2014. The report, whose goal was to declare the Israeli settlements are legal contra accepted interpretations of international law, and to set the grounds for the construction of more settlements, was the pinnacle of legal, administrative, and construction procedures that together comprised a long process of land-grab in the territories. Since the Oslo Accord of 1993, the settler population

has more than tripled: from 105,400 in 1994, to more than 350,000 in 2013. More than 116 settlements and outposts were established between 1993 and 2005. Note that this data does not include East Jerusalem and its neighborhoods (*Peace Now* and *Amana—The Settlement Movement*).

20 In 2000 Ehud Barak, then prime minister, coined this expression that has since become the backbone of Israel's both formal and informal approach toward the conflict.

21 Otto Mayr, *Authority, Liberty, and Automatic Machinery in Early Modern Europe* (Baltimore: Johns Hopkins University Press, 1986).

22 The idea of "tempered government" becomes very common in the eighteenth century, and its structural backbone is the notion of "checks and balances" that seeks to facilitate precisely such a moderate movement of and between different extensions of power. "It will not be denied," argues Madison in the Federalist 48, "that power is of an encroaching nature, and that it ought to be effectually restrained from passing the limits assigned to it." Government appears here as an apparatus composed of different communicating branches (borrowing from the "communicating vessels" principle) operating along the physical model of self-regulation. Montesquieu's principle of checks and balances is perhaps the most well-known version of this principle. According to this model, power's own movement toward more power, can be restrained only by the movement of another power. Therefore, each branch of power must endure in its movement to allow an "*internal regulation of governmental rationality.*" Foucault, *The Birth of Biopolitics: Lectures at the Collège De France, 1978–79* (New York: Palgrave Macmillan, 2008), 10 (my italics).

23 Barry Hindess argues that liberalism sees the population of a state "as encompassing a variety of self-regulating domains—the sphere of economic activity, the workings of civil society, the organization of domestic life, processes of population growth, and so on"; see "The Liberal Government of Unfreedom," *Alternatives: Global, Local, Political* 26, no. 2 (2001): 96.

24 First formulated as a systematic theory of international relations, the notion of the balance of power sought to promote such a system of self-regulation between states. Note that in all cases "balance" was not stasis, but an ongoing process of balancing and counterbalancing, that is, a movement back and forth between the different powers that should restrain the unleashing of the brutal movement of war.

25 See chapter 3.

26 So Burke can tell us that a good government has a "plastic nature"; that it merely needs to establish certain conditions in the image of some ruling principles, and then "[leave] it afterwards to its own operation." *Reflections on the Revolution in France* (Oxford; New York: Oxford University Press, 2009), 170. Thus, in both the sphere of the individual and in the sphere of governance, liberalism largely imagined individual freedom as a self-regulated movement of bodies.

27 Such a characterization of movement, here quoted from Nicholas De Genova and Na-

thalie Peutz's description of free movement, is quite common. "Mobility also means promiscuity," Giovanna Procacci provides another formulation, as "indecipherable couplings, difficult to use as cohesive supports for the social fabric; spontaneous solidarities which elude 'legal' or 'contractual' definition, evading any attempt to orient them towards the goal of the social project." De Genova and Peutz, *The Deportation Regime: Sovereignty, Space, and the Freedom of Movement* (Durham, NC: Duke University Press, 2010), 58–59; and Procacci, "Social Economy and the Government of Poverty," in *The Foucault Effect: Studies in Governmentality*, eds. Colin Gordon, Graham Burchell, Peter Miller (Chicago: University of Chicago Press, 1991), 161.

28 Foucault, *Security, Territory, Population*, 49.

29 Foucault's point goes further here: while it is "undeniable," "that this ideology of freedom really was one of the conditions of development of modern or, if you like, capitalist forms of economy, . . . it is not altogether sure that this was what was really aimed at or sought after in the first instance." Foucault, *Security, Territory, Population*, 48.

30 Foucault, *Security, Territory, Population*, 40; 41–42. The example of the vaccine is probably the most celebrated one: to overcome an epidemic everyone is infected with a reduced, diluted version of the disease. By getting slightly sick, the body develops antibodies and the epidemic thus fights itself. Marx's analysis of financial and commerce crises in his *Manifesto* is another clear example, and the challenge of airport security I mentioned in the preface is yet another. Recall the CEO I quoted in the preface, who seemed to assume that large-scale crises (such as a bomb at an airport) are both rare and inevitable. The challenge, as he put it, was not to prevent such crises altogether (that would paralyze the airport), but to maximize the movement of airplanes and passengers while minimizing the explosion of bombs, even if this maximization means that every once in a while a bomb will explode.

31 Foucault, *Security, Territory, Population*, 48.

32 Foucault, *Security, Territory, Population*, 48, 49, 65, respectively.

Chapter 3. *The Fence That "Ill Deserves the Name of Confinement"*

1 "Stretched" not merely since Burke is often seen as a conservative rather than a liberal (after all, in many ways his political analysis is close to that of liberals of his time, even if at times his conclusions might be different); but since Burke's critique of reason itself sets him radically apart from the Kantian, or even Lockean model.

2 Gerald Dworkin, *The Theory and Practice of Autonomy* (Cambridge: Cambridge University Press, 1988), 15.

3 Donna Haraway, "Situated Knowledges: The Science Question in Feminism and the Privilege of Partial Perspective," *Feminist Studies* 14, no. 3. (Autumn 1988): 575–99.

4 Hannah Arendt, *On Revolution* (London: Penguin Classics, 1990), 32; see also Arendt, *Men in Dark Times* (London: Cape, 1970), 224.

5 Linda M. G. Zerilli, *Feminism and the Abyss of Freedom* (Chicago: University of Chicago Press, 2005), 43.
6 In a paraphrase, or as an addition to Foucault's "take life or let live"; see *Society Must Be Defended: Lectures at the Collège De France, 1975–76* (New York: Picador, 2003), 241.
7 The shift in the operation of power Mill identifies in the first chapter of *On Liberty* and that is described in the introduction is quite analogous to the shift Foucault identifies between sovereignty and disciplinary power.
8 The concept appears as part of a self-referring tradition only in the nineteenth century, and many argue that this tradition crystallized (even if still not self-consciously, to borrow Jennifer Pitts's formulation) only in the eighteenth century. Yet, Pitts aptly argues that, "liberalism has been usefully evoked to describe overlapping strands of thought long prior to the term's invention at the turn of the nineteenth century"; see *A Turn to Empire: The Rise of Imperial Liberalism in Britain and France* (Princeton, NJ: Princeton Unversity Press, 2005), 3; and Foucault, *The Birth of Biopolitics: Lectures at the Collège De France, 1978–79* (New York: Palgrave Macmillan, 2008). C. B. Macpherson further claims that the roots of liberalism can be traced down to the framework of possessive individualism, which he identifies as the heart of the theories of both Hobbes and Locke; see *The Political Theory of Possessive Individualism: Hobbes to Locke* (Oxford; New York: Oxford University Press, 1985). David Johnston begins his account of the history of the liberal tradition with Locke, Smith, and Hobbes in *The Idea of a Liberal Theory: A Critique and Reconstruction* (Princeton, NJ: Princeton University Press, 1994); see also Knud Haakonssen, *Traditions of Liberalism: Essays on John Locke, Adam Smith, and John Stuart Mill* (St. Leonards, Australia: Centre for Independent Studies, 1988). Others, however, insist that we cannot talk coherently about liberalism before the eighteenth century (Foucault, *The Birth of Biopolitics*).
9 John Rogers, *The Matter of Revolution: Science, Poetry, and Politics in the Age of Milton* (Ithaca, NY: Cornell University Press, 1996), xi.
10 Schematically, the Aristotelian model of sphere-shaped movement that dominated natural philosophy throughout the Middle Ages was replaced with two competing models—Harvey's circular model and other vitalist versions on the one hand, and the mechanical model whose quintessential representative was Descartes on the other.
11 Steven Shapin and Simon Schaffer make a compelling case it cannot in *Leviathan and the Air-Pump Hobbes, Boyle, and the Experimental Life* (Princeton, NJ: Princeton University Press, 1989).
12 Rogers, *The Matter of Revolution*, 3.
13 For the primacy of movement in Hobbes see also Thomas A. Spragens, *The Politics of Motion: The World of Thomas Hobbes* (Lexington: University Press of Kentucky, 1973); W. Von Leyden, *Seventeenth-Century Metaphysics: An Examination of Some Main Concepts and Theories* (London: Gerald Duckworth, 1968), 38–41; or the classic studies of

Frithiof Brandt, *Thomas Hobbes' Mechanical Conception of Nature* (Copenhagen: Levin & Munksgaard, 1927).

14 Hobbes, *Leviathan* (Cambridge: Cambridge University Press, 1996), 46. "So that Sense in all cases, is nothing els but originall fancy, caused (as I have said) by the pressure, that is, by the motion, of externall things upon our Eyes, Ears, and other organs thereunto ordained" (14); "All fancies are Motions within us" (20); "Contemnt being nothing else but immobility" (39); "The words *Appetite*, and *Aversion* . . . signifie the motions, one of approaching, the other of retiring" (38); and "whatsoever is the object of any mans Appetite or Desire; that is it, which he for his part calleth *Good*; And the object of his Hate, and Aversion, *Evill*" (39). Even the difference between a dream and reality is based on motion: "The motion when we are awake, beginning at one end; and when we Dream, at another" (18).

15 Hobbes, *Leviathan*, 4.

16 Rogers, *The Matter of Revolution*, 5; see also Spragens, *The Politics of Motion*, chapter 6. Michel Verdon argues along parallel lines that Hobbes's state of nature was a political thought-experiment that paralleled Galileo's thought-experiment of motion in a vacuum. It was this experiment, which relied on a break from Aristotelian cosmology (in which things and people had a proper place and "could fulfill [their] 'being' only by occupying that . . . position and not by moving") that enabled Hobbes to put forth the postulation of equality. "Rectilinear inertial motion is only possible in a homogeneous Cartesian universe where space is . . . not differentiated ontologically. Hobbes reached the same conclusion in his social cosmology: in the 'state of nature,' for free and inertial motion to be possible at all, all individuals must be equal"; see "On the Laws of Physical and Human Nature: Hobbes' Physical and Social Cosmologies," *Journal of the History of Ideas* 43, no. 4 (1982): 656, 659, respectively.

17 Hobbes, *Leviathan*, 145, 147, respectively (my italics)

18 Thomas Hobbes, *De Cive* 9.9, translated by Quentin Skinner in his *Hobbes and Republican Liberty* (Cambridge: Cambridge University Press, 2008) 116–17. The *English Works* suggests a slightly different formulation: "And every man hath more or less Liberty, as he hath more or less space in which he employs himself: as he hath more Liberty, who is in a large, than he that is kept in a close prison." *The English Works of Thomas Hobbes of Malmesbury* (London: J. Bohn, 1839), ii: 120.

19 Hobbes, *Leviathan*, 146.

20 Skinner, *Hobbes and Republican Liberty*, 163, 164, respectively.

21 This split is probably most explicit in Hobbes's account of representation in chapter 16. Hobbes points to two cases: in one, the subjects grant the sovereign—the person who bears their person—unlimited authority. In this case the person represents them in their entirety; they are the authors of everything he does. Hobbes seems to foreground this case in the book, arguing that each and every action of the sovereign is also the subjects' and thus the sovereign can never be blamed for

violating a contract. However, chapter 16 presents another possibility: "Otherwise, when they limit him in what, and how farre, he shall represent them, none of them owneth more, than they gave him commission to Act" (Hobbes, *Leviathan*, 114). In this case the sovereign only represents parts of the subjects. In some of his capacities (we can assume, at the very least, in matters concerning war and security) the subject and the sovereign are one, but there are elements within the subject that remain unincorporated into the sovereign. This split can account for some of the tensions in Hobbes's notions of freedom to which this chapter points.

22 Hobbes, *Leviathan*, 122.
23 Hobbes, *Leviathan*, 124.
24 Hobbes, *Leviathan*, 9.
25 Hobbes, *Leviathan*, 152.
26 Hobbes, *English Works*, iv: 215. In regard to this group, it may be interesting to note that in *The Elements of Law*, where Hobbes upheld a different notion of liberty that was not equivalent to free movement, freedom of movement—the right of "commodious passage from place to place" and the "means of transportation of things necessary"—was one of the two elements of natural liberty situated under this category of undeniable rights.
27 Hobbes, *Leviathan*, 147.
28 Hobbes, *Leviathan*, 114.
29 Hobbes, *Leviathan*, 34.
30 Hobbes, *Leviathan*, 239–40.
31 Nancy J. Hirschmann, *Gender, Class, and Freedom in Modern Political Theory* (Princeton, NJ: Princeton University Press, 2008), 64.
32 Such a reading will not merely be anachronistic; it will also stand in a radical contrast to the many readings seeing the Hobbesian subject as lacking any interiority, not to say a complex and multilayered structure. See for example Vanita Seth, *Europe's Indians: Producing Racial Difference, 1500–1900* (Durham, NC: Duke University Press, 2010), 67; and Stephen Greenblatt, "Psychoanalysis and Renaissance Culture," in *Literary Theory/Renaissance Texts*, eds. Patricia Parker and David Quint (Baltimore: Johns Hopkins University Press, 1986), 210–24.
33 Accordingly, even though Hobbes argues that "The World (I mean not the Earth onely [sic] . . . but the *Universe*.) is Corporeall, that is to say, Body . . . and that which is not Body, is not part of the Universe: And because the Universe is All, that which is not part of it, is *Nothing*; and consequentially *no where*" (Hobbes, *Leviathan*, 463), we can read moments in him as suggesting that *as* subjects we are merely rights-bearing entities. Hence rises the problem to which I pointed above.
34 Hobbes, *Leviathan*, 121.
35 "For the passions of men, are commonly more potent than their reason." Hobbes, *Leviathan*, 131.
36 Hobbes, *Leviathan*, 141.

37 No matter what the motivation for the action is—be it fear, desire, or reason—the last "appetite in the Deliberation" is the will (Hobbes, *Leviathan*, 44–45). If one had considered an action but never executed it, we can not say he willed it; rather than "will," the phenomenon considered in this case is "Inclination" (45).

38 The etymologic origin of "servitude," Hobbes tells us in crucial parentheses, may not be from the verb "to serve" but from "to save"—to preserve the condition of life itself. The servant is thus the image of all saved men—all men who were saved from the war of all against all in the state of nature by a powerful master/sovereign. The servant, then, is as free as all other men, and indeed—he *is* all other men (Hobbes, *Leviathan*, 141).

39 Hobbes, *Leviathan*, 141 (my italics).

40 Greenblatt, "Psychoanalysis and Renaissance Culture."

41 Once the technology of this logic would consolidate, once the state would develop the means to monopolize movement, the modern state would take the form Torpey identifies: a system that has "expropriated from individuals and private entities the legitimate 'means of movement,' particularly through but by no means exclusively across international boundaries"; see *The Invention of the Passport: Surveillance, Citizenship, and the State* (Cambridge: Cambridge University Press, 2000), 4. In Hobbes's time this monopoly cannot even be fully imagined, yet Hobbes nevertheless envisages an embryotic form of this logic.

42 Once again, this reading may be taken as merely another perspective of Hobbes's critique of republicanism (his claim that any objection subjects might have to the sovereign's action is rendered contradictory by the fact they are part of the sovereign itself). Yet reading Hobbes's critique from this particular angle shows how it endeavors to solve the tension in his account(s) of freedom and to assert the freedom of the subject *as such*, rather than deny this freedom, as most readings propose.

43 Shapin and Schaffer, *Leviathan and the Air-Pump Hobbes*, 92–99, 152.

44 As Claudia Baracchi notes in a different context, we can see "war as coextensive with motion, indeed, as the moving of humans." *Of Myth, Life, and War in Plato's Republic* (Bloomington: Indiana University Press, 2002), 153. For a more elaborated discussion see chapter 5.

45 It is almost as if Hobbes's materialism had failed him in his extensive political enterprise: the construction of the largest artifact of all—the state—as a unitary being.

46 Gil Anidjar had made a similar point regarding blood—itself, he remarks, a fluid concept. Anidjar rejects these distinctions and refuses to "be content to treat blood as a *material* or physiological substance, as a *symbolic* repository into which social energies are merely poured, or as a *metaphorical* marker that inherently structures the understanding." "Do we measure—and how—the literalization of the metaphor, the concreteness of the symbol," Anidjar asks, calling us to see the "instabil-

ity of the metaphoric in its relation to the literal, indeed, to the political." Instead, he wants to use blood as a "prism" through which to examine other questions. Blood thus becomes "a category of historical analysis," much like what I propose to do with flows of different kinds here; see *Blood: A Critique of Christianity* (Columbia University Press, 2014), 39, 44, 101, 339n265.

47 Many readers of earlier drafts of this text have proposed I shall mark more clearly the distinction between the metaphorical use of movement and movement as a physical phenomenon. My argument here is that such a marking is not merely unproductive; it is impossible.

48 Of course minds, or souls (as things, discursive objects, or figures of speech) can move and be moved in nonspatial ways (we often call these movements "e-motion").

49 Mary Wollstonecraft, *The Vindication of the Rights of Women* (Mineola, NY: Dover 1996), 43, 77.

50 Michel Foucault, *The History of Sexuality*, Vol. 1 (New York: Vintage Books, 1990).

51 Wollstonecraft, *Vindication*, 77, 41, 42 respectively (my italics).

52 Barbara Arneil, "Disability, Self Image, and Modern Political Theory," *Political Theory* 37, no. 2 (2009): 224.

53 Notably, Uday Mehta, Nathan Tracov, and Nancy Hirschmann have directed political theory back to this text, arguing that it is a significant text to understanding Locke's political thought.

54 John Locke, *Some Thoughts Concerning Education and, of the Conduct of the Understanding* (Indianapolis: Hackett, 1996), §11.

55 Hirschmann, *Gender, Class, and Freedom in Modern Political Theory*, 88.

56 "Reason is the endpoint of Locke's physical prescription"—the center of the first half of *Thoughts Concerning Education*. Nancy Hirschmann, "Intersectionality before Intersectionality Was Cool," in *Feminist Interpretations of John Locke*, eds. Nancy Hirschmann, Kirstie McClure (University Park: The Pennsylvania State University Press, 2007), 167.

57 Locke, *Some Thoughts Concerning Education*, §11.

58 Locke, *Some Thoughts Concerning Education*, §12.

59 Immanuel Kant, "What Is Enlightenment," 40.

60 Kant, "What Is Enlightenment," 20.

61 This taming of the body and taming of the mind to move properly can be seen as an analogy to the entire project of the first critique: of taming reason itself to not "overstep" the limits of experience or sensibility. In a way, the problem with speculative reason is the complete inversion (but hence also the mirror reflection) of the man who hesitates to walk his first independent steps: it is too eager to proceed and transgress its natural boundaries, and is therefore almost bound to go astray and stumble over contradictions. Hence, it is not surprising that the enemies of metaphysics as the former "queen of all the sciences" are compared by Kant to

"nomadic tribes, who hate a permanent habitation and settled mode of living." *Critique of Pure Reason* (Mineola, NY: Dover Publications, 2003), vii–viii. Ultimately, man—or reason—should be able to set his own boundaries. This is the meaning of autonomy; acting out of respect for the law one sets to herself. But to be able to set the proper law, and, moreover, to be able to *desire* that law, the individual must be produced in a certain way—his reason, as well as desire, must be tamed and shaped. Mehta's reading in Locke to which I shall arrive shortly, or Foucault's understanding of discipline are apt here.

62 Arneil, "Disability, Self Image, and Modern Political Theory," 226.

63 John Locke, *Two Treatises of Government* (New Haven, CT: Yale University Press, 2003), ii, §22.

64 This conception has become essential to liberalism. Kant is perhaps the most obvious example here, even if his notion of the law (as a self-constituted rule) is quite different than Locke's. The predominance of this conception is what allows Benjamin Constant to dedicate the chapter on personal liberty in his *Principles of Politics* almost exclusively to arbitrary power. Nevertheless, it is interesting to note that when he specifies the most injurious forms of executing arbitrary power he points to arrest and exile: preventing or forcing movement. *Political Writings* (Cambridge: Cambridge University Press, 1988), 294; see also Friedrich A. von Hayek, *The Constitution of Liberty* (Chicago: University of Chicago Press, 1978), 12.

65 Locke mentions "motion" one time in the entire text, yet neither in relation to concrete bodies nor to liberty. This motion is the motion of the body-politic; its context is that of war—a situation seen by Locke as standing in opposition to freedom (see chapter 4): "because war and peace giving a different motion to the force of such public body none can make war or peace but that which has the direction of the force of the whole body, and that in politic societies is only the supreme power." Locke, *Two Treatises*, ii §131.

66 Brown, *Walled States, Waning Sovereignty* (New York: Zone Books, 2010), 44.

67 Uday Singh Mehta, *The Anxiety of Freedom: Imagination and Individuality in Locke's Political Thought* (Ithaca, NY: Cornell University Press, 1992), 85, 100, respectively.

68 Kirstie Morna McClure, *Judging Rights: Lockean Politics and the Limits of Consent* (Ithaca, NY: Cornell University Press, 1996), 9.

69 As I argued in the introduction, stability and movement complement rather than contradict each other.

70 McClure, *Judging Rights*, 7. In this analysis McClure continues the tradition to which I pointed at the beginning of the section on Hobbes.

71 Locke, *Two Treatises*, ii, §57: We cannot desire to go off a cliff, of course, and yet so often we do. This, indeed, is the crucial task of education: to render our desires rational, to carve our wants so that the barrier that is the law will become transparent, or better: internalized, so that this "hedge" would not "abolish or restrain," but rather "preserve and enlarge Freedom:" . . . "law, in its true notion, is not so

much the limitation, as the direction of a free and intelligent agent to his proper interest."
72. Hirschmann is thus accurate in observing that for Locke, "all limitations of freedom are simultaneously expressions of it." *Gender, Class, and Freedom in Modern Political Theory*, 100.
73. Locke, *Two Treatises*, ii, §119.
74. Locke, *Two Treatises*, ii, §36. This very famous formulation echoes a much less famous claim by Hobbes, which should not be left unnoticed: "The multitude of poor, and yet strong people still increasing, they are to be transplanted into Countries not sufficiently inhabited, where . . . they are . . . to court each little Plot with art and labour, to give them their sustenance in due season." Hobbes, *Leviathan*, 239.
75. Locke, *Two Treatises*, ii, §119.
76. John Locke, *An Essay Concerning Human Understanding* (London; New York: Penguin, 1997), II.21.8.
77. Locke, *Essay*, II.21.10.
78. Locke, *Essay*, II.21.4 (my italics).
79. Locke, *Essay*, II.13.14; II.8.9, respectively; see also II.8.17.
80. For an analysis of this notion of abstract movement in Locke see P. J. White, "Materialism and the Concept of Motion in Locke's Theory of Sense-Idea Causation," *Studies in History and Philosophy of Science* 2.2 (1971): 132.
81. Locke, *Essay*, II.21.13. Relying on a different understanding of the mechanics within which the will operates, Hobbes, unsurprisingly, proposes the same claim: "from the use of the word *Free Will* no Liberty can be inferred of the will, desire, or inclination, but the Liberty of the man; which consisteth in this, that he finds no stop, in doing what he has the will, desire, or inclination to doe." Hobbes, *Leviathan*, 146.
82. T. H. Green, *Lectures on the Principles of Political Obligation, and Other Writings* (Cambridge: Cambridge University Press, 1986), 228, 37 respectively.
83. One may say that the Cartesian subject was fully integrated into political thought—perhaps even political institutions—but there is a shortcoming to this framing. To draw on Balibar's claim, Descartes does not appeal to the concept of subjectivity when he refers to the cogito: "Descartes does not name the thinking substance or 'thinking thing' subject," he argues contra Heidegger. The abstraction of the subject is thus not merely a "return" to Descartes or some "importation" of Descartes into political theory, but rather a later development of liberal political ontology. "Citizen/Subject," in *Who Comes after the Subject?*, eds. Peter Connor Eduardo and Jean-Luc Nancy (New York: Routledge, 1991), 33–57.
84. Samantha Frost, *Lessons from a Materialist Thinker: Hobbesian Reflections on Ethics and Politics* (Stanford, CA: Stanford University Press, 2008).
85. P. S. Atiyah, *The Rise and Fall of Freedom of Contract* (Oxford; New York: Clarendon Press; Oxford University Press, 1985), 212–13.

86 It is therefore not surprising that many of these moments occurred in tandem with another mode of disturbing the political surface of liberalism: gendering the liberal subject.

87 Maurice Merleau-Ponty, *Phenomenology of Perception* (New York: Routledge, 1974), 198.

88 William Blackstone, *Commentaries on the Laws of England* (Chicago: University of Chicago Press, 1979), 130.

89 Blackstone, *Commentaries*. It is worthwhile noting that this right was translated in Blackstone's frame into a confined and local movement. Blackstone did not see in immigration, for example, part of the natural right for liberty (134, 137); see also Frederick G. Whelan, "Citizenship and the Right to Leave," *The American Political Science Review* 75, no. 3 (1981): 645. Susan Staves has argued that while immigration laws and other laws concerning mobility across and within borders were rapidly changing in Blackstone's time to facilitate increasing mobility, he still thought of citizenship (or subjecthood) as natural and stable. "Chattel Property Rules and the Construction of Englishness, 1660–1800," *Law and History Review* 12.1 (1994), 127–28.

90 By limbs, Blackstone says he "only understand[s] those members which may be useful to [a man's] in fight." Limbs are the "gift" given to man to "enable man to protect himself from external injuries in a state of nature" (*Commentaries*, 126).

91 Blackstone, *Commentaries*, 131.

92 Blackstone, *Commentaries*, 125; Hobbes, *English Works*, i, 407.

93 It is not accidental, I proposed, that when Merleau-Ponty seeks to demonstrate and illustrate the agency of the body itself—the model of a subject who is a body rather than a subject in a body—he focuses on the movement of limbs and their extensions. A detailed work of comparing this schema of movement to the one assumed in liberalism would be a worthy project in this context, yet beyond the scope of this chapter.

94 The term "an anecdote" appears here in the Foucauldian meaning, as a small story that nonetheless captures something essential in the logic I set to delineate. For one of the most insightful analyses on the use of anecdotes in Foucault see Adi Ophir, "The Semiotics of Power: Reading Michel Foucault's Discipline and Punish," *Manuscrito* XII 2 (1989): 9–34.

95 "Performance," in Judith Butler's meaning of the concept; see, for example, *Gender Trouble: Feminism and the Subversion of Identity* (New York: Routledge, 1990).

96 Elizabeth Cady Stanton, *Eighty Years and More; Reminiscences, 1815–1897* (New York: Schocken Books, 1971), 201.

97 Ida Harper, a member of this group and the biographer of Susan B. Anthony, makes this connection between the bloomer and a wider woman's rights campaign explicitly: "[this costume] was worn chiefly by women who preached doctrines for which the public was no better prepared than for dress reform"; see *The Life and Work of Susan B. Anthony* (Indianapolis; Kansas City: Bowen-Merrill, 1899), 113.

98 Stanton, *Eighty Years and More*, 201.
99 Charles Neilson Gattey, *The Bloomer Girls* (New York: Coward-McCann, 1968), 60.
100 Elizabeth Wilson, *Adorned in Dreams: Fashion and Modernity* (New Brunswick, NJ: Rutgers University Press, 2003), 27–30; Kaja Silverman, "Fragments of a Fashionable Discourse," in *On Fashion*, eds. Shari Benstock and Suzanne Ferriss (New Brunswick, NJ: Rutgers University Press, 1994, 183–84).
101 Cited in Harper, *The Life and Work of Susan B. Anthony*, 119. Although she had already abandoned the bloomer at that point, Anthony replied, sharing Smith's analysis: "I stand alone in my opinion of the dress question—I can see no business avocation, in which woman, in her present dress, can possibly earn equal wages with man—& feel that it is folly for us to make the demand until, we adapt our dress to our work—I every day, feel more keenly the terrible bondage of these long skirts—I own that the want of Moral Courage, caused me to turn to them—And I can but doubt my own strength, in that it has failed me . . ." Elizabeth Cady Stanton and Susan B. Anthony, *The Selected Papers of Elizabeth Cady Stanton and Susan B. Anthony* (New Brunswick, NJ: Rutgers University Press, 1997), 321.
102 This is not to say that thinking without this matrix is impossible, but that it is impossible within the liberal ontology.

Chapter 4. The Problem of "Excessive" Movement

1 Scott, *Seeing Like a State: How Certain Schemes to Improve the Human Condition Have Failed* (New Haven, CT: Yale University Press, 1998), 1.
2 While the "extensive administrative infrastructure necessary to carry out such regulation" would only consolidate toward the end of the nineteenth century, this chapter focuses on the seventeenth century. It is also not strictly situated in Europe—the cradle of the modern nation-state, but in what may be described as its primary tentacle at the time: America; see John C. Torpey, *The Invention of the Passport*, 7.
3 William Walters, "Secure Borders, Safe Haven, Domopolitics," *Citizenship Studies* 8, no. 3 (2004): 244. Walters argues that the current European regime of immigration does not seek "to arrest mobility, but to tame it; not to build walls but systems capable of utilizing mobilities." Walters marks this politics of mobility as "domopolitic"—politics that is organized by the dual principle of "domus/domare": domos, as house or home, which is etymologically connected to the verb domare, which means to tame, but also to conquer or subdue. This notion is a different attempt to point to the duality I seek to capture here. The positive aspects, if I may say so (freedom in my case, and in Walters a sense of belonging, a place of one's own, a status as a citizen, but also institutions such as social security or more open immigration policies) are entangled with a force, an act of domination. The latters are perceived as necessary in order to tame (and thus allow) what is perceived as a threat to "the sanctity of the home," as Walters argues,

and/or to a particular order (security), to an imagined community or homogeneity (248, 241–42 respectively).
4 Plato, Republic (Indianapolis: Hackett, 1992), 558A, 561D.
5 In the seventeenth century, the patterns of exclusion and "othering" processes were still not stabilized within racial categories; see Uday Singh Mehta, Liberalism and Empire: A Study in Nineteenth-Century British Liberal Thought (Chicago: University of Chicago Press, 1999); Vanita Seth, Europe's Indians: Producing Racial Difference, 1500–1900 (Durham, NC: Duke University Press, 2010); and Peter Linebaugh and Marcus Rediker, The Many-Headed Hydra: Sailors, Slaves, Commoners, and the Hidden History of the Revolutionary Atlantic (Boston: Beacon Press, 2000).
6 Étienne Balibar, "Racism as Universalism," in Masses, Classes, Ideas: Studies on Politics and Philosophy before and after Marx (New York: Routledge, 1994); Mehta, Liberalism and Empire.
7 Jennifer L. Morgan, Laboring Women: Reproduction and Gender in New World Slavery (Philadelphia: University of Pennsylvania Press, 2004).
8 Serhat Karakayali and Enrica Rigo, "Mapping the European Space of Circulation," in The Deportation Regime: Sovereignty, Space, and the Freedom of Movement, eds. Nicholas De Genova and Nathalie Peutz (Durham, NC: Duke University Press, 2010), 129.
9 Plato, Republic, 558a.
10 Plato, Republic, 561d (my italics).
11 Plato, Republic, 327b-c.
12 Plato, Republic, 328c.
13 Adi Ophir points to the fact that it takes about ten hours to read the dialog aloud, but after the speakers stopped in the first book at Cephalus' home, no change of setting is indicated (Plato's Invisible Cities: Discourse and Power in the Republic (Savage, MD: Barnes & Noble, 1991), 105–6.
14 Plato, Republic, 432e; 369b, 394d; 432b, d-e respectively.
15 J. A. O. Larsen, "Demokratia," Classical Philology 68, no. 1 (1973): 45; Kurt A. Raaflaub, "Origins of Democracy in Ancient Greece" (Berkeley: University of California Press, 2007), 158. As Jacques Rancière notes in this context, "the 'poor,' however," "does not designate an economically disadvantaged part of the population; it simply designates the category of peoples who do not count, those who have no qualifications to part-take in arche, no qualification for being taken into account" (Disagreement: Politics and Philosophy (Minneapolis: University of Minnesota Press, 1999); see also Giorgio Agamben, for a similar claim, though differently situated in both time and language: Rome and Latin rather than Greece and Greek; in Homo Sacer: Sovereign Power and Bare Life (Stanford, CA: Stanford University Press, 1998), 176–77.
16 Stuart Elden, "Another Sense of Demos: Kleisthenes and the Greek Division of the Polis," Democratization 10, no. 1 (2003): 135.
17 See Michel Verdon, "On the Laws of Physical and Human Nature: Hobbes' Physical

and Social Cosmologies," *Journal of the History of Ideas* 43, no. 4 (1982)." Thus for Aristotle, rest "enjoyed an ontological primacy; rest was the repose of something that had reached its end or fulfillment. Rest was a mark of wholeness and completion, a completion towards which motion was striving. In a sense, then, rest was really the 'cause' of movement"; movements could be explained by the attempt to reach these spatial homes." See also Thomas A. Spragens, *The Politics of Motion: The World of Thomas Hobbes* (Lexington: University Press of Kentucky), 1973, 66, 82, and 61–63.

18 Claudia Baracchi, *Of Myth, Life, and War in Plato's Republic* (Bloomington; Indiana University Press, Combined Academic, 2002), 23–24.

19 Plato, *Republic*, 514a.

20 In a similar vein, Hannah Arendt maintains that within this paradigm, which begins with Plato but is by no means limited to him, "the human faculty of motion had been assigned to the soul" rather than the body. The soul "was suppose to move the body as well as itself." "What Is Freedom?" in *Between Past and Future: Eight Exercises in Political Thought* (New York: Penguin, 1977), 158.

21 Baracchi, *Of Myth, Life, and War in Plato's Republic*, 25.

22 Much like James Scott, John Urry shows that this meaning is still preserved within current notions of mobility; see *Mobilities* (Malden, MA: Polity, 2007), 8.

23 Plato, *Republic*, 563d.

24 And it was, indeed, "himself." Sally Shuttleworth's work on menstrual bleeding reveals the connection between the exclusion of women from liberal egalitarianism and assumptions regarding nonregulatable, excessive motion; see "Female Circulation: Medical Discourse and Popular Advertising in the Mid-Victorian Era," in *Body/Politics: Women and the Discourses of Science*, eds. Mary Jacobus et al. (New York; London: Routledge, 1990), 47–68.

25 Thomas Hobbes, *Leviathan* (Cambridge: Cambridge University Press, 1996), 141–42, see also 154.

26 As Vanita Seth (following Greenblatt) pointedly argues, the Hobbesian individual lacks any interiority. He is but a mask. Since Hobbes thought of the individual as "the source of chaos," he could be imagined as "the instigator of order" only if his very individuality is denied and a radical uniformity is assumed (*Europe's Indians*, 67). Seth argues that the move from the state of nature to a civil state does not include, in Hobbes, a "shift in the constitution of the individual" (71) that may allow him to think of a subject whose "interiority" can be a source of order rather than discord. Perhaps the lack of such a shift can be explained by the fact that the Hobbesian subject is always already social (this is Macpherson's claim), but perhaps such shifts can nevertheless be found. Nancy Hirschmann traces some changes, even if minimal, that the law produces within the individual. Fear operates also internally and produces certain tendencies of behavior; *The Subject of Liberty: Toward a Feminist Theory of Freedom* (Princeton, NJ: Princeton University Press, 2003). Or perhaps, we

should get rid of the structure of interiority altogether when thinking of Hobbes, as Frost proposes, and allow Hobbes's materiality to form a subject whose dimensions and facets are all external; see *Lessons from a Materialist Thinker: Hobbesian Reflections on Ethics and Politics* (Stanford, CA: Stanford University Press, 2008). Either way, these transformations in the subject—internal or a function of new conditions of living together (as Seth or Macpherson suggest in different ways)—are not merely minimal; they are also quite flat. Hence my claim above: we can begin to see a model developed here, but it still remains limited to the surface.

27 Richard Peters, *Hobbes* (London: Penguin, 1956), 94.
28 Hobbes, *Leviathan*, 145 (my italics).
29 Torpey, *The Invention of the Passport*; Cresswell, *On the Move: Mobility in the Modern Western World* (New York: Routledge, 2006); and in very different ways Gilles Deleuze and Félix Guattari, *A Thousand Plateaus: Capitalism and Schizophrenia* (London: Athlone Press, 1988).
30 Iris Marion Young, "Feminist Reactions to the Contemporary Security Regime," *Hypatia* 18, no. 1 (2003): 228.
31 Hobbes, *Leviathan*, 91.
32 *De Cive*, in Thomas Hobbes, *The English Works of Thomas Hobbes of Malmesbury* (London: J. Bohn, 1839), II, 127.
33 Torpey, *The Invention of the Passport*.
34 "All actions which men doe in Common-wealths, for *fear* of the law, are actions, which the doers had *liberty* to omit." Hobbes, *Leviathan*, 146.
35 And movement is the element that ties the two together. The constant collisions of particles that Spragens sees as analogous to the violent colliding of bodies in the state of nature manifests our vulnerability to the movements of others; see *The Politics of Motion*; and John Rogers, *The Matter of Revolution: Science, Poetry, and Politics in the Age of Milton* (Ithaca, NY: Cornell University Press, 1996). For further analysis see chapter 3. Samantha Frost (*Lessons from a Materialist Thinker*, 7) claims that Hobbes constitutes his subject "intersubjectively and in relation to the material environment." Throughout her reading of Hobbes, Frost describes an almost Butlerian subject—whose language, desires, and even thoughts are to a great degree given to others (or perhaps come about only *with* others—a point to which we shall return in chapter 5). And it is perhaps Judith Butler, more than anyone else, who makes clear the degree of our vulnerability to violence that is inherent in this intersubjectivity. As I have noted, this way of thinking about movement as violence does not work counter to the reading of movement as freedom in the previous chapter.
36 Hobbes, *Leviathan*, 88–89; Foucault, *Society Must Be Defended: Lectures at the Collège De France, 1975–76* (New York: Picador, 2003), chapter 4.
37 Hobbes, *Leviathan*, 88–89.
38 In Seth the claim that the commonwealth grants time receives a different meaning:

Time, she argues, remains empty without society. It is only within a social existence that time becomes a mediator of the human condition: "Thus, at the moment of contract, the individual does not leave the past and create a history. Instead, he creates history out of nothing. He creates time as the God of Genesis created man" (Europe's Indians, 72).

39 Fear, according to Hobbes, is an "Aversion": "an endeavour . . . fromward something . . . with opinion of Hurt from the object" (Leviathan, 38, 41).

40 Leviathan, 38 (my italics).

41 Spragens, The Politics of Motion, 65.

42 Carlo Galli's arrives at a similar conclusion from an analysis of the space of sovereignty. Within the commonwealth, "individual mobility remains, but it is devoid of its absolute and natural dimension, which generates conflict. The state, in short, serves the purpose of giving cohabitation stability, but it does not impose fixity or rootedness on the Subject"; see Political Spaces and Global War (Minneapolis: University of Minnesota Press, 2010), 31. Spragens, too, emphasized the role of space in this restriction of movement: "the task of politics in the Hobbesian world . . . is preeminently the task of *containment*—containment of the natural forces which produce a life that is . . . 'solitary, poore, nasty, brutish, and short'" (The Politics of Motion, 193, my italics).

43 Hirschmann, Gender, Class, and Freedom in Modern Political Theory.

44 Hobbes, Leviathan, 239.

45 Hobbes, Leviathan, 91.

46 Whereas much has been written about Locke and America, fewer have dedicated scholarly attention to Hobbes's engagement with the colonial project. In this context it is important to note that not only Locke had financial interest in the colonies, (see endnote 66), Hobbes, too, was financially invested in the Virginia Company; see Richard Tuck, The Rights of War and Peace: Political Thought and the International Order from Grotius to Kant (Oxford; New York: Oxford University Press, 1999), 128.

47 "The savage people of many places of America . . . live at this day in that brutish manner" (Hobbes, Leviathan, 89). Carl Schmitt suggests that the entire paradigm of homo homini lupus must be understood in relation to the new world: "in the 16th and 17th centuries, the homo homini lupus was revived, and the formula acquired a concrete meaning with amity lines, because now it was localized—it's acquired its own space": America. The Nomos of the Earth in the International Law of the Jus Publicum Europaeum (New York: Telos, 2003), 96.

48 Quentin Skinner, Hobbes and Republican Liberty (Cambridge: Cambridge University Press, 2008), 99–103; see also Tuck, The Rights of War and Peace, 137.

49 De Cive, 96, in Skinner's Hobbes and Republican Liberty, 98.

50 From a different perspective that also results in a different analysis, Carole Pateman similarly argues that the social contract is a "settler contract," that had to assume

the paradigm of *terra nullius* to be valid see The Settler Contract," in *Contract and Domination*, eds. Charles Mills and Carole Pateman (Malden, MA: Polity, 2007).
51 Schmitt, *The Nomos of the Earth*, 96.
52 Seth, *Europe's Indians*, 75–76.
53 Hobbes, *Leviathan*, 89. Charles Mills explains this seeming contradiction by arguing that the spatio-racial mark of Europe must be added into its latter part: "The non-European state of nature is thus actual, a wild and racialized place. . . . The European state of nature, by contrast, is either hypothetical or, if actual, generally a tamer affair, a kind of garden gone to seed, which may need some clipping but is really *already* partly domesticated." *The Racial Contract* (Ithaca, NY: Cornell University Press, 1997), 46. At least from a certain perspective, my argument here supports, rather than contradicts his.
54 Mehta, *Liberalism and Empire*, 46. Jan Pieterse Nederveen and Bhikhu C. Pareka, however, rightly note that "the contradiction is not just between liberal thought and liberal practice, but within liberal thought itself." *The Decolonization of Imagination: Culture, Knowledge, and Power* (London: Zed Books, 1995), 82.
55 Mehta, *Liberalism and Empire*, 63.
56 Thus, in effect this universal minimum materializes hierarchically. Indeed, Étienne Balibar suggests that "as soon as universalism *ceases* to be a mere word, a would-be philosophy, and becomes an effective system of concepts, it necessarily incorporates in its very center its *opposite*, [even] its *extreme* opposite." Thus, "no *definition* of the human . . .—something which is crucial for universalism, or universalism as humanism—has ever been proposed which would not imply a latent hierarchy" ("Racism as Universalism," in *Masses, Classes, Ideas: Studies on Politics and Philosophy before and after Marx* (New York: Routledge, 1994), 197.
57 And the distinction here is important: Nancy Hirschmann aptly argues that "we must distinguish between capacities, defined as the natural potential to think rationally if people receive adequate education, and abilities, that is, what one actually can do." *Gender, Class, and Freedom in Modern Political Theory*, 85.
58 "The Savages of America, are not without some good Morall Sentences; also they have a little Arithmetick, to adde, and divide in Numbers not too great." Hobbes, *Leviathan*, 459.
59 Hobbes, *Leviathan*, 459 (my italics).
60 Hobbes, *Leviathan*.
61 Hobbes, *Leviathan*.
62 Hobbes, *Leviathan*.
63 And yet this geographic split is fragile. Ultimately, "Hobbes's 'Other' is . . . an equal: we ourselves *are* the 'savages'"; Galli, *Political Spaces and Global War*, 28. While noting at one moment that America is a concrete location wherein his state of nature can be found, he also revokes this claim. Any society, including (and perhaps primarily) his England, can at any moment disintegrate. Yet as we've seen, this

collapse is not complete. In light of a separation, even if unstable, between Europe (although not Europeans) and the New World, a distinction between an other and a self is nonetheless looming.

64 A striking example of such a divide can be found in Rebecca Stein's work on tourism. Stein contrasts images of Jewish Israeli travels to Arab countries with Arab tourists making a parallel journey into Israel in the post-Oslo years. "While the Jewish Israeli tourist was portrayed as an heroic traveler, freely traversing borders into Arab lands, the Arab tourist seeking entry to Israel was the object of considerable anxiety." "'First Contact' and Other Israeli Fictions: Tourism, Globalization, and the Middle East Peace Process," *Public Culture* 14, no. 3 (2002): 517. Unlike the free individual whose individuality, as well as freedom, is reaffirmed in the act of crossing borders (in the case of the Jewish Israeli), Arab tourists were often depicted as "an underclass mob," very much in the tradition of colonial voyage stories (531). The movement of tourism in the case of the latter, Stein suggests, is being documented as a crime (532).

65 A parallel split, which will not be pursued here, is worth thinking about in this context. Parallel to the configuration of some movements as nonfree by the virtue of the danger embedded in them, some movements are thus configured by portraying the movers as passive victims. Nowhere is this portrayal clearer, I suspect, than in the discussion of trafficking in women (and children) for the sex industry. Here, global location (global wealth distribution, as well as the dispersion of racial, ethnic, and national identities) is coupled with gender (and age) to set the movement of the classic liberal subject apart from a set of other(ed) movements. For a critique of such a schism in the assumptions regarding freedom, slavery, and movement (particularly immigration) see Wendy Chapkis, "Soft Glove Punishing Fist: The Trafficking Victims Protection Act of 2000," in *Regulating Sex: The Politics of Intimacy and Identity*, eds. Laurie Schaffner and Elizabeth Bernstein (New York: Routledge, 2005), 51–66.

66 More than his writing—and probably tightly related to his intellectual interest—America had occupied Locke's personal and financial interests. Both directly and via his patron, Anthony Ashley Cooper (who became the first Earl of Shaftesbury), Locke served for about a decade in both private and public colonial administrating roles, and was heavily invested in the slave trade of both the Bahamas Company and the Royal African Company. Probably most famous is his contribution to drafting, and later revising, the *Fundamental Constitutions of Carolina* in 1669–70. For detailed accounts on Locke's personal involvement with the colonial project see: David Armitage, *The Ideological Origins of the British Empire* (Cambridge: Cambridge University Press, 2000); David Armitage, "John Locke, Carolina, and the Two Treatises of Government," *Political Theory* 32, no. 5 (2004); Maurice William Cranston, *John Locke: A Biography* (London: Longmans Green, 1957); Duncan Ivison, "Locke, Liberalism and Empire," in *The Philosophy of John Locke: New Perspectives*, ed.

Peter R. Anstey (London: Routledge, 2003), 86–105; Vicki Hsueh, "Cultivating and Challenging the Common: Lockean Property, Indigenous Traditionalisms, and the Problem of Exclusion," *Contemporary Political Theory* 5 (2006).

67 Armitage, *The Ideological Origins of the British Empire*, 97. See also Said, *Orientalism* (New York: Pantheon Books, 1978); Nederveen Pieterse and Parekh, *The Decolonization of Imagination*. Armitage ascribes this justification of imperial expansion to the marginality of the religion-based mode of justification within the formation of the British Empire. Unlike the Spanish Empire, the ideological grounds of the British Empire never relied on religion per se. Especially in Locke, whose *Letter on Toleration* rejected the idea that possession can be based on religious grounds alone, there was a need to provide another anchor to justify settlement overseas.

68 Armitage, *The Ideological Origins of the British Empire*, 97.

69 Pateman, "The Settler Contract."

70 Seth, *Europe's Indians*, 82–83, 13, respectively.

71 Seth, *Europe's Indians*, 64, 4, respectively.

72 I obviously play here with Balibar's formulation, but am not fully committed to his analysis of this subject and his intellectual heritage. My aim is to point to the configuration at the core of the demarcated *polis*—the right-bearing entity that often subsumes the category "subject."

73 Seth, *Europe's Indians*, 99.

74 Locke, *An Essay Concerning Human Understanding* (New York: Penguin, 1997), II.21.8.

75 In his 2004 essay, David Armitage argues that Locke probably wrote this chapter as he was engaged in revising the *Fundamental Constitution of Carolina*, and that "there was an immediate and identifiable colonial context" for his theory of property; see "John Locke, Carolina, and the Two Treatises of Government," 602. Duncan Ivison further proposes that we should see the two contexts as entangled, and be able to address the relevance of both, perhaps even how they work in tandem; see "Locke, Liberalism, and Empire," in *The Philosophy of John Locke: New Perspectives*, ed. Peter R. Anstey (London: Routledge, 2003), 86, 105. See also Barbara Arneil, *John Locke and America: The Defence of English Colonialism* (Oxford: Oxford University Press, 1996), 118–32.

76 James Tully, *An Approach to Political Philosophy: Locke in Contexts* (Cambridge: Cambridge University Press, 1993), 129.

77 "The connection between agrarian labour and colonialism is profound," argues Arneil. "When we talk about liberal colonialism, we are centrally concerned with settlement and agrarian labour." "Liberal Colonialism, Domestic Colonies and Citizenship," *Journal of the History of Political Thought* 33, no. 2 (2012): 497.

78 Locke, *Two Treatises of Government* (New Haven, CT: Yale University Press, 2003), ii: §32.

79 Locke, *Two Treatises of Government*, ii: §43. A few paragraphs beforehand Locke provides the more moderate ratio of one to ten, or perhaps to a hundred (ii: §37).

80 Locke, *Two Treatises of Government*, ii: §28.
81 Locke, *Two Treatises of Government*, ii: §26.
82 William W. Bassett, "The Myth of the Nomad in Property Law," *Journal of Law and Religion* 4, no. 1 (1986): 134.
83 Bassett, "The Myth of the Nomad in Property Law, 150.
84 Hirschmann, "Intersectionality before Intersectionality Was Cool," in *Feminist Interpretations of John Locke*, eds. Nancy Hirschmann and Kirstie McClure (University Park: The Pennsylvania State University Press, 2007), 165. Hirschmann's main axis of analysis here is class. It would be interesting to follow the intersectional proposition she puts forward in the essay and think of this denial of rationality based on the lack of property in conjunction with a denial that circulates around both property and race, as in the case of indigenous Americans.
85 Locke, *Two Treatises of Government*, ii: §37.
86 Locke, *Two Treatises of Government*, ii: §26.
87 Locke, *Two Treatises of Government*, ii: §37.
88 Locke, *Two Treatises of Government*, ii: §4.
89 Most explicitly Locke, *Two Treatises of Government*, §ii: 93, 136, 222; see also Wendy Brown, *Walled States, Waning Sovereignty* (New York: Zone Books, 2010), 44.
90 However note that when Locke applies "laws of reason" to the situations within which his Indians are given, it is not altogether clear whether the reason he refers to is *theirs* (as acting agents) or *ours* (as interpreters). Take, for example, Locke's statement in §30: "Thus this law of reason makes the deer that Indian's who hath killed it; it is allowed to be his goods who hath bestowed his labour upon it, though before it was the common right of every one." Locke makes this claim as part of his argument that it is labor rather than consent that grants property rights, but it is unclear whether he asks us to use our own reason to determine the legitimacy of deer appropriation here, or whether he makes an argument about the "Indian's" capacity of doing the same.
91 Schmitt, *The Nomos of the Earth*, 75.
92 "Is a man under the law of nature? What made him free of that law? What gave him a free disposing of his property, according to his own will, within the compass of that law? I answer, a state of maturity, wherein he might be supposed capable to know that law, that so he might keep his actions within the bounds of it. When he has acquired that state, he is presumed to know how far that law is to be his guide, and how far he may make use of his freedom, and so comes to have it." Hence: "We are borne free, as we are borne rational," he states. "Not that we have actually the exercise of either: age, that brings one, brings with it the other too." Locke, *Two Treatises of Government*, ii: §59, 61.
93 In the *Treatises* the list is composed merely from the former two, yet it is not Locke's list, but the list of Richard Hooker whom Locke cites (11: §60). In the *Essay* this list appears several times, this time in Locke's own words.

94 Uday Singh Mehta, *The Anxiety of Freedom: Imagination and Individuality in Locke's Political Thought*, Contestations (Ithaca, NY: Cornell University Press, 1992), 107, 10. It is possible to further speculate that beyond the tendency of the madman to refuse *epistemological* confinement, thereby breaking the link that grounds perceptions in "things," the mind of the madman is also *moved* too easily, thereby becoming emotionally unstable.

95 It is worthwhile noting here that the savage's spatial problem went beyond the locality of enclosure. On top of a presumed inability to be "properly" located (that is, anchored to a demarcated locus), Locke identifies in the *Essay* the savages' failure of rationality also as a function of concrete location. Locke's refutation of innate ideas is a telling illustration. To demonstrate that the mind is originally empty (his famous *tabula rasa* principle) he proposes: "Had you or I been born at the Bay of Soldania, possibly our thoughts, and notions, had not exceeded those brutish ones of the Hottentots that inhabit there: and had the Virginia king Apochancana been educated in England, he had, perhaps, been as knowing a divine [one of the supposedly-innate ideas Locke considers], and as good as a mathematician, as any in it." Most of the indigenous Americans Locke has "spoken with . . . were otherwise of quick and rational parts enough," so it is not altogether clear why presenting the relevant experience to them would not allow their mind to be of equal capacity to that of a mature Englishman. Why, in other words, should king Apochancana be educated *in* England and not simply like an Englishman; Locke, *An Essay Concerning Human Understanding*, I.4.12, II.XVI.6. Perhaps the spatial proposition—"in"—is but a slip of the tongue, yet it is quite consistent with the lattice connecting rationality and spatiality in Locke. Moreover, this might be seen as an early articulation of the principle Ann Stoler identified in later, more developed and systematized imperial apparatuses: education in the motherland (or fatherland) was seen as crucial to the management and sustainability of colonial rule; see *Along the Archival Grain: Epistemic Anxieties and Colonial Common Sense* (Princeton, NJ: Princeton University Press, 2009), chapter 3. This local cultivation of sentiments, she argues, can be traced back to Locke, and to his "contention that moral thinking was embodied in the dispositions of the everyday, in the habits of comportment that had to be learned." These were tightly anchored in the particular space in which education took place (96–97).

96 Arneil, "Liberal Colonialism, Domestic Colonies and Citizenship." Indeed, Ann Stoler defines the colony as "a principle of managed mobilities" through which "the value of human kinds" is assessed. "Colony," *Political Concepts: A Critical Lexicon* 1 (2012).

97 Vicki Hsueh shows that Locke was well aware that this assumption, which stood at the base of his theory of colonial appropriation, was not founded and perhaps even false. Locke, she demonstrates, was familiar with the fact that "Carolina colonists under [his] secretarial observation learned types of stationary planting, cultivation,

and gathering from various local indigenous tribes—in essence, adapting the skills and knowledges of local tribes to develop some measure of the productivity and stability attributed to the presumptively progressive, 'Civilized' actors articulated by the *Two Treatises*." Such information may indicate that the dichotomy presented in the *Treatises* between two modes of relation to the land (enclosure and "waste") was a product of "rewriting and ultimately writing away a history of colonial dependencies, insecurities, and contingencies." Hsueh, "Cultivating and Challenging the Common," 203; see also Armitage, "John Locke, Carolina, and the Two Treatises of Government." Parekh further claims that the famous section concerning over-accumulation in the *Second Treatise*: "if either the Grass or his Inclosure rotted on the ground, or the Fruit of his planting perished without gathering, and laying up, this part of Earth, notwithstanding his Inclosure, was till to be looked on as Waste, and might be the Possession of any other" (II: 38), was written not as a critique of the idle rich, but as part of justifying dispossession of indigenous Americans from enclosed lands. Parekh argues that this argument was made to support settler's claims that the practice of letting land rot and compost every three years rendered it, even when enclosed, available for European grab since it was not fully exploited; see Nederveen Pieterse and Parekh, *The Decolonization of Imagination*, 85. According to these or Bassett's arguments, the notion of excessive movement can be seen as but a cynical hook upon which to hang certain identity categories. Indeed, the concrete patterns of movement in these cases seem to be irrelevant, to the degree that a myth of movement had to be fabricated to function as such a justification mechanism. Without disregarding the merit of this reading, this chapter seeks not to unmask the façade, but to examine what the myth preforms and produces.

98 Accordingly, "the European ideas about productivity and efficiency" deemed the land "uncivilized" from the perspective of Europeans, and thus available for settlement despite the fact it was "not really vacant." Margaret Kohn and Keally D. McBride, *Political Theories of Decolonization: Postcolonialism and the Problem of Foundations* (New York: Oxford University Press, 2011), 103. The tie between the absence of systematic cultivation of the land and its "emptiness" was emphasized by Locke (much like Grotius before him) via the notion of "the right of husbandry." Carole Pateman analyzes significant aspects of this combination in "The Settler Contract."

99 Famously: "A land without a people for a people without a land."

100 Locke refers to the law as a hedge that "hedges us in only from bogs and precipices," Locke, *Two Treatises*, ii: §57.

101 The first and second chapters provided some examples for this structure, and there are others available. Let us take as another example the system of permits. In order to pass through a checkpoint a Palestinian has to have a certain permit. These are issued by the DCO (District Command Officer). Yet most of the DCO's offices are located in such a way that necessitates most Palestinians to cross a checkpoint—the very checkpoint they need the permit to cross—in order to get to them.

Thus, in order to cross the checkpoint one needs a permit; in order to get the permit one needs to cross the checkpoint. There are many other examples.

102 Ivison, however, argues that "Locke wrote with an eye to both the domestic and international consequences of his arguments" ("Locke, Liberalism and Empire"). Indeed, in her later work, Arneil seeks to demonstrate that Locke's "twin ideological commitments to agrarian labour and reason, combined with breaking free of custom and 'progress/improvement' through segregation from civil society, are the key constitutive terms in Locke's liberal colonialism." This colonialism, however, was domestic no less than external: "these fundamental beliefs have profound implications not only for indigenous people . . . but equally for the idle and irrational at home, in England." "Liberal Colonialism, Domestic Colonies and Citizenship," 502.

103 Linebaugh and Rediker quote here Richard Hakyluyt, who had been making such arguments in support of colonization early in the seventeenth century (The Many-Headed Hydra, 16). See also Locke's reference to "beggars swarming in the streets," in "An Essay on the Poor Law," 187. We still find this rhetoric as late as the nineteenth century; see Bruce L. Kinzer, England's Disgrace?: J. S. Mill and the Irish Question (Toronto: University of Toronto Press, 2001).

104 Linebaugh and Rediker argue that the outcomes of this "profound and far-reaching cause" (i.e., enclosures) were a shift from subsistence-based, to commercial agriculture; an increase in wage labor; a growth in urban population; an institutionalization of markets; a growth of globalized trade; and a resultant establishment of a colonial system (The Many-Headed Hydra, 16).

105 Linebaugh and Rediker, The Many-Headed Hydra, 44.

106 P. S. Atiyah, The Rise and Fall of Freedom of Contract (Oxford: Oxford University Press, 1985), 85–86.

107 This is a significant outcome of the sixteenth and seventeenth centuries' acts of enclosures, much more so than it would be in the Parliamentary enclosures of the eighteenth century, which gave some form of land compensation to the poor.

108 The home, the enclosed land of the liberal subject—both as an ideology and as a technology of power—is accordingly formed as a mirror image of this movement: "The bourgeoisie will get its initial power and class characteristic . . . less from commerce and industry than from the strategic implantation that establishes the 'fox domicile' as a social and momentary value." Paul Virilio, Speed and Politics: An Essay on Dromology (New York: Columbia University, 1986), 34.

109 Torpey, The Invention of the Passport, 8. See also De Genova and Mae Peutz, The Deportation Regime, 57. Karakayali and Rigo argue that the immobility of feudalism is itself a fiction, or perhaps better put, an idea whose constant attempts of actualization (that is, the production of sedentarism) were a function of constant repression, see "Mapping the European Space of Circulation."

110 Procacci, "Social Economy and the Government of Poverty, in The Foucault Effect:

Studies in Governmentality, eds. Colin Gordon, Graham Burchell, Peter Miller (Chicago: University of Chicago Press 1991), 158, 61 (my italics). Perhaps this is why by the seventeenth century, the poor were put into the same category as the "unemployed..., the prisoners, and... the insane" all had to be assigned a home within the "enormous houses of confinement"; see Foucault, *Madness and Civilization: A History of Insanity in the Age of Reason* (New York: Vintage Books, 1973), 38–39. While according to Mary Poovey this distinction between poverty and pauperism is a product of the nineteenth century, traces of this configuration of the poor's movement as a threat to social order—and of poverty as vagrancy—can be traced back to the sixteenth century; see *Making a Social Body: British Cultural Formation, 1830–1864* (Chicago: University of Chicago Press, 1995).

111 Cherbuliez; cited in Procacci, "Social Economy and the Government of Poverty," 160.

112 Foucault, *Madness and Civilization*, 39–50; Atiyah, *The Rise and Fall of Freedom of Contract*, 67–68, 527–28; and Locke "Essay on the Poor Law."

113 The Poor Law act of 1575 tied together "the punishment of vagabonds" with "the relief of the poor," and "prescribed the construction of *houses of correction*" [italics in original] to deal with both problems simultaneously (Foucault, *Madness and Civilization*, 43). Atiya shows how the model is almost overturned by the nineteenth century in the New Poor Law (1834): "the workman was given freedom of contract, freedom of movement, in return for the loss of his right to subsistence from the State, except in case of extreme deprivation" (*The Rise and Fall of Freedom of Contract*, 527). Nevertheless, the logic of confinement subsists; Walters sees the camp (primarily deportation camps) as a contemporary incarnation of the same logic; see "Deportation, Expulsion, and the International Police of Aliens," *Citizenship Studies* 6, no. 3 (2002): 286.

114 Torpey, *The Invention of the Passport*, 8. Of course, this desire to confine the poor does not end with the shift in the model of work to which Atiya points (in the above footnote) and that increased freedom of movement of industrial workers. From the seventeenth century until today, we can witness the desire to "produce 'fixed concentrations of population' (for example, anti-vagabondage laws, the poor law, and later, public housing), then camps and deportations"; all "represent components" of an ongoing "sedentarization campaign" (Walters, "Deportation, Expulsion, and the International Police of Aliens," 286). Contemporary reforms of welfare in the United States often appeal to a similar logic of sedentarization, aspiring to confine welfare recipients, ideally organized within "normative families," in stable locations (homes); see Anna Marie Smith, *Welfare and Sexual Regulation* (Cambridge: Cambridge University Press, 2007).

115 Foucault, *Madness and Civilization*.

116 Locke, "Essay on the Poor Law," 184.

117 Locke, "Essay on the Poor Law," 187. Locke proposes increasingly severe punish-

ments for beggars violating these spatial restrictions, so that, for example, if someone "above fourteen years old shall be found begging out of her own parish (if she be an inhabitant of a parish within five miles' distance of that she is found begging in)," she will be returned to her parish and delivered "to the overseer of the poor" on her expense. If, however, such a female is found "at a greater distance than five miles from the place of her abode," or if "she is found begging without a lawful pass" for the second time within the same distance, she will be sent to the "house of correction, there to be employed in hard work three months." Such strict spatial regulations were beginning to be installed, at least formally, by demanding beggars to wear a badge of the parish to which they belonged for identification (9). The most mobile vagrants (those found far away from their parish) were to be confined in the ultimate site of landless, uprooted movement: they were to be put on board of a ship and sent to the sea (185–6):

> not to the house of correction . . . , nor to the place of habitation . . . , but, if it is in a maritime country, . . . they be sent to the next seaport town, there to be kept at hard labour, till some of his majesty's ships, coming in or near there, give an opportunity of putting them on board, where they shall serve three years to serve on naval ships, at soldier's pay. . . . , and be punished as deserters if they go on shore without leave, or, when sent on shore, if they either go further or stay longer than they have leave.

118 Locke, *Essay*, II.xxxiii.6; see also Emily C. Nacol, "Poverty, Work and 'the People' in Locke's Political Thought," 10th APT *Annual Conference* (Columbia: University of South Carolina, 2012).

119 Hirschmann, *Gender, Class, and Freedom in Modern Political Theory*, 83; see also C. B. Macpherson, *The Political Theory of Possessive Individualism: Hobbes to Locke* (Oxford; New York: Oxford University Press, 1985), 226.

120 "We are born to be, if is be please, rational creatures, but it is use and exercise only that makes us so," argues Locke. The best way to train the mind is mathematics, and it should therefore "be taught all those who have the time and opportunity" (and in the subsequent section Locke poses the formulation "fortunes and time"). This, Locke observes, should probably occur in childhood, since "it will not be done without industry and application, which will require more time and pains than grown men, settled in their course of life, will allow to it, and therefore very seldom is done." However, the requirement of "fortune and time" also means it is not the prospect of all children: the children of "a poor countryman" or "the Americans" do not usually enjoy this opportunity; see Locke, *The Conduct of the Understanding* (London: W. Blackader, 1800), §6.

121 Locke, *The Conduct of the Understanding*, § 6.

122 Locke, *Essay*, 2.21.67

123 This is where both projects meet and converge with the previous colonial reading.

As Sandro Mezzadara observes: "The concept of property itself is in John Locke an 'anthropological' concept." After establishing the property of the self—a product of securing a bodily border, a capacity to rationality, a domination of one's passion and disciplining "himself in order to be able to do that labor which constitutes in turn the foundation of every 'material' property"—the individual "is able to become a citizen." In this process, this figure also produces its own borders, that is, a series of figures that are bound to be the "others" of citizenship: the woman (who, in Locke's view, is by nature destined to subordinate herself to the authority of the man within the family), the atheist, the foolish, the idle poor, and the American Indian. "Citizen and Subject: A Postcolonial Constitution for the European Union?" *Situations: Project of the Radical Imagination* 1, no. 2 (2006): 33.

124 Walters, "Deportation, Expulsion, and the International Police of Aliens," 270–71.
125 On the ties between the two as they take shape in Locke via mobility regimes (in promoting early incarnations of domestic farm- and labor-colonies, as well as the colonization in America) see Arneil, "Liberal Colonialism, Domestic Colonies and Citizenship."
126 Locke, *Two Treatises of Government*, ii: §36.
127 Akin to the mirrored image of nomadism, this image of freedom was to a great degree mythical. Locke's idea of moving poor populations (and criminals) to the new colonies was vastly applied in the seventeenth century (and in Spain and Portugal as early as the fifteenth century), yet it was a project of removing and transporting populations, rather than a project of free immigration. In 1597 the Vagrancy Act legalized deportation, and petty offences were punished by expropriation to the new colonies to supply working hands to the colonizing companies; see Linebaugh and Rediker, *The Many-Headed Hydra*; Walters, "Deportation, Expulsion, and the International Police of Aliens."
128 Hume, and following him, Smith, would question this assumption of freedom, in the different context of tacit consent: "Can we seriously say, that a poor peasant or artisan has a free choice to leave his country, when he knows no foreign language or manners, and lives, from day to day, by the small wages which he acquires? We may as well assert that a man, by remaining in a vessel, freely consents to the dominion of the master; though he was carried on board while asleep, and must leap into the ocean and perish, the moment he leaves her." The ability to move and the fact of staying put is not enough to deduce freedom, Hume argues here, pointing to other social factors; David Hume, "On the Original Contract" in *The Philosophical Works* (Edinburgh; London: Adam Black and William Tait, 1826), III: 520. See also Adam Smith, *Lectures on Jurisprudence*, eds., R. L. Meek, D. D. Raphael and P. G. Stein (Oxford: Clarendon Press, 1978), 403.

Chapter 5. The "Substance and Meaning of All Things Political"

1 Uday Singh Mehta, *The Anxiety of Freedom: Imagination and Individuality in Locke's Political Thought*, Contestations (Ithaca, NY: Cornell University Press, 1992).
2 Sandro Mezzadra's idea of the *metaborder* is a good example for this simultaneity of separation and connection. The metaborder separating the metropolis and the colonies (a border that is both spatial and temporal: the colony is an elsewhere and a past) is necessary for the set of distinctions that conditions the colonial order. And yet this metaborder reproduces itself within the metropolises of the "postcolonial" world, dividing and connecting the spaces within Europe, echoing a colonial past that has not yet passed, and re-creating matrixes of colonial control within the cities of Europe. "Citizen and Subject: A Postcolonial Constitution for the European Union?" *Situations: Project of the Radical Imagination* 1, no. 2 (2006): 31–42.
3 The movement and confinement of women, men, children, servants, food, sex, sewage, or manufacturing activities produced the domestic and public sphere. The circulation of merchants, farmers, workers, sailors, traders, investors, consumers, produces, or money correlates to the formation of the city and farmland, among other divisions. And finally, there are the movements and halts set upon the movements of colonized, colonizers, or those who cannot quite fall into any of these categories (vagrants, convicted felons, unindustrialized poor).
4 Different theorists within mobility studies imagine the shared space—"the social," "the state," or simply "the movement"—as characterized by streams of escalating movements. For most, this is an attribute of modern political space, which is seen as "a space of movement. But [also as] a space that is itself in movement." Carlo Galli, *Political Spaces and Global War* (Minneapolis: University of Minnesota Press, 2010), 7. Along similar lines, John Urry calls for replacing the understanding of society as a relatively stable entity (relying on definitions such as "the social as society" or a concept of society that is confined within the nation-state) with the idea of "the 'social as mobility.'" John Urry, *Sociology Beyond Societies: Mobilities for the Twenty-First Century* (London and New York: Routledge, 2000), 2. See also: Urry, *Mobilities*; Virilio, *Speed and Politics*; Marshall Berman, *All That Is Solid Melts into Air: The Experience of Modernity* (New York: Simon and Schuster, 1982). However, the trend in mobile studies to see the emphasis on movement as essentially modern misses the fact that classic political thought too, often conceives social/political entities as moving collectivities or collectivities forming via movement.
5 At least from the seventeenth century, bound Chinese feet functioned as a metonym for China: backward, tyrannical, and essentially immobile (contrasted with an image of a progressive Europe). The bound foot—gendered, deformed, foreign, and at times exotic—was used as an index of a lack of freedom demonstrated (but also executed and secured) via a hindered mobility. I examine the many uses of the term in Western thought elsewhere; see Hagar Kotef, "Little Chinese Feet Encased in Iron Shoes," in *Political Theory*, forthcoming.

6 Kant's metaphor of the man emerging into enlightenment as a man who has to accustom his body "to such free movement," and who eventually learns to "walk firmly," is a telling example (Immanuel Kant, "What Is Enlightenment," see my analysis in chapter 3). This metaphor captures a mode of being in the world that by the nineteenth century came to embody "bourgeois self-consciousness." Andrew Hewitt, Social Choreography: Ideology as Performance in Dance and Everyday Movement, Post-Contemporary Interventions (Durham, NC: Duke University Press, 2005), 81.

7 This was the main claim of the previous chapter, especially in the analysis focusing on Locke. But such a mode of argumentation does not remain confined to the seventeenth century and to the relation between England and the New World.

8 Catherine Kudlick, "Disability History: Why We Need Another 'Other,'" The American Historical Review 108, no. 3 (2003): 766.

9 Thomas Hobbes, Leviathan (Cambridge: Cambridge University Press, 1996), 120, 114, respectively.

10 Elias Canetti, Crowds and Power (London: Gollancz, 1962).

11 Michael Hardt and Antonio Negri, Multitude: War and Democracy in the Age of Empire (New York: Penguin, 2004).

12 According to Peter Linebaugh and Marcus Rediker we can see this conceptualization of a multiple body already in the sixteenth century. A figure through which the threatening multitude of the dispossessed was configured, the hydra was a myth often referred to in order "to describe the difficulty of imposing order on increasingly global system of labor"; see The Many-Headed Hydra: Sailors, Slaves, Commoners, and the Hidden History of the Revolutionary Atlantic (Boston: Beacon, 2000), 3. Accordingly, Hobbes notes in Behemoth that the heads of the Hydra cannot be bought (that is, cannot be incorporated into the new order from within this order's logic). Such attempts of reconciliation would only cause more heads of rebellion to emerge. Instead, the heads must be cut off; The English Works of Thomas Hobbes of Malmesbury (London: J. Bohn, 1839), VI: 245.

13 Doreen B. Massey, For Space (London: Thousand Oaks, CA: Sage, 2005), 7.

14 Massey, For Space; see also Henri Lefebvre, The Production of Space (Malden, MA: Blackwell, 1991).

15 Ash Amin describes an episode—an event, in his terms—of a man losing consciousness on a train. The event, he argues, momentarily brought the passengers together, united in a community by a sense of anxiousness, precariousness, and an urgency of care: "in the singularity of the event we had become a unitary public, affected in the same way by the situation, and in ways that would endure as a reminder of both our fragility and cooperative power." Paper presented at the "City/Space Workshop," Tel Aviv, 2013.

16 The example of the Zionist movement, to which I briefly return below, is one such example of mass movements of different individuals and communities to form a new political reality, to create a new nation, and to permanently alter space.

17 Adi Ophir, "State," *Mafteakh: Lexical Journal for Political Thought* 3 (2011): 69. Ophir argues that "the modern state . . . came into the world as an intellectual construct, a sort of Kantian idea, i.e., a concept with no adequate representation in the world of experience" (72).

18 Wendy Brown unfolds the ties between the "psychic-political desires" of "late modern subjects" and the materiality of some of these enclosures (specifically, wall-building). It is precisely the inability to fully enclose—to protect, to separate, the "vulnerability and unboundedness, permeability and violation"—of both subjects and states that keeps producing the desire to enclose. *Walled States, Waning Sovereignty* (New York: Zone Books, 2010), 107–8.

19 John Torpey, *The Invention of the Passport: Surveillance, Citizenship, and the State* (Cambridge: Cambridge University Press, 2000); Max Weber, *Politics as a Vocation* (Philadelphia: Fortress Press, 1965).

20 Virilio, *Speed and Politics*, 43.

21 Hobbes, *Leviathan*, 9.

22 As Hannah Arendt identifies, this paradigm begins with Plato. Within this paradigm "the human faculty of motion had been assigned to the soul, which was supposed to move the body as well as itself." "What Is Freedom?" in *Between Past and Future: Eight Exercises in Political Thought* (New York: Penguin, 1977), 158.

23 Hobbes, *Leviathan*, 9.

24 Hobbes, *Leviathan*, 158.

25 Adriana Cavarero, *Stately Bodies: Literature, Philosophy, and the Question of Gender* (Ann Arbor: University of Michigan Press, 2002), 165, 66.

26 Cavarero, *Stately Bodies*, 173.

27 Thomas A. Spragens, *The Politics of Motion: The World of Thomas Hobbes* (Lexington: University Press of Kentucky, 1973). See also chapter 3 here.

28 For example, Arendt, *The Human Condition* (Chicago: University of Chicago Press, 1998).

29 Foucault's famous inversion suggests that "politics is the continuation of war by other means"; see *Society Must Be Defended: Lectures at the Collège De France, 1975–76* (New York: Picador, 2003), 15.

30 Hobbes, *Leviathan*, 38, 41.

31 Hobbes, *Leviathan*, 149. See also Galli: "if 'the Law of Nations, and the Law of Nature, is the same thing,' then the State's exclusive objective—vital but limited—of putting an end to internal civil war means that the enclosed space of the State will remain open to the ever-present possibility of war between States" (*Political Spaces and Global War*, 32).

32 Hobbes, *Leviathan*, 175.

33 Total liberty in Hobbes is always violence (at least potentially so) as it is the right for *everything*. In a way it is the full liberty Hegel has identified as the empty liberty of total annihilation; death. Because it encapsulates the state of nature, this liberty is the luring possibility of the end of life.

34 Claudia Baracchi, *Of Myth, Life, and War in Plato's Republic* (Bloomington; Indiana University Press, 2002), 153.
35 Baracchi, *Of Myth, Life, and War in Plato's Republic*, 164–65.
36 Carl Schmitt, *Political Theology: Four Chapters on the Concept of Sovereignty* (Chicago: University of Chicago Press, 2005).
37 Hannah Arendt, *The Origins of Totalitarianism* (New York: Meridian Books, 1958), 398.
38 On the fantasy of enclosure lying at the origin and contemporary infrastructure of sovereignty see Brown, *Walled States*, esp. chapter 2. On the idea of the border as a container see Avery Kolers, *Land, Conflict, and Justice: A Political Theory of Territory* (Cambridge: Cambridge University Press, 2009). Ophir proposes that the state is "an imagined enclosure of the political body." While it is "a never-ending task," this enclosure is nonetheless "a crucial one." It is a precondition "for all the other developments. The ability to impose a clear distinction between inside and outside and to prevent people, messages, and objects from coming and going unsupervised allows a constant growth of the governable domain and enables all the mechanisms that enact surveillance, control, tracking, and regulating to improve their capacities for penetration and intervention within this closed domain" ("State," 75, 82).
39 John Agnew, "Borders on the Mind: Re-Framing Border Thinking," *Ethics & Global Politics* 1, no. 4 (2008); Stuart Elden, *The Birth of Territory* (Chicago: University of Chicago Press, 2013). According to Merav Amir, sovereignty is the *effect* of the performativity of borders: of various border-praxes that simulate (and in that produce, but also trouble) borders. "Borders as Praxis," forthcoming.
40 This claim about the relation between the inside and outside of the state does not necessitate a conceptualization hinging on sovereignty, however. It applies also to other models of thinking on power and political relations. Foucault can thus argue: "when it is a question of an independent power facing other powers, government according to *raison d'État* has limited objectives. But there is no limit to the objectives of government when it is a question of managing a public power that has to regulate the behavior of subjects . . . the correlative of this limitation of the International objective of government according to *raison d'État*, of this limitation in international relations, is the absence of a limit in the exercise of government in the police state." *The Birth of Biopolitics: Lectures at the Collège De France, 1978–79* (New York: Palgrave Macmillan, 2008), 7.
41 Note that what we see with Hobbes is not the practical impossibility to realize a desire of full closure that defines the state, but rather a dual even if self-contradictory desire.
42 A "sanguification," in Hobbes's words, which Gil Anidjar situates in a much wider framework of flows in *Blood: A Critique of Christianity* (Columbia University Press, 2014).
43 Napoleon, "expresses it clearly" when he argued that "Aptitude for war is aptitude

for movement." Virilio, *Speed and Politics*, 47. Many others have argued that military problems are "essentially [problems] of motion, its facilitation and its prevention." Reviel Netz, *Barbed Wire: An Ecology of Modernity* (Middletown, CT: Wesleyan University Press, 2004), 63.

44 Hobbes works here within a long tradition wherein religion and economy are entangled via blood. See Gil Anidjar, "Christian and Money (The Economic Enemy)," *Ethical Perspectives: Journal of the European Ethics Network* 12, no. 4 (2005), 497–519.

45 Hobbes, *Leviathan*, 174.

46 Hobbes, *Leviathan*, 174 (my italics).

47 Hobbes, *Leviathan*, 175.

48 Mark Neocleous makes a similar claim in arguing that the organic image of the political body is not foreign to liberal thinking. Contra Claude Lefort, Philippe Lacoue-Labarthe, Jean-Luc Nancy, or Simon Critchley who argue that in liberal democracies the corporeal image of the state gives way to the primacy of individual bodies (and their property), Neocleous proposes that this image is dominant also in liberal thought. The notion of the social body gaining dominancy in the eighteenth century is, according to him, at one and the same time the bourgeois mode of corporalization of the collective body-politic, and the correlative of fascist imagination of society. Mark Neocleous, *Imagining the State* (Philadelphia: Open University Press, 2003). Marshall Berman indeed contends that in modernity all these distinctions are fluid; see *All That Is Solid Melts into Air: The Experience of Modernity* (New York: Simon & Schuster, 1982).

49 Quoted in Virilio, *Speed and Politics*, 66.

50 Partly, this is one of the elements that render this empire "liberal." Virilio, echoing Hobbes's statement, yet drawing his argument from quite different sources, sees the movement of violence ("violence can be reduced to nothing but movement," he argues) as an essentially bourgeois enterprise: a project of mobilizing the bodies of the different historical incarnations of working class poor to serve as either weapons or targets (*Speed and Politics*, 62).

51 Hugo Grotius's main argument in *Mare Liberum* was that all nations can freely trade in the sea, contra a monopoly of trade set by Portugal and later England; see *The Freedom of the Seas* (New York: Oxford University Press, 1916). For a thorough analysis of this argument and its historical context see Philip Steinberg, *Social Construction of the Ocean* (Cambridge: Cambridge University Press, 2001).

52 See various examples also in David Armitage, *The Ideological Origins of the British Empire* (Cambridge: Cambridge University Press, 2000), esp. chapters 4 and 6.

53 Nicholas Barbon (1690), cited in Armitage, *The Ideological Origins*, 143.

54 Armitage, *The Ideological Origins*, 147. Armitage argues that the discourse of political economy (emerging as a distinct discipline in the nineteenth century, but can be traced back to the seventeenth) bridged these seemingly contradicting characters of liberal European states.

55 Carl Schmitt, *The Nomos of the Earth in the International Law of the Jus Publicum Europaeum* (New York: Telos, 2003), 43. Even though this freedom was theoretically a freedom of navigation and labor (fishing) alongside war (the "three very different spheres of human activity" to which the sea was supposedly opened), violence always triumphed: "the peaceful fisherman has the right to fish peacefully precisely where the belligerent sea power is allowed to lay its mines, and the neutral party is allowed to sail freely in the area where the warring parties have the right to annihilate each other with mines, submarines, and aircraft."

56 Schmitt, *The Nomos of the Earth*, 94. A claim Schmitt makes in regard to the New World—oceans alongside land. The "free space" and "free" sea were free from any limitation set upon expansion, appropriation, and occupation. See also Virilio: "The right of the sea very quickly became the right to crime, to a violence that was also freed from every constraint. . . . Soon, the 'empire of the seas' replaces the open sea" (*Speed and Politics*, 65).

57 Accordingly, "the most inflectional book on naval strategy ever written, *The Influence of Seapower on History 1660–1783*" sets "naval warfare in the framework of economic competition between nations"; see Paul Q. Hirst, *Space and Power: Politics, War and Architecture* (Malden, MA: Polity, 2005), 68. This also meant that there was a prevalent perception according to which "liberalism is an English policy"; a policy that, "as a general rule is [a] policy suited to maritime nations." Surrounded by land, Germany, for example, thought that its own imperial desires necessitated a nonliberal structure (Foucault, *The Birth of Biopolitics*, 108). In other words: the sea was the medium through which empire took a liberal form.

58 Ian Baucom, *Specters of the Atlantic: Finance Capital, Slavery, and the Philosophy of History* (Durham, NC: Duke University Press, 2005), 35–36.

59 "It is almost impossible to stand on the defensive in the sea and await enemies. Ships have to move and fixed positions cannot be built on the high seas." The empire thus took the form of nomad warring tribes. Like the steppe, the sea "was potentially a single extensive space across which nomads and their animals [or ships and their sailors] could move relatively freely." Hirst, *Space and Power*, 53.

60 This should be added to the factors that lead Gilles Deleuze and Félix Guattari to argue that "war is against the state, and makes it impossible." And yet here we see that this undoing is integral to the very structure of the state. Accordingly, the clause opening Deleuze and Guattari's statement—"just as Hobbes saw clearly that the State was against war"—is not entirely wrong but very partial: the Hobbesian state is indeed against the war of the state of nature, or the civil war, but it is (to remain with their terms) "a war machine." *A Thousand Plateaus: Capitalism and Schizophrenia* (London: Athlone Press, 1988), 357.

61 Deleuze and Guattari, *A Thousand Plateaus*, 364.

62 Galli, *Political Spaces and Global War*, 40.

63 While there are clear differences between the two, he argues, there are also impor-

tant continuities: "the rulers of composite monarchies faced problems that would be familiar to the administrators of any empire: the need to govern distant dependencies from a powerful center; collisions between metropolitan and provincial legislatures; the necessity of imposing common norms of law and culture over diverse and often resistant populations; and the consequent reliance of the central government of the co-operation of local elites." Armitage, *The Ideological Origins of the British Empire*, 23.

64 Galli can thus argue that Hobbesian politics manifests "a hostility towards boundaries, and an indifference to space." *Political Spaces and Global War*, 29.

65 Galli, *Political Spaces and Global War*, 40.

66 Hobbes, *Leviathan*, 398.

67 For a systematic analysis of the ways in which different technological and spatial factors have contributed to this speed, but also for a critique of the linear assumption according to which speed is always growing see Hirst, *Space and Power*, esp. ch. 6.

68 Virilio, *Speed and Politics*, 68.

69 Eyal Weizman, *The Least of All Possible Evils: Humanitarian Violence from Arendt to Gaza* (New York; London: Verso, 2012), 3.

70 Yotam Feldman, *The Lab* (a documentary, 2013).

71 Hirst, *Space and Power*, 120. Accordingly, urban warfare "is a revolutionary warfare," as the city fragments and to some degree diffuses the movement of military violence (or is it the violence of the military's movement?).

72 Here, however, enters the moderating effect of legitimacy to which Weizman refers: bombing civilians from the air, for example, is less sustainable for long periods of time (and the question what counts as "long" or who counts as a "civilian" may receive different answers that are functions of many geographies and politics of violence).

73 On the history of barricading and the spatial reaction see Mark Traugott, *The Insurgent Barricade* (Berkeley: University of California Press, 2010). According to Traugott, since the sixteenth century barricades were a symbol, not merely a technic, of revolution.

74 In 1971, as part of the counterinsurgency campaign in Gaza, Ariel Sharon ordered the construction of wide roads in several refugee camps in the Strip. Bulldozers cut through buildings to allow the new passageways, that not merely facilitated the free and relatively protected movement of military units, but also enabled Israel to dissect the different neighborhoods at will. For an analysis of how roads can be used for the purpose of restricting movement and isolating land cells, see Ariel Handel, "Where, Where to and When in the Occupied Palestinian Territories: An Introduction to a Geography of Disaster" in *The Power of Inclusive Exclusion*, ed. Adi Ophir et al. (New York: Zone Books, 2009). The quotes in the text's body, however, are taken from a different context: they are part of Engels's description of the new

European cities reshaped after 1848 in his introduction to Marx's *The Class Struggle in France 1848–1850*.

75 According to the Human Rights organization B'Tselem, thousands of houses have been destroyed since 2001, particularly in the Gaza Strip, as part of "stripping" acts aimed at constructing security zones. Thousands of acres of agricultural fields and natural vegetation were destroyed in the name of securing areas from which Palestinians might be able to attack Israel or Israeli soldiers (including fields where small growth—such as tomatoes or squash—could not really provide hiding space for potential insurgents). The numbers are mounting with every military operation in Gaza, and putting them in print seems a futile task, yet the strategy remains: demolition, destruction, uprooting; refugees whose homes—more or less temporary—and means of existence are systematically taken. Israel systematically demolishes Palestinians' homes and habitats for other reasons as well (primarily claims of illegal construction, in areas wherein almost any construction of Palestinians is deemed illegal). Since 1967 Israel has demolished more than twenty-eight thousand houses in the oPt; data from ICAHD: The Israeli Committee against House Demolitions.

76 The wall is the most brutal example of this. Always presented as a means to prevent terror, the wall was originally meant to be constructed roughly on the green line. It was promoted above all by the Zionist left and center, as part of a slow partition plan, and objected to by the right until 2003. In Sharon's execution, however, the wall was pushed farther and farther to the east, tightly surrounding Palestinian cities, entering deep into Palestinian territories. Together with the security measures surrounding the settlements, the wall, as well as many other fences and obstacles, splits Palestinian territories into dozens of walled or fenced enclaves. A detailed description of the public debates and plans concerning the construction of the wall are provided by Shaul Arieli and Michael Sfard in *The Wall of Folly* (Tel Aviv: Yediot Hachronot, 2008). Ariel Handel provides an analysis of the settlements as "gating communities": communities surrounded by fences, whose fences are stretched far beyond their municipal areas, and in fact gate all other communities. Handel, "Gated/Gating Community: The Settlements Complex in the West Bank," *Transactions of the Institute of British Geographers* (forthcoming).

77 From the time when the siege policy became effective, a tunnel-based economy has developed in Gaza. Most tunnels (dug under the border between Egypt and Gaza) are controlled by Hamas and serve to smuggle food, people, money, goods, and weapons. According to the Human Rights organization Gisha, the "tunnel industry" is "one of the biggest sources of economic activity in Gaza" (www.gisha.org). The estimations are that currently between six hundred to one thousand tunnels lead to and from the Strip. For an account of the tunnels and their role in the Gaza economy see Omar Shaban's analyses in *Pal-Think: Gaza Based Think and Do Tank* (http://palthink.org/en/). For an analysis of Israel's interest in the tunnels'

existence and some of their political effects, particularly the establishment and strengthening of Hamas's government see Merav Amir, "Matters of Siege: How and Why the Closure of Gaza Fails" (forthcoming).

78 However, reconstruction can be a delicate, double-edged political task in this context. Weizman describes the arguments concerning the reconstruction of Jennin: "The UNRA engineer . . . wanted to 'take advantage of the destruction and widen the road to 4–6 meters across.'" Yet while he had the interest of the camp in mind, the camp's popular committee resisted the change, arguing that the wide roads would also serve the Israeli army by allowing tanks to move freely without "getting stuck between the buildings"; see *Hollow Land: Israel's Architecture of Occupation* (New York: Verso, 2007), 2004.

79 Naveh in an interview to Yotam Feldman, *The Lab*.

80 It is worthwhile to quote here at length Naveh's words to Weizman (*Hollow Land*, 198):

> This space that you look at, this room that you look at, is nothing but your interpretation of it. Now, you can stretch the boundaries of your interpretation, but not in an unlimited fashion, after all, it must be bound by physics, as it contains buildings and alleys. The question is, how do you interpret the alley? Do you interpret the alley as a place, like every architect and every town planner does, to walk through, or do you interpret the alley as a place forbidden to walk through? This depends only on interpretation. We interpreted the alley as a place forbidden to walk through, and the door as a place forbidden to pass through, and the window as a place forbidden to look through, because a weapon awaits us in the alley, and a booby trap awaits us behind the doors. This is because the enemy interprets space in a traditional, classical manner, and I do not want to obey this interpretation and fall into his traps. Not only do I not want to fall into his traps, I want to surprise him! This is the essence of war. I need to win. I need to emerge from an unexpected place. . . . This is why we opted for the methodology of moving through walls. . . . Like a worm that eats its way forward, emerging at points and then disappearing.

81 Weizman, *Hollow Land*, 70, 209.

82 And it is precisely this infiltration, this ability to permeate all meanings and territories that Baucom identifies in regard to the logic of monetary value that itself was a product of a colonial organization of Atlantic circulation and itself, as he shows, cost the life of many. Capital, then, becomes another form of the maritime-colonial matrix of violence. Baucom, *Specters of the Atlantic*.

83 "Flying checkpoint" is the official name given to provisory temporary checkpoints. The literal translation from their Hebrew name is something like "checkpoints by surprise" or "surprise checkpoints." Often, they take the form of a jeep blocking the road and random security checks. These checkpoints are part of the logic of "breaking the routine" that was presented in the first chapter. On top of concrete

security alerts, they are often used to demonstrate military presence and to make sure potential Palestinian resistance cannot predict military patterns.
84 Closed military zones appear and disappear in the oPt, often according to declarations of local officers. They can miraculously surface wherever there is a demonstration, an activity of international, local, or Israeli left organizations. They more permanently emerge in areas to which Palestinian towns and villages may expand. They can pop up one day next to an area that has been inhabited for years, thereby limiting all movement of the local population, or they can emerge amid this area, thereby justifying house demolition. They are sometimes there only vis-à-vis specific people: a closed military zone can be declared, and applied to confine the movement of Palestinians and other activists, but the settler's movement in the very same place would not be interrupted.
85 Handel, "Where, Where to and When in the Occupied Palestinian Territories."
86 Stoler provides a definition for colony in general ("Colony") but also warns us against this very endeavor, specifically when considering the colonies of what she prefers to call "imperial formations." Empires do not come in one form, she argues (and we can assume that neither do their colonies). Rather, they "are macropolities whose technologies of rule thrive on the production of exceptions and their uneven and changing proliferation." "On Degrees of Imperial Sovereignty," Public Culture 18, no. 1 (2006): 128. When we consider Israel as an instance of colonial rule we should accordingly keep two points in mind: a. that it is exceptional, and b. that so is any other.
87 Stoler, "Colony." As Sari Hanafi claims in regard to Israel/Palestine, borders are "portable, porous, and hazy," they are "border[s] in motion," constantly redrawn and shifting; see "Spacio-Cide and Bio-Politics: The Israeli Colonial Conflict from 1947 to the Wall," in Against the Wall: Israel's Barrier to Peace, ed. M. Sorkin (New York: New Press, 2005), 251–61.
88 Hilla Dayan, "Regimes of Separation: Israel/Palestine," in The Power of Inclusive Exclusion: Anatomy of Israeli Rule in the Occupied Palestinian Territories, eds. Adi Ophir, Michal Givoni, and Sari Hanafi (New York: Zone Books, 2009).
89 Lindsay Bremner, "Border/Skin," in Against the Wall: Israel's Barrier to Peace, ed. Michael Sorkin (New York: New Press, 2005), 132. Bremner claims that "under apartheid, borders were not things one crossed but places one stayed in." These borders "were designed to be porous, to regulate the body in motion. They produced a narrative not of closure, but of hundreds and thousands of entries and crossings" (131).
90 Scholars of security studies argue in recent years that this has become the structure of borders much more generally: borders become ubiquitous, the logic of sharply separating an interiority from an externality no longer works, and what used to be clear separations between military, police, and other security agencies begin to blur; see Étienne Balibar, Politics and the Other Scene (New York: Verso, 2002), 84.

According to some, this is a relatively recent crisis of borders (for example Didier Bigo, "Möbius Ribbon of Internal and External Security(Ies)," in *Identities, Borders, Orders Rethinking International Relations Theory*, eds. D. Jacobson, Y. Lapid, and M. Albert (Minneapolis: University of Minnesota Press, 2005), 103. This claim can be taken to suggest that the European space takes upon itself the logic of the colony. According to others, this is part of the very logic of borders, not a contemporary feature characteristic to security regimes. Such a claim is at times accompanied by contending that, at the deepest structural levels, the nation-state and the colony must be understood in tandem; see Mezzadra, "Citizen and Subject?"; Merav Amir, "Borders as Praxis," forthcoming.

91 This is not to say that every place is, de facto, a border at any given time, but that the border can emerge anywhere.

92 Different regimes of halts, checkpoints, segregated passages, enclosed areas, curfews, and other limitations set upon movement are central to different colonial administrations. According to Fanon: "The first thing the colonial subject learns is to remain in his place and not overstep its limits. Hence the dreams of the colonial subject are muscular dreams, dreams of action, dreams of aggressive vitality. I dream I am jumping, swimming, running, and climbing. I dream I burst out laughing, I am leaping across a river and chased by a pack of cars that never catches up with me." *The Wretched of the Earth*, 15. The immobility of the colonized world can find its resolution only in one's sleep—as an unarticulated and unrealizable desire when the body is motionless.

93 Handel, "Where, Where to and When in the Occupied Palestinian Territories," 214.

94 Once again, Naveh makes the principle lucid in his vision of the separation wall—perhaps the most visible and stable simulation of border between Israel and the West Bank. Referring to the debates concerning the wall's route, Naveh said that "Whatever path they [the politicians] can agree to build the fence [wall] along is okay with me—as long as I can cross [it]" (cited in Weizman, *Hollow Land*, 217). The wall should limit the movement of the occupied/colonized but must not prevent the movement of occupiers/colonizers and of occupation/colonization.

95 The analogy between the liberal state and the liberal body was unfolded, even if at times latently, throughout this book. Both bodies are autonomous, presumably enclosed, and take form via the model of moderated, regulated movement. Both are entities whose freedom is movement and vice versa. Both are constituted at the intersection of two projects that are often in tension: on the one hand, the project of autonomy as a project of closure, constantly engaged in protecting and sealing boundaries; and on the other hand a project of maximized movement that often goes beyond these borders, which sometimes has "reproductive" functions (to stick to Hobbes's terminology), and which thus calls into question the stability of borders. Via the reading of Hobbes in this chapter, I offered a critique of this closure and this motion; parallel critiques have been made in regard to the liberal,

autonomous subject. For some examples see Judith Butler, *Undoing Gender* (New York; London: Routledge, 2004); Butler, *Precarious Life: The Powers of Mourning and Violence* (London; New York: Verso, 2004); Carole Pateman, "Women and Consent," *Political Theory* 8, no. 4 (1980); and Luce Irigaray, *This Sex Which Is Not One* (Ithaca, NY: Cornell University Press, 1985). Wendy Brown provides important keys in completing this analogy from a critical perspective in *Walled States, Waning Sovereignty*.

96 Juxtaposing the arguments regarding the space of colonies here with the chapter on the imaginary line can begin to outline such an analogy between bodies whose ability to assume the model of moderated movement is constantly undone: the colonial space as either completely immobile or in an excessive flux, that then constructs the subject-position of the colonized as those who can never abide by the (shifting) rule of movement.

97 In *Palestinian Walks*, Raja Shehadeh shows how hill walking is a form of resistance. It is a way of inhabiting land amid an ongoing effort to limit, deny, and take control over that land. *Palestinian Walks: Forays into a Vanishing Landscape* (New York: Scribner, 2008). Simple acts of enjoying nature become a part of a struggle when movement is so severely hindered, when the right over land is at stake, and a struggle over that right produces massive transformation of the landscape. Since 2010, one of the main sites of Palestinian civil, nonviolent uprising is Nebi Salih, a small village next to Ramallah, whose nearby spring, Ein al-Qaws ("the Bow") was taken over by settlers from a nearby settlement. Every weekend, a group of people tries to walk to the spring, which used to serve the residences of the village. This simple act, which has brought about many violent incidents as the settlers and army try to deny the Palestinians' access, has become an icon of Palestinian resistance.

98 For a brilliant analysis of the role flows of sewage play in the occupation see *Hollow Land*, interlude, 1967.

99 Even the highest walls can be bypassed. They "may augment the technologies, cost, social organization, experiences, and meaning of what they purport to lock out, but they are relatively ineffective as interdiction." Brown, *Walled States, Waning Sovereignty*, 109–10. See also M. J. Dear, *Why Walls Won't Work: Repairing the US-Mexico Divide* (New York: Oxford University Press, 2013). In the West Bank bypassing a checkpoint is part of the daily routine of many who try to work in Israel due to the lack of employment in Palestinian areas. Beyond this mode of everyday resistance (as James Scott has termed it), bypassing checkpoints has also become part of a declared mode of resistance—of breaking a law as part of objecting to its very legality. A collaboration of Israeli and Palestinian groups has initiated a movement called the Disobedient Women (in Hebrew Lo Met'zaitot) that resists the checkpoints by bypassing them illegally, making these acts public after each group of Palestinians is safely back in their homes.

100 As of 2009, potentiality had become the main mode of restricting movement in the West Bank: many checkpoints are open to free movement, but soldiers are watch-

ing and monitoring them, ready to close them at any moment. Most constructions were left intact even after the checkpoint was officially removed—allowing reestablishing a tight regime of movement instantly. Moreover, the army's reliance on "flying checkpoints" means that at every moment any point in space can become a checkpoint.

101 Ann Stoler, *Along the Archival Grain: Epistemic Anxieties and Colonial Common Sense* (Princeton, NJ: Princeton University Press, 2009), chapter 3; and *Race and the Education of Desire: Foucault's History of Sexuality and the Colonial Order of Things* (Durham, NC: Duke University Press, 1995).

102 Deborah B. Gould, *Moving Politics: Emotion and Act Up's Fight against Aids* (Chicago: University of Chicago Press, 2009); Michael Hardt, "Love as a Political Concept," a paper presented in the "Concepts Workshop" (Duke University, Durham, NC: Franklin Humanities Institute 2010).

103 Gould, *Moving Politics*, 3. Gould sees affect itself as an "unbound . . . unattached, free-floating mobile energy" (20).

104 "To act, in its most general sense, means to take an initiative, to begin . . . , to set something into motion." Arendt, *The Human Condition*, 177.

105 Michael Hardt, "Today's Bandung?," in *A Movement of Movements: Is Another World Really Possible?*, ed. Tom Mertes (New York: Verso, 2004), 236.

106 Charles Tilly, *Social Movements, 1768–2004* (Boulder, CO: Paradigm, 2004). Tilly argues that displays of worthiness, unity, numbers, and commitments (or in his term "WUNC displays") by the movements' participants are one of the three key elements rendering a group of actors or political processes into a social movement.

107 The group seeks to simulate and produce different (social/political) movements by well-orchestrated (physical) movements in key public spaces.

108 In an interview accessible online via Artis video series (http://vimeo.com/37963094).

109 Elias Canetti, *Crowds and Power* (London: Gollancz, 1962), 16.

110 Or fear it somewhat less. Canetti seems to be blind here to gender differences and to the radically different experience of women in crowds.

111 And it is telling that Canetti claims that if this equality is to be realized and experienced, the crowd should have a shared *direction* (*Crowds and Power*, 29).

112 Arendt, *The Promise of Politics*, 117, my italics.

113 Hence *Pravda* identified in 1976 that "Parading in the streets is a worker's best possible preparation for the battle for power" (cited in Virilio *Speed and Politics*, 44).

114 Arendt, *Human Condition*, 221.

115 Arendt, *Human Condition*, 224, citing Plato's *Republic*, 443E.

116 Arendt would argue that this is a necessary condition to sustain the plurality, which is a condition to sustain action, and thus politics. Any other mode of representation would either disintegrate the very possibility of political life by dispersing people, or replace action with rule, and politics with "stability, security, and productivity" (*Human Condition*, 222).

117 Linebuagh and Rediker (*The Many-Headed Hydra*) suggest that the unity of the Hobbesian sovereign, its ability to reign by subjecting everyone to a single sword, was necessary in order to unite a potentially rioting plurality: the plurality of all those who could not subsist in the new economic system of the late sixteenth and seventeenth centuries. The hydra—a symbol of resistance and civil war, indeed of plurality as civil war—took in Hobbes a different figure, a different body of another mythical animal: the Behemoth. See also Carl Schmitt, *The Leviathan in the State Theory of Thomas Hobbes: Meaning and Failure of a Political Symbol* (Westport, CT: Greenwood, 1996).

118 The flow of people, ideas, and objects, which allowed "new forms of cooperation ... from mutinies and strikes to riots and insurrections and revolution," shows also how nonstatist bodies work against and counter to the state, and reveals the various continuities between efforts of social change, civil wars, and revolutions; see Linebaugh and Rediker, *The Many-Headed Hydra*, 4. For more on the analogies between social movements and rebellions or civil wars see also Sidney Tarrow, "Inside Insurgencies: Politics and Violence in an Age of Civil War," *Perspectives on Politics* 5, no. 3 (2007).

119 Hobbes, *Leviathan*, 114. "For it is the Unity of the Representer, not the Unity of the Represented, that maketh the Person One," he continues.

120 W. J. T. Mitchell, "Image, Space, Revolution: The Arts of Occupation," *Critical Inquiry* 39, no. 1 (2012): 9.

121 Tilly, *Social Movements, 1768–2004*. The term was used to refer to the Socialist and Communist movements.

122 Giorgio Agamben, "Movement," 2005; lecture transcription at http://www.generation-online.org. A somewhat more elaborated analysis of Schmitt's use of the term can be found in the introduction of this book.

123 This is not to argue, alongside Agamben that "democracy ends when movements emerge"; that "revolutionary traditions on the left agree with Nazism and Fascism"; or that movement, as a "decisive political concept," demises the people's power ("Movement"). The many examples above, (to which we can add many others) attest to the democratic power of movements. In this context it may be worthwhile noting that Neocleous makes an almost opposite claim in arguing that both fascism and liberalism draw on the image of the political body as an organism that must be protected, whereas the movements of the left (to which Agamben refers as analogous to fascism) are marked by him as an *alternative* to these models of movement in politics. Neocleous's call to "rethink some of the connections between bourgeois democracy and fascism" (*Imagining the State*, 24) is well made (by him as well as others) and deserves careful attention; see Berman, *All That Is Solid Melts into Air*; Agamben, *Homo Sacer: Sovereign Power and Bare Life* (Stanford, CA: Stanford University Press, 1998); and Foucault, *Society Must Be Defended*. Juxtaposing this claim and Agamben's critique, however, shows that this model of movement is shared

by a wider range than the liberal-fascist arch proposes. This structural parallelism, which was central and productive within critical thought since the Second World War, may no longer be sufficient in thinking about political relations and organizations today.

124 Carl Schmitt, *State, Movement, People: The Triadic Structure of the Political Unity; The Question of Legality* (Corvallis, OR: Plutarch Press, 2001), 18.

125 Mitchell, "Image, Space, Revolution," 9. It is often space, rather than face, that represents many social/political movements—Mitchell claims in regard to the 2011 uprisings.

126 The occupation movement is not exceptional in this duality—in the quintessential reliance on the ability to move (in space—but also to change things), and the need of a confined space. Another example at point is the Zionist movement of the nineteenth century, which took form also via the myth and practice of mostly maritime voyages (legal and illegal) of Jewish immigrants to Palestine. The several hundred ships; the image, language, and historical memory of exodus; the youth movements abroad that prepared people for the voyage also by breaking and denying bonds to existing communities—all marked a movement toward a desired stability: a home, a permanent residence, a nation state in "Zion"/Palestine.

127 Arendt, *The Origins of Totalitarianism*, 293–97. In its extreme formulation, this becomes clear in Arendt's account of the refugees. Arendt argues that what the stateless people have lost is not specific rights but the right to take place, to reside, which conditions the possibility of political existence: the possibility to form a community, a political fabric, and, therefore, a precondition for the possibility to act.

128 Mitchell, "Image, Space, Revolution," 13.

129 Even her demarcation of the political—as a site wherein new things can emerge, where freedom is thus possible, where men leave their imprint by making something new—calls for stability: "When [the world] is violently wretched into a movement in which there is no longer any sort of permanence," she argues, it "becomes inhuman." Arendt, *Men in Dark Times* (London: Cape, 1970), 10–11.

130 Within the Schmittian claim that "All significant concepts of the modern theory of the state are liquidated theological concepts, not only because of their historical development, but also because of their systematic fluidity," Gil Anidjar emphasizes the notion of flows. Therefore, he argues, "A scholarly and let us say, critical exploration of those concepts, the blood that runs through them shall have to follow closely and fluently their motion and their flows." Anidjar, *Blood*, viii; Schmitt, *Political Theology*, 36.

131 Mapping the mechanisms that render some forms of violence as legitimate and some as unlawful, some as tolerable and some as not, some as visible and some as hidden, is crucial to finding ways out from the monopolies of violence that can no longer be thought of simply as the monopolies of the states. Ultimately, within

the economy of violences, there are good reasons to advocate nonviolence, but we should also bear in mind that sometimes, the lack of a violent resistance partakes in perpetuating conditions much more violent.

132 For example, within this framework, the colony is often portrayed as either excessively mobile (a territory in flux, as we saw here, a population that is constructed as unable to regulate its movement, as we saw earlier), or as completely immobile (a regime of closures, walls, sieges, permits). This structure, that we see in the oPt and that has been in place also in many other colonial contexts, was identified by Fanon as one of the attributes of colonialism (The Wretched of the Earth). It is a portrayal of a political order that fails to obtain a balance between movement and stability, thereby marking spaces and bodies that call for coercive restraint or of erupting military force.

133 For some examples of these changes see Hagar Kotef and Merav Amir, "(En)Gendering Checkpoints: Checkpoint Watch and the Repercussions of Intervention." Signs: Journal of Women in Culture and Society 32, no. 4 (2007): 975–76.

134 Thus, when Schmitt aptly argues that the freedom of the "non-European soil of the rest of the earth" meant that it was "free to be occupied by European states" (Nomos of the Earth, 142), what he says is also that the freedom of Europe is the freedom to occupy the rest of the world.

135 "A colony as a common noun," she argues, "is a place where people are moved in and out, a place of livid, hopeful, desperate, and violent—willed and unwilled—circulation. It is marked by unsettledness, and regulated, policed migration. A colony as a political concept is not a place but a principle of managed mobilities, mobilizing and immobilizing populations, dislocating and relocating peoples according to a set of changing rules and hierarchies that orders social kinds: those eligible for recruitment, for subsidized or forced resettlement, for extreme deprivation or privilege, prioritized residence or confinement." Stoler, "Colony."

136 Stoler, "Colony."

Conclusion

1 Netz, Barbed Wire: An Ecology of Modernity (Middletown, CT: Wesleyan University Press, 2004), xi.

2 Netz, Barbed Wire, xi.

3 Consider here the two ways by which the system is broken in the case described in the beginning of this book: either in its absence (in the bank there is a marked yellow line that one should not pass until the clerk calls her to approach; in the case of the imaginary line there is no line and still it must not be crossed) or in its presence that is never symbolic (an electric iron turnstile instead of a line).

4 Erin Manning, Politics of Touch: Sense, Movement, Sovereignty (Minneapolis: University of Minnesota Press, 2007); Donna Haraway, "Situated Knowledges: The Science

Question in Feminism and the Privilege of Partial Perspective," *Feminist Studies* 14, no. 3 (Autumn, 1988): 575–99; Elizabeth Grosz, *Volatile Bodies Towards a Corporeal Feminism* (Bloomington: Indiana University Press, 1994); Judith Butler, *Bodies That Matter* (New York: Routledge, 1993).

5 Michelle Alexander outlines the incarnations of systems of racial control and confinement in the United States from slavery to segregation to mass incarceration. Often, these systems had to produce an appearance—or a reality—of uncontrollable movement to justify their operations. After the civil war, when a "large number of former slaves roamed the highways," several southern states adopted severe vagrancy laws that were applied to black people, and rendered criminal and thus confinable all those who did not have permanent jobs. Such laws inflated images of African Americans' "unruly" movement, tied their movement to criminality, and ultimately served to justify new systems of incarceration and forced labor. A system of mass incarceration, supported by practices of racial profiling, stop-and-frisk, and imbalanced drug laws that target African Americans for scrutiny and harsher sentencing, has replaced segregation as a new system of racial control. At the same time, denial of public housing to felons leaves many African-American men homeless, thus ultimately facilitating their return to prison. See Michelle Alexander, *The New Jim Crow: Mass Incarceration in the Age of Colorblindness* (New York: New Press, 2010), 187, 28, 57. Hence, the phenomenon of being guilty of "driving while black" captures a core aspect of the way racial threat is perceived and controlled in the United States: The movement (the freedom) of those who should stay put (be enslaved) is by itself threatening.

6 Sally Shuttleworth shows that in the nineteenth century, women's exclusion from the political and economic spheres was justified in part by defining their bodies as existing within "a condition of excess" produced by their bodily "flows." Their inability to regulate and control bodily flows presumably undermined their rational capacities, making them incapable of participating as equal in a "rational" social order; see "Female Circulation: Medical Discourse and Popular Advertising in the Mid-Victorian Era" in *Body/Politics: Women and the Discourses of Science*, ed. Mary Jacobus et al., (New York: Routledge), 1990. Of all flows, menstruation occupied the front stage. Thomas Laquer proposes that the focus on menstruation and the tie between this bodily flow and the unpredicted, frantic behavior of animals in heat served as the "basis for a case against women's participation in public activities, which required steady, day-to-day concentration. Women were too bound to their bodies [itself, a recent phenomenon, as Laquer so well illustrates] to take part in such endeavors"; especially since this body was itself in flux. The paradigm of heat in other mammals allowed configuring menstruation within a framework of unstable, erupting flows, rather than with the order of a cyclical movement; see *Making Sex: Body and Gender from the Greeks to Freud* (Cambridge, MA: Harvard University Press, 1990), 216, 218.

7 In the Israeli Negev—a large desert area in the south of Israel—there are currently forty-five unrecognized villages in which more than 76,000 of the 180,000 Arab Bedouin minority in Israel reside. Beyond the denial of any basic infrastructure (such as electricity, water, sewage, or education) these villages are constantly evacuated and destroyed by the state, rebuilt by the local population, and then demolished again. This ongoing cycle has taken place ever since the aftermath of the 1948 war, and renders these villages *settlements in motion*. The Israeli government insists that due to their presumably nomadic character, these non-Jewish citizens have no land tenure. This "nomadism," however, is often produced by the state: since 1947 Israel has expelled tribes from their villages and repeatedly moved them en masse from one location to another. Again we see that the production of nomadism allows the image of an empty land, free for other movements: the free movement of (Jewish) citizens; the state's movement of expansion. The foundations of the Bedouin's struggle are therefore questions of settlement, nomadism, and control over lands, which are not merely façades, but rather the material form through which questions of citizenship are negotiated. For more information, see the Regional Council of Unrecognized Villages at http://rcuv.wordpress.com/; Negev Coexistence Forum for Civil Equality; and Human Rights Watch report "Off the Map," http://www.hrw.org/en/reports/2008/03/30/map; Ahmad Amara, Ismael Abu-Saad, and Oren Yiftachel, *Indigenous (in)Justice: Human Rights Law and Bedouin Arabs in the Naqab/Negev* (Cambridge, MA: Human Rights Program at Harvard Law School, 2012). See also Suhad Bishara and Haneen Naamnih, "Nomads against Their Will: The Attempted Expulsion of the Arab Bedouin in the Naqab: The Example of Atir–Umm Al-Hieran," Adalah (The Legal Center for Arab Minority Rights in Israel), 2011.

BIBLIOGRAPHY

Agamben, Giorgio. *Homo Sacer: Sovereign Power and Bare Life*. Stanford, CA: Stanford University Press, 1998.
Agamben, Giorgio. "Movement," 2005. http://www.generation-online.org/p/fpagamben3.htm.
Agnew, John. "Borders on the Mind: Re-Framing Border Thinking." *Ethics & Global Politics* 1, no. 4 (2008): 175–91.
Alexander, Michelle. *The New Jim Crow: Mass Incarceration in the Age of Colorblindness*. New York: New Press, 2010.
Amara, Ahmad, Ismael Abu-Saad, and Oren Yiftachel. *Indigenous (in)Justice: Human Rights Law and Bedouin Arabs in the Naqab/Negev*. Cambridge, MA: Human Rights Program at Harvard Law School, 2012.
Amir, Merav. "Borders as Praxis," forthcoming.
Amir, Merav. "Matters of Siege: How and Why the Closure of Gaza Fails," forthcoming.
Anidjar, Gil. *Blood: A Critique of Christianity*. New York: Columbia University Press, 2014.
Anidjar, Gil. "Christian and Money (The Economic Enemy)." *Ethical Perspectives: Journal of the European Ethics Network* 12 no. 4 (2005).
Arbel, Tal. "Mobility Regimes and the King's Head: A History of Techniques for the Control of Movement in the Occupied West Bank." Paper presented at "Commemorative Occupations: Chechnya, Iraq, Palestine, Governing Zones of Emergency," Harvard University, February 25–26, 2006.
Arendt, Hannah. *The Origins of Totalitarianism*. New York: Meridian Books, 1958.
Arendt, Hannah. *Men in Dark Times*. London: Cape, 1970.

Arendt, Hannah. "What Is Freedom?" In *Between Past and Future: Eight Exercises in Political Thought.* New York: Penguin, 1977.
Arendt, Hannah. *On Revolution.* London: Penguin Classics, 1990.
Arendt, Hannah. *The Human Condition.* Chicago: University of Chicago Press, 1998.
Arendt, Hannah. *The Promise of Politics.* New York: Schocken Books, 2005.
Arieli, Shaul and Michael Sfard. *The Wall of Folly.* Tel Aviv: Yediot Hachronot, 2008.
Armitage, David. *The Ideological Origins of the British Empire.* Cambridge: Cambridge University Press, 2000.
Armitage, David. "John Locke, Carolina, and the Two Treatises of Government." *Political Theory* 32, no. 5 (2004): 602–27.
Arneil, Barbara. *John Locke and America: The Defence of English Colonialism.* Oxford: Oxford University Press, 1996.
Arneil, Barbara. "Disability, Self Image, and Modern Political Theory." *Political Theory* 37, no. 2 (2009): 218–42.
Arneil, Barbara. "Liberal Colonialism, Domestic Colonies and Citizenship." *Journal of the History of Political Thought* 33, no. 2 (2012): 492–523.
Atiyah, P. S. *The Rise and Fall of Freedom of Contract.* Oxford: Oxford University Press, 1985.
Azoulay, Ariella, and Adi Ophir. "The Monster's Tail." In *Against the Wall: Israel's Barrier to Peace.* Edited by M. Sorkin. New York: New Press, 2005.
Azoulay, Ariella, and Adi Ophir. *This Regime Which Is Not One: Occupation and Democracy between the Sea and the River (1967—).* Tel Aviv: Resling, 2008.
Azoulay, Ariella, and Adi Ophir. *The One-State Condition: Occupation and Democracy in Israel/Palestine.* Stanford, CA: Stanford University Press, 2012.
Azoulay, Ariella and Adi Ophir, *Bad Days: Between Disaster and Utopia* [in Hebrew]. Tel Aviv: Resling Publishing, 2002.
B'Tselem. "Builders of Zion: Human Rights Violations of Palestinians from the Occupied Territories Working in Israel and the Settlements." Written by Lein, Yehezkel, and Najib Abu-Rokaya. 1999. Accessed March 2014. www.http://www.btselem.org.
B'Tselem. "Forbidden Roads: Israel's Discriminatory Road Regime in the West Bank." 2004. Accessed June 2014. http://www.btselem.org.
B'Tselem. "Ground to a Halt: Denial of Palestinian's Freedom of Movement in the West Bank." 2007. Accessed June 2014. http://www.btselem.org.
Balibar, Étienne. "Citizen/Subject." In *Who Comes after the Subject?* Edited by Peter Connor Eduardo and Jean-Luc Nancy. New York: Routledge, 1991.
Balibar, Étienne. "Racism as Universalism." In *Masses, Classes, Ideas: Studies on Politics and Philosophy before and after Marx.* New York: Routledge, 1994.
Balibar, Étienne. *Politics and the Other Scene.* New York: Verso, 2002.
Balibar, Étienne. "Cosmopolitanism and Secularism: Controversial Legacies and Prospective Interrogations." *Grey Room* 44 (2011): 6–25.
Baracchi, Claudia. *Of Myth, Life, and War in Plato's Republic.* Chesman; Bloomington; Indiana University Press, Combined Academic, 2002.

Barda, Yael. *The Bureaucracy of the Occupation: The Regime of Movement Permits 2000—2006*. Tel Aviv: Hakibbutz Hameuchad, The Van Leer Jerusalem Institute, 2012.
Bassett, William W. "The Myth of the Nomad in Property Law." *Journal of Law and Religion* 4, no. 1 (1986): 133–52.
Baucom, Ian. *Specters of the Atlantic: Finance Capital, Slavery, and the Philosophy of History*. Durham, NC: Duke University Press, 2005.
Bauman, Zygmunt. *Globalization: The Human Consequences*. New York: Columbia University Press, 1998.
Ben-Ari, Eyal. *From Checkpoints to Flow-Points: Sites of Friction between the Israel Defense Forces and Palestinians*. Gitelson Peace Publication. Jerusalem: Harry S. Truman Research Institute for the Advancement of Peace, Hebrew University of Jerusalem, 2005.
Benvenisti, Meron. *Intimate Enemies: Jews and Arabs in a Shared Land*. Berkeley: University of California Press, 1995.
Berman, Marshall. *All That Is Solid Melts into Air: The Experience of Modernity*. New York: Simon & Schuster, 1982.
Bigo, Didier. "Security and Immigration: Toward a Critique of the Governmentality of Unease." *Alternatives: Global, Local, Political* 27 (2002).
Bigo, Didier. "Möbius Ribbon of Internal and External Security(Ies)." In *Identities, Borders, Orders Rethinking International Relations Theory*. Edited by D. Jacobson, Y. Lapid, and M. Albert. Minneapolis: University of Minnesota Press, 2005.
Bigo, Didier. "Detention of Foreigners, States of Exception, and the Social Practices of Control of the Banopticon." In *Borderscapes: Hidden Geographies and Politics at Territory's Edge*. Edited by Carl Grundy-Warr and Prem Kumar Rajaram. Minneapolis: University of Minnesota Press, 2007.
Bishara, Azmi. *Yearning in the Land of Checkpoints*. Tel Aviv: Babel Press, 2006.
Bishara, Suhad, and Haneen Naamnih. "Nomads against Their Will: The Attempted Expulsion of the Arab Bedouin in the Naqab: The Example of Atir–Umm Al-Hieran." Adalah, 2011.
Blackstone, William. *Commentaries on the Laws of England*. Chicago: University of Chicago Press, 1979.
Brandt, Frithiof. *Thomas Hobbes' Mechanical Conception of Nature*. Copenhagen: Levin & Munksgaard, 1927.
Bremner, Lindsay. "Border/Skin." In *Against the Wall: Israel's Barrier to Peace*. Edited by Michael Sorkin. New York: New Press, 2005.
Brown, Wendy. *Walled States, Waning Sovereignty*. New York: Zone Books, 2010.
Burke, Edmund. *Reflections on the Revolution in France*. Oxford: Oxford University Press, 2009.
Butler, Judith. *Gender Trouble: Feminism and the Subversion of Identity*. New York: Routledge, 1990.
Butler, Judith. *Bodies That Matter: On the Discursive Limits of Sex*. New York: Routledge, 1993.
Butler, Judith. *Precarious Life: The Powers of Mourning and Violence*. London; New York: Verso, 2004.

Butler, Judith. *Undoing Gender*. New York and London: Routledge, 2004.
Canetti, Elias. *Crowds and Power*. London: Gollancz, 1962.
Castells, Manuel. *The Rise of the Network Society*. Malden, MA: Blackwell, 2000.
Cavarero, Adriana. *Stately Bodies: Literature, Philosophy, and the Question of Gender*. Ann Arbor: University of Michigan Press, 2002.
Cavarero, Adriana. *Horrorism: Naming Contemporary Violence*. New York: Columbia University Press, 2009.
Chapkis, Wendy. "Soft Glove Punishing Fist: The Trafficking Victims Protection Act of 2000." In *Regulating Sex: The Politics of Intimacy and Identity*. Edited by Laurie Schaffner and Elizabeth Bernstein. New York: Routledge, 2005.
Constant, Benjamin. *Political Writings*. Cambridge: Cambridge University Press, 1988.
Cranston, Maurice William. *John Locke: A Biography*. London: Longmans and Green, 1957.
Cresswell, Tim. *On the Move: Mobility in the Modern Western World*. New York: Routledge, 2006.
Dayan, Hilla. "Regimes of Separation: Israel/Palestine." In *The Power of Inclusive Exclusion: Anatomy of Israeli Rule in the Occupied Palestinian Territories*. Edited by Adi Ophir, Michal Givoni, and Sari Hanafi. New York: Zone Books, 2009.
Dear, M. J. *Why Walls Won't Work: Repairing the Us-Mexico Divide*. Oxford: Oxford University Press, 2013.
De Genova, Nicholas, and Nathalie Mae Peutz. *The Deportation Regime: Sovereignty, Space, and the Freedom of Movement*. Durham, NC: Duke University Press, 2010.
Deleuze, Gilles, and Félix Guattari. *A Thousand Plateaus: Capitalism and Schizophrenia*. London: Athlone Press, 1988.
Dossa, Shiraz. "Human Status and Politics: Hannah Arendt on the Holocaust." *Canadian Journal of Political Science / Revue canadienne de science politique* 13, no. 2 (1980): 309–23.
Dworkin, Gerald. *The Theory and Practice of Autonomy*. Cambridge; New York: Cambridge University Press, 1988.
Elbaz, Sagi. *Minority Opinion in Israeli Media*. Tel Aviv: Dionun, 2013.
Elden, Stuart. "Another Sense of Demos: Kleisthenes and the Greek Division of the Polis." *Democratization* 10, no. 1 (2003): 135–56.
Elden, Stuart. *The Birth of Territory*. Chicago: University of Chicago Press, 2013.
Esmeir, Samera. Paper presented at "Crisis in Gaza and Prospects for Peace," University of California, Berkeley, March 2009.
Fanon, Frantz. *The Wretched of the Earth*. New York: Grove Press, 2004.
Foucault, Michel. *Madness and Civilization: A History of Insanity in the Age of Reason*. New York: Vintage Books, 1973.
Foucault, Michel. *Discipline and Punish: The Birth of the Prison*. New York: Vintage Books, 1979.
Foucault, Michel. *The History of Sexuality*, vol. 1. New York: Vintage Books, 1990.
Foucault, Michel. *Society Must Be Defended: Lectures at the Collège De France, 1975–76*. New York: Picador, 2003.

Foucault, Michel. *Security, Territory, Population: Lectures at the Collège De France, 1977–78.* New York: Palgrave Macmillan, 2007.

Foucault, Michel. *The Birth of Biopolitics: Lectures at the Collège De France, 1978–79.* New York: Palgrave Macmillan, 2008.

Freeden, Michael. *Liberal Languages: Ideological Imaginations and 20th Century Progressive Thought.* Princeton: Princeton University Press, 2005.

Freudendal-Pedersen, Malene. *Mobility in Daily Life: Between Freedom and Unfreedom.* Burlington, VT: Ashgate, 2009.

Frost, Samantha. *Lessons from a Materialist Thinker: Hobbesian Reflections on Ethics and Politics.* Stanford, CA: Stanford University Press, 2008.

Galli, Carlo. *Political Spaces and Global War.* Minneapolis: University of Minnesota Press, 2010.

Gattey, Charles Neilson. *The Bloomer Girls.* New York: Coward-McCann, 1968.

Gazit, Shlomo. *The Carrot and the Stick: Israel's Policy in the Administered Territories, 1967–1968.* Washington, DC: B'nai B'rith Books, 1985.

Gordon, Neve. *Israel's Occupation.* Berkeley: University of California Press, 2008.

Gordon, Neve. "Democracy and Colonialism." *Theory & Event* 13, no. 2 (2010).

Gould, Deborah B. *Moving Politics: Emotion and Act Up's Fight against Aids.* Chicago: University of Chicago Press, 2009.

Green, Thomas Hill. *Lectures on the Principles of Political Obligation, and Other Writings.* Cambridge: Cambridge University Press, 1986.

Greenblatt, Stephen. "Psychoanalysis and Renaissance Culture." In *Literary Theory/Renaissance Texts.* Edited by Patricia Parker and David Quint. Baltimore: Johns Hopkins University Press, 1986.

Gregory, Derek. *The Colonial Present: Afghanistan, Palestine, and Iraq.* Malden, MA: Blackwell, 2004.

Grosz, Elizabeth. *Volatile Bodies Towards a Corporeal Feminism.* Indianapolis: Indiana University Press, 1994.

Grotius, Hugo. *The Freedom of the Seas.* Oxford: Oxford University Press, 1916.

Haakonssen, Knud. *Traditions of Liberalism: Essays on John Locke, Adam Smith, and John Stuart Mill.* St. Leonards, Australia: Centre for Independent Studies, 1988.

Habermas, Jürgen. *The Structural Transformation of the Public Sphere: An Inquiry into a Category of Bourgeois Society.* Cambridge, MA: MIT Press, 1991.

Hammami, Rema. "On the Importance of Thugs: The Moral Economy of a Checkpoint." *Middle East Report* 231 (2004): 26–34.

Hanafi, Sari. "Spacio-Cide and Bio-Politics: The Israeli Colonial Conflict from 1947 to the Wall." In *Against the Wall: Israel's Barrier to Peace.* Edited by M. Sorkin. New York: New Press, 2005.

Handel, Ariel. "Where, Where to and When in the Occupied Palestinian Territories: An Introduction to a Geography of Disaster." In *The Power of Inclusive Exclusion*, edited by Adi Ophir et al. New York: Zone Books, 2009, 179–222.

Handel, Ariel. "Gated/Gating Community: The Settlements Complex in the West Bank." *Transactions of the Institute of British Geographers* (forthcoming).

Haraway, Donna. "Situated Knowledges: The Science Question in Feminism and the Privilege of Partial Perspective." *Feminist Studies* 14, no. 3 (Autumn 1988): 575–99.

Hardt, Michael. "Today's Bandung?" In *A Movement of Movements: Is Another World Really Possible?* Edited by Tom Mertes. New York: Verso, 2004.

Hardt, Michael. "Love as a Political Concept." Paper presented at "Concepts Workshop," Duke University, Durham, NC, Franklin Humanities Institute, November 29, 2010.

Hardt, Michael, and Antonio Negri. *Multitude: War and Democracy in the Age of Empire.* New York: Penguin, 2004.

Harper, Ida. *The Life and Work of Susan B. Anthony.* Kansas City: Bowen-Merrill, 1899.

Hass, Amira. "Israel's Closure Policy: An Ineffective Strategy of Containment and Repression." *Journal of Palestine Studies* 31, no. 3 (2002): 5–20.

Hass, Amira. "The Natives' Time Is Cheap." *Ha'aretz*, February 23, 2005.

Hayek, Friedrich A. von. *The Constitution of Liberty.* Chicago: University of Chicago Press, 1978.

Hewitt, Andrew. *Social Choreography: Ideology as Performance in Dance and Everyday Movement.* Durham, NC: Duke University Press, 2005.

Hindess, Barry. "The Liberal Government of Unfreedom." *Alternatives: Global, Local, Political* 26, no. 2 (2001): 93–111.

Hirschmann, Nancy. *The Subject of Liberty: Toward a Feminist Theory of Freedom.* Princeton, NJ: Princeton University Press, 2003.

Hirschmann, Nancy. "Intersectionality before Intersectionality Was Cool." In *Feminist Interpretations of John Locke.* Edited by Nancy Hirschmann and Kirstie McClure. University Park: The Pennsylvania State University Press, 2007.

Hirschmann, Nancy. *Gender, Class, and Freedom in Modern Political Theory.* Princeton, NJ: Princeton University Press, 2008.

Hirst, Paul Q. *Space and Power: Politics, War and Architecture.* Malden, MA: Polity, 2005.

Hobbes, Thomas. *The English Works of Thomas Hobbes of Malmesbury.* London: J. Bohn, 1839.

Hobbes, Thomas. *Leviathan.* Cambridge: Cambridge University Press, 1996.

Hobhouse, L. T. *Liberalism and Other Writings.* Cambridge: Cambridge University Press, 1994.

Hsueh, Vicki. "Cultivating and Challenging the Common: Lockean Property, Indigenous Traditionalisms, and the Problem of Exclusion." *Contemporary Political Theory* 5 (2006): 193–214.

Human Rights Watch. "Off the Map: Land and Housing Rights Violations in Israel's Unrecognized Bedouin Villages." 2008. Accessed June 2014. http://www.hrw.org/en/reports/2008/03/30/map.

Hume, David. "On The Original Contract." In *The Philosophical Works.* London: Adam Black and William Tait, 1826.

Hume, David. *An Inquiry Concerning Human Understanding*. Indianapolis: Hackett, 1993.
Institute for Policy and Strategy, "National Strength and Security Balance." In Third Annual Conference on "The New Strategic Landscape: Trends, Challenges, Responses." Edmond Benjamin De Rothschild Herzliya Conferences Series, 2002.
Irigaray, Luce. *This Sex Which Is Not One*. Ithaca, NY: Cornell University Press, 1985.
Ivison, Duncan. "Locke, Liberalism and Empire." In *The Philosophy of John Locke: New Perspectives*. Edited by Peter R. Anstey. London: Routledge, 2003.
Johnston, David. *The Idea of a Liberal Theory: A Critique and Reconstruction*. Princeton, NJ: Princeton University Press, 1994.
Kant, Immanuel. *Critique of Pure Reason*. Mineola, NY: Dover Publications, 2003.
Kant, Immanuel. "What is Enlightenment." 1784. Available, among other places, at http://www.columbia.edu/acis/ets/CCREAD/etscc/kant.html
Kaplan, Caren. "Transporting the Subject: Technologies of Mobility and Location in an Era of Globalization." PMLA 117, no. 1 (2002): 32–42.
Karakayali, Serhat, and Enrica Rigo. "Mapping the European Space of Circulation." In *The Deportation Regime*. Edited by Nicholas De Genova and Nathalie Peutz. Durham, NC: Duke University Press, 2010.
Kinzer, Bruce L. *England's Disgrace?: J. S. Mill and the Irish Question*. Toronto: University of Toronto Press, 2001.
Klausen, Jimmy Casas. "Hannah Arendt's Antiprimitivism." *Political Theory* 38, no. 3 (2010): 394–423.
Kohn, Margaret, and Keally D. McBride. *Political Theories of Decolonization: Postcolonialism and the Problem of Foundations*. Oxford: Oxford University Press, 2011.
Kolers, Avery. *Land, Conflict, and Justice: A Political Theory of Territory*. Cambridge: Cambridge University Press, 2009.
Kotef, Hagar. "Little Chinese Feet Encased in Iron Shoes," *Political Theory* forthcoming.
Kotef, Hagar, and Merav Amir. "(En)Gendering Checkpoints: Checkpoint Watch and the Repercussions of Intervention." *Signs: Journal of Women in Culture and Society* 32, no. 4 (2007): 973–96.
Kudlick, Catherine. "Disability History: Why We Need Another 'Other.'" *The American Historical Review* 108, no. 3 (2003): 763–93.
Laqueur, Thomas Walter. *Making Sex: Body and Gender from the Greeks to Freud*. Cambridge, MA: Harvard University Press, 1990.
Larsen, J. A. O. "Demokratia." *Classical Philology* 68, no. 1 (1973): 45.
Lavi, E. "The Palestinians and Israel: Between Agreement and Crisis—the Next Round." *Adkan Astrategi* [in Hebrew] 12, no. 4 (2010): 67–80.
Lefebvre, Henri. *The Production of Space*. Cambridge, MA: Blackwell, 1991.
Linebaugh, Peter, and Marcus Rediker. *The Many-Headed Hydra: Sailors, Slaves, Commoners, and the Hidden History of the Revolutionary Atlantic*. Boston: Beacon, 2000.
Locke, John. *The Conduct of the Understanding*. London: W. Blackader, 1800.

Locke, John. *Some Thoughts Concerning Education; and, of the Conduct of the Understanding.* Indianapolis: Hackett, 1996.

Locke, John. *An Essay Concerning Human Understanding.* New York: Penguin, 1997.

Locke, John. "An Essay on the Poor Law," in *Political Essays.* Cambridge: Cambridge University Press, 1997, 182–198.

Locke, John. *Two Treatises of Government.* New Haven, CT: Yale University Press, 2003.

Lomasky, Loren. "Liberalism Beyond Borders." In *Liberalism: Old and New.* Edited by Ellen Frankel Paul, Fred Miller Jr., and Jeffrey Paul. Cambridge: Cambridge University Press, 2007.

Lorde, Audre. *Sister Outsider.* Berkeley: Crossing Press, 1984.

Macpherson, C. B. *The Political Theory of Possessive Individualism: Hobbes to Locke.* Oxford: Oxford University Press, 1985.

Malkki, Liisa. "National Geographic: The Rooting of Peoples and the Territorialization of National Identity among Scholars and Refugees." *Cultural Anthropology* 7, no. 1 (1992): 24–44.

Manning, Erin. *Politics of Touch: Sense, Movement, Sovereignty.* Minneapolis: University of Minnesota Press, 2007.

Maoz, Eilat. "The Privatization of the Checkpoints and the Late Occupation." Accessed June 2014. whoprofits.org.

Marx, Karl. *Capital: A Critique of Political Economy,* vol. 1. London: Penguin Books in association with New Left Review, 1981.

Marx, Karl, and Friedrich Engels. *The Class Struggle in France 1848–1850.* Literary Licensing, 2013.

Marx, Karl, and Friedrich Engels. "Manifesto of the Communist Party." In *The Marx-Engels Reader.* Edited by Robert Tucker. New York: Norton, 1978.

Massey, Doreen B. *For Space.* Thousand Oaks, CA: Sage, 2005.

Mayr, Otto. *Authority, Liberty, and Automatic Machinery in Early Modern Europe.* Baltimore: Johns Hopkins University Press, 1986.

McClure, Kirstie Morna. *Judging Rights: Lockean Politics and the Limits of Consent.* Ithaca, NY: Cornell University Press, 1996.

Mehta, Uday Singh. *The Anxiety of Freedom: Imagination and Individuality in Locke's Political Thought?* Ithaca, NY: Cornell University Press, 1992.

Mehta, Uday Singh. *Liberalism and Empire: A Study in Nineteenth-Century British Liberal Thought.* Chicago: University of Chicago Press, 1999.

Melville, Herman. *Moby Dick.* Oxford: Oxford University Press, 1988.

Merleau-Ponty, Maurice. *Phenomenology of Perception.* London: Routledge and Kegan Paul, 1974.

Mezzadra, Sandro. "Citizen and Subject: A Postcolonial Constitution for the European Union?" *Situations: Project of the Radical Imagination* 1, no. 2 (2006): 31–42.

Mill, John Stuart. *On Liberty and Other Writings.* Cambridge: Cambridge University Press, 1989.

Mills, Charles. *The Racial Contract*. Ithaca, NY: Cornell University Press, 1997.

Mitchell, W. J. T. "Image, Space, Revolution: The Arts of Occupation." *Critical Inquiry* 39, no. 1 (2012): 8–32.

Morgan, Jennifer L. *Laboring Women: Reproduction and Gender in New World Slavery*. Philadelphia: University of Pennsylvania Press, 2004.

Nacol, Emily C. "Poverty, Work and 'the People' in Locke's Political Thought." Paper presented at the "10th APT Annual Conference," University of South Carolina, October 12, 2012.

Nederveen Pieterse, Jan, and Bhikhu C. Parekh. *The Decolonization of Imagination: Culture, Knowledge, and Power*. London: Zed Books, 1995.

Neocleous, Mark. *Imagining the State*. Philadelphia: Open University Press, 2003.

Netz, Reviel. *Barbed Wire: An Ecology of Modernity*. Middletown, CT: Wesleyan University Press, 2004.

Newman, David. "Boundaries, Borders, and Barriers: Changing Geographic Perspectives on Territorial Line." In *Identities, Borders, Orders: Rethinking International Relations Theory*. Edited by Mathias Albert, David Jacobson, and Yosef Lapid. Minneapolis: University of Minnesota Press, 2001.

Norton, Anne. "Heart of Darkness: Africa and African Americans in the Writings of Hannah Arendt." In *Feminist Interpretations of Hannah Arendt*. Edited by Bonnie Honig. University Park: Pennsylvania State University Press, 1995.

Nyers, Peter. "Abject Cosmopolitanism: The Politics of Protection in the Anti–Deportation Movement." *Third World Quarterly* 24, no. 6 (2003): 1069–93.

Ophir, Adi. "The Semiotics of Power: Reading Michel Foucault's Discipline and Punish." *Manuscrito* XII 2, 1989: 9–34.

Ophir, Adi. *Plato's Invisible Cities: Discourse and Power in the Republic*. Savage, MD: Barnes & Noble, 1991.

Ophir, Adi. "State." *Mafteakh: Lexical Journal for Political Thought* 3 (2011).

Orna Ben-Naftali, Aeyal M. Gross, and Keren Michaeli. "Illegal Occupation: Framing the Occupied Palestinian Territory." *Berkeley Journal of Int'l Law* 23, no. 3 (2005): 551–614.

Pateman, Carole. "Women and Consent." *Political Theory* 8, no. 4 (1980): 149–68.

Pateman, Carole. "The Settler Contract." In *Contract and Domination*. Edited by Charles Mills and Carole Pateman. Malden, MA: Polity, 2007.

Peled, Yoav, and Gershon Shafir. *Being Israeli: The Dynamics of Multiple Citizenship*. Cambridge: Cambridge University Press, 2002.

Peters, Richard. *Hobbes*. London: Penguin Books, 1956.

Pitts, Jennifer. *A Turn to Empire: The Rise of Imperial Liberalism in Britain and France*. Princeton, NJ: Princeton Unversity Press, 2005.

Plato. *Republic*. Indianapolis: Hackett, 1992.

Poovey, Mary. *Making a Social Body: British Cultural Formation, 1830–1864*. Chicago: University of Chicago Press, 1995.

Portes, Alejandro, and Rubén G. Rumbaut. *Immigrant America: A Portrait*. Berkeley: University of California Press, 2006.

Pradeep Jeganathan. "Checkpoints: Anthropology, Identity and the State," in *Anthropology at the Margins of the State*, eds. Veena Das and Deborah Poole (Santa Fe: School of American Research Press, 2004), 67–80.

Procacci, Giovanna. "Social Economy and the Government of Poverty." In *The Foucault Effect: Studies in Governmentality*. Edited by Colin Gordon, Graham Burchell, and Peter Miller. Chicago: University of Chicago Press, 1991.

Raaflaub, Kurt A. "Origins of Democracy in Ancient Greece." Berkeley: University of California Press, 2007.

Raijman, Rebeca, and Adriana Kemp. "Labor Migration, Managing the Ethno-National Conflict, and Client Politics in Israel." In *Transnational Migration to Israel in Global Comparative Context*. Edited by Sarah S. Willen. Lanham, MD: Rowman & Littlefield, 2007.

Rana, Junaid. "The Language of Terror." In *State of White Supremacy: Racism, Governance, and the United States*. Edited by Moon-Kie Jung, João H. Costa Vargas, and Eduardo Bonilla-Silva. Stanford, CA: Stanford University Press, 2011.

Rancière, Jacques. *Disagreement: Politics and Philosophy*. Minneapolis: University of Minnesota Press, 1999.

Rawls, John. *Political Liberalism*, expanded ed. New York: Columbia University Press, 2005.

Rogers, John. *The Matter of Revolution: Science, Poetry, and Politics in the Age of Milton*. Ithaca, NY: Cornell University Press, 1996.

Said, Edward. *Orientalism*. New York: Pantheon Books, 1978.

Said, Edward. "Zionism from the Standpoint of Its Victims." *Social Text*, no. 1 (1979): 7–58.

Sassen, Saskia. *The De-Facto Transnationalizing of Immigration Policy*. Florence: Robert Schuman Centre at the European University Institute, 1996.

Sassen, Saskia. *Guests and Aliens*. New York: New Press, 1999.

Sassen, Saskia. *Territory, Authority, Rights: From Medieval to Global Assemblages*. Princeton, NJ: Princeton University Press, 2006.

Sayigh, Yezid. "The Palestinian Paradox: Statehood, Security and Institutional Reform." *Conflict, Security & Development* 1 (April 2001).

Sayigh, Yezid. "Inducing a Failed State in Palestine." *Survival: Global Politics and Strategy* 49, no. 3, 2007.

Schmitt, Carl. *The Leviathan in the State Theory of Thomas Hobbes: Meaning and Failure of a Political Symbol*. Westport, CT: Greenwood, 1996.

Schmitt, Carl. *The Nomos of the Earth in the International Law of the Jus Publicum Europaeum*. New York: Telos, 2003.

Schmitt, Carl. *Political Theology: Four Chapters on the Concept of Sovereignty*. Chicago: University of Chicago Press, 2005.

Schmitt, Carl. *State, Movement, People: The Triadic Structure of the Political Unity: The Question of Legality.* Corvallis, OR: Plutarch, 2001.

Scott, James C. *Seeing Like a State: How Certain Schemes to Improve the Human Condition Have Failed.* New Haven, CT: Yale University Press, 1998.

Seth, Vanita. *Europe's Indians: Producing Racial Difference, 1500–1900.* Durham, NC: Duke University Press, 2010.

Shamir, Ronan. "Without Borders? Notes on Globalization as a Mobility Regime." *Sociological Theory* 23, no. 2 (2005): 197–217.

Shapin, Steven, and Simon Schaffer. *Leviathan and the Air-Pump Hobbes, Boyle, and the Experimental Life.* Princeton, NJ: Princeton University Press, 1989.

Shehadeh, Raja. *Palestinian Walks: Forays into a Vanishing Landscape.* New York: Scribner, 2008.

Shenhav, Yehuda, and Ya'el Berda. "The Colonial Foundations of the Racialized Theological Bureaucracy: Juxtaposing the Israeli Occupation of Palestinian Territories with Colonial History." In *The Power of Inclusive Exclusion: Anatomy of Israeli Rule in the Occupied Palestinian Territories.* Edited by Michal Givoni, Adi Ophir, and Sari Hanafi. New York: Zone Books, 2009.

Shuttleworth, Sally. "Female Circulation: Medical Discourse and Popular Advertising in the Mid-Victorian Era." In *Body/Politics: Women and the Discourses of Science.* Edited by Mary Jacobus et al., New York: Routledge, 1990.

Silverman, Kaja. "Fragments of a Fashionable Discourse." In *On Fashion.* Edited by Shari Benstock and Suzanne Ferriss. New Brunswick, NJ: Rutgers University Press, 1994.

Skinner, Quentin. *Hobbes and Republican Liberty.* Cambridge: Cambridge University Press, 2008.

Smith, Adam. *Lectures on Jurisprudence.* Edited by R. L. Meek, D. D. Raphael, and P. G. Stein. Oxford: Clarendon Press, 1978.

Smith, Anna Marie. *Welfare and Sexual Regulation.* Cambridge: Cambridge University Press, 2007.

Spragens, Thomas A. *The Politics of Motion: The World of Thomas Hobbes.* Lexington: University Press of Kentucky, 1973.

Stanton, Elizabeth Cady. *Eighty Years and More; Reminiscences, 1815–1897.* New York: Schocken Books, 1971.

Stanton, Elizabeth Cady, and Susan B. Anthony. *The Selected Papers of Elizabeth Cady Stanton and Susan B. Anthony.* New Brunswick, NJ: Rutgers University Press, 1997.

Staves, Susan. "Chattel Property Rules and the Construction of Englishness, 1660–1800." *Law and History Review* 12.1 (1994).

Stein, Rebecca L. "'First Contact' and Other Israeli Fictions: Tourism, Globalization, and the Middle East Peace Process." *Public Culture* 14, no. 3 (2002): 515–44.

Steinberg, Philip. *Social Construction of the Ocean.* Cambridge: Cambridge University Press, 2001.

Stoler, Ann. *Race and the Education of Desire: Foucault's History of Sexuality and the Colonial Order of Things*. Durham, NC: Duke University Press, 1995.

Stoler, Ann. "On Degrees of Imperial Sovereignty." *Public Culture* 18, no. 1 (2006): 125–46.

Stoler, Ann. *Along the Archival Grain: Epistemic Anxieties and Colonial Common Sense*. Princeton, NJ: Princeton University Press, 2009.

Stoler, Ann. "Colony." *Political Concepts: A Critical Lexicon* 1 (2012).

Tadiar, Neferti Xina M. *Things Fall Away: Philippine Historical Experience and the Makings of Globalization*. Durham, NC: Duke University Press, 2009.

Tarrow, Sidney. "Inside Insurgencies: Politics and Violence in an Age of Civil War." *Perspectives on Politics* 5, no. 3 (2007): 587–600.

Tilly, Charles. *Social Movements, 1768–2004*. Boulder, CO: Paradigm, 2004.

Torpey, John C. *The Invention of the Passport: Surveillance, Citizenship, and the State*. Cambridge: Cambridge University Press, 2000.

Traugott, Mark. *The Insurgent Barricade*. Berkeley: University of California Press, 2010.

Tuck, Richard. *The Rights of War and Peace: Political Thought and the International Order from Grotius to Kant*. Oxford: Oxford University Press, 1999.

Tully, James. *An Approach to Political Philosophy: Locke in Contexts*. Cambridge: Cambridge University Press, 1993.

Urry, John. *Sociology Beyond Societies: Mobilities for the Twenty-First Century*. London: Routledge, 2000.

Urry, John. *Mobilities*. Malden, MA: Polity, 2007.

Verdon, Michel. "On the Laws of Physical and Human Nature: Hobbes' Physical and Social Cosmologies." *Journal of the History of Ideas* 43, no. 4 (1982): 653–63.

Virilio, Paul. *Speed and Politics: An Essay on Dromology*. Los Angeles: Semiotext(e), 1986.

Von Leyden, W. *Seventeenth-Century Metaphysics: An Examination of Some Main Concepts and Theories*. London: Gerald Duckworth, 1968.

Walters, William. "Deportation, Expulsion, and the International Police of Aliens." *Citizenship Studies* 6, no. 3 (2002): 265–92.

Walters, William. "Secure Borders, Safe Haven, Domopolitics." *Citizenship Studies* 8, no. 3 (2004): 237–60.

Walters, William. "Border/Control." *European Journal of Social Theory* 9, no. 2 (2006): 187–203.

Weber, Max. *Politics as a Vocation*. Philadelphia: Fortress, 1965.

Weizman, Eyal. *Hollow Land: Israel's Architecture of Occupation*. New York: Verso, 2007.

Weizman, Eyal. *The Least of All Possible Evils: Humanitarian Violence from Arendt to Gaza*. New York; London: Verso, 2012.

Whelan, Frederick G. "Citizenship and the Right to Leave." *The American Political Science Review* 75, no. 3 (1981): 636–53.

White, P. J. "Materialism and the Concept of Motion in Locke's Theory of Sense-Idea Causation." *Studies in History and Philosophy of Science* 2.2 (1971).

Wilson, Elizabeth. *Adorned in Dreams: Fashion and Modernity*. New Brunswick, NJ: Rutgers University Press, 2003.

Wollstonecraft, Mary. *The Vindication of the Rights of Women*. Mineola, NY: Dover, 1996.

Ya'alon, Moshe. "The Strategic Environment and the Principles of Responses." The Third Herzliya Conference. Herzliya, Israel: Interdisciplinary Center (IDC), 2002.

Young, Iris Marion. "Feminist Reactions to the Contemporary Security Regime." *Hypatia* 18, no. 1 (2003): 228.

Zerilli, Linda M. G. *Feminism and the Abyss of Freedom*. Chicago: University of Chicago Press, 2005.

INDEX

Note: Italicized numbers indicate a figure; n indicates an endnote

ability and disability, 14, 74, 76, 85
Agamben, Giorgio, 12–13, 197–98nn122–123
airports, *vii–ix*, 10, 11, 44, 146n41, 160n30
America: attachment to the land of the indigenous Indians of, 26; colonial as a site of excessive movement, 8, 9; European land-grabbing from the indigenous populace of, 87; Hobbes's financial interests in, 173n46; Hobbes's view of as a "no man's land," 97–98; Hobbes's view of as a place of excessive movement, 96–97; the immigration to as a product of mobility and immobility in Europe, 107–8; Locke's analysis of colonial versus Indian land use in, 103–6, 176n75, 178–79n97; Locke's financial interests in, 173n46, 175–76n66; Locke's view of as a place of excessive movement, 78, 101, 110–11, 183n125; Locke's view of as archetypical of the "state of nature," 101, 174–75n63; Locke's view of as a vacant place, 78, 101, 102–3, 110–11; nineteenth-century suffragists in, 65; racial discrimination in, 1, 10, 142–43n8, 200–201n5
American Indians: as archetypes of mankind in the state of nature, 102, 171–72n26, 199n133; colonial justifications for land-grabbing from, 102–5, 107, 109–11, 176n75, 177n84, 177n90, 182–83n123; Hobbes's portrayal of as barbarians and savages, 97, 99–100, 154n15, 173n47, 174n58; Locke's portrayal of as barbarians and savages, 101, 105, 182n120, 182–83n123; Locke's portrayal of as prototypes of the free and rational man, 98–99, 102, 105, 177n90, 178n95; the Myth of Nomadism, 5, 26, 78, 103–4, 106

Amir, Merav, 29, 43–45, 151–52n2, 154n19, 187n39, 191–92n77, 193–94n90
apartheid, 37, 193n89; apartheid roads in the oPt, 151–52n5, 155–56nn2–3; Israeli segregation practices against Bedouins, 200–201n7; Israeli segregation practices against Palestinians, 28, 32, 52–56, 157n9
Arendt, Hannah: on freedom of movement, 1, 14–16, 62, 142n1, 147n67, 171n20, 186n22; on plurality, 15–16, 117, 130, 142n1, 147n67, 196n116, 196–97n116; and racism, 199n133; on unitary, collective movement, 118–19, 130–31, 132, 198n127, 198n129
Aristotle, 161n10, 162n16, 170–71n17
Armitage, David, 101, 106, 122, 176n67, 176n75, 188n54
Arneil, Barbara, 74, 76, 105–6, 106–7, 176n77, 180n102, 183n125
Atiyah, P.S., 80

Baracchi, Claudia, 92, 118, 144n19, 164n44
barricades, 127, 190m73
Bedouins, 3, 201–2n7
beggars. *See* poor; vagabondage; vagrancy
Beit Furik, 54–56
Bigo, Didier, 10–11, 148n84
Blackstone, William, 2, 65, 81–82, 168nn89–90
blood: circulation as a basis for sociopolitical metaphor, 65, 119–20, 164–65n46, 187n42, 188n44, 198n130; menstrual, 171n24, 201n6
bloomer, 83–85, 168–69n97, 169n101
body: and liberal thinking, 17–18, 37, 81, 83, 188n48, 194–95n95, 197–98n123; and the symbolism of freedom, 17, 59, 66–69, 79–82, 112–13, 142n1, 160n30; as the locus of fear, 19, 69, 95–96, 100; as the pivotal point between movement and stability, 8, 76–77, 80–83, 89, 185n6; collective movements of bodies, 13–14, 26, 113–15, 129, 131, 197n118; and gender, 5, 17, 65, 73–75, 83–86, 171n24, 201n6; Hobbes on the, 66–68, 82, 100, 113–22, 163n33; images of by Hobbes versus Blackstone, 82; the liberal subject as a moving, 4, 8–9, 17, 62–63, 65, 80–82, 168n93; life as a motion of limbs, 67, 74, 81–82, 116, 168n90, 168n93; Locke on the, 74–75, 79, 109, 166n65; of the nonautonomous or individualized subject, 14–16, 112–13; replacement of by the soul, 17–18, 25, 65, 108, 147n69, 171n20, 186n22; self-regulation of the, 9, 14–15, 62, 112, 159n26, 165–66n61; traits of liberalism's "Others," 9, 21, 23, 25, 108, 188n50, 199n132; traits of the liberal subject, 9, 25, 82–83, 88–89; Wollstonecraft on the dual nature of the, 73–74. *See also* corporeality
body-politic: individual as a metaphor for the larger, 113, 116, 188n48; movement of the, 8, 26, 117, 120–23, 129–30, 166n65; political space as a, 14–16, 70–72, 91, 112–22, 125–32, 185n12, 187n38
bourgeois, 15, 180n108, 185n6, 188n48, 188n50, 197–98n123
Brown, Wendy, 10, 19, 77, 186n18, 187n38, 194–95n95
Butler, Judith, 14, 138, 172n35

camps: deportation, 11, 23, 64, 181nn113–14; detention, 1; Palestinian refugee, 124, 190–91n74, 192n78

Canetti, Elias, 130, 196nn110–111
capital. *See* trade
Cavarero, Adriana, 19, 116–17
checkpoints: as an embedded failure system, 21–22, 29–35, 38, 42–44, 48–51, 179–80n101, 192–93n83; Beit Furik, 54–56; as disciplinary sites, 37–38; dual political definition of Palestinians at, 40–41, 49–50; flying, 125, 192–93n83, 195–96n100; harassment routines of, 31–33, 38, 42–47, 56–57, 125, 179–80n101; imaginary line, 24, 29–42, 44, 153n11, 200n3; in the Israeli-occupied Palestinian territories, 20–23, 24, 27–28, 151–52n5, 154n24, 195–96n100; language discrimination at, 27, 38, 40, 42; Nablus, 42, 54, 56, 152–53n7; Qalandia, 43–45, 47; and racism, 10, 32–38, 46–49, 100, 152n7, 155–56n3, 194n92; separation as one underlying strategy at, 28, 34, 36, 45, 47; in Sri Lanka, 32; as targets of peaceful resistance, 195n99; terminals as, 30, 41–50, 154n24; threat of violence at, 36–37, 39, 42, 48, 153n13; turnstiles at, 34, 36, 44–47, 46, 154–55n26; white line to control human rights activists, 24, 38–41. *See also* occupied Palestinian territories (oPt); Palestinians
Checkpoint Watch (CPW), 38–41, 42, 43, 56, 154n19
children: Locke on freedom of movement for, 74–75; Locke on poor, 105, 108–9, 182n120; subjection of to unwanted movement, 128, 184n3; as victims of discrimination, 46, 47
China, 7, 74–75, 113, 143–44n16, 144n18, 184n5
circulation: controlled as a complement to freedom, 6, 87–88, 93; crises and movements as open, unimpeded flows, 16, 59, 120–21, 129, 187n42, 197n118, 198n130; excessive flows, 171n24, 199–200n136, 200–201nn5–6; of goods and capital, 13, 184n3, 192n82; of ideas, 17, 147nn70–71; overlap of literal and figurative meanings of, 65, 87, 119–21, 124, 127–28, 147nn70–71, 164–65n46; state control over, 1–2, 14, 20–23, 26, 27–28, 60
civil society, 90, 159n23, 180n102
colonization: as a capitalist movement, 8, 107, 120, 192n82; as a complement to liberalism, 25, 63, 89, 142–43n8, 180n102; as a mechanism for managing excessively moving groups, 106–7, 110–11, 112, 125–28, 176n77, 178n96, 180nn103–4; the colony as a principle of mobility, 8, 134, 178n96, 199–200n36; the colony as territory in flux, 114–15, 125–28, 134, 179n98, 183nn86–87, 193–94n90, 199n132; the colony as the epitomization of wild, dangerous movement, 2, 8, 9, 57, 89, 194nn92–94, 199–200n136; configuration of colonized subjects as inferior beings, 5, 9, 25, 35, 88, 127–28; decolonization movements, 131, 132, 134; and English enclosure, 106–7, 110, 180nn102–4, 183nn125–28; excessive movement of colonized subjects, 10, 100, 110, 153–54n14, 156n7; Fanon on plight of the colonized subject, 153–54n14, 194n92, 199n132; function of as a tool for forcing movement, 12–13, 15, 37, 100, 123, 184n3; hierarchical relationship between metropole and colony, 88, 112, 127–28, 137, 178n95, 184n2, 189–90n63; Hobbes's ideas concerning colonial America, 90, 97, 122, 173n46;

colonization (*continued*)
land appropriation as basis for, 87, 88, 101–7, 110–11, 176n67; Locke's justifications for European land-grabbing in America, 103, 110, 173n46, 175–76nn66–67, 176n75, 178–79nn97–98, 182–83n123–27; the oPt and colonial apparatuses, 26, 125–27, 134, 193–94n90, 193nn86–87, 194n94, 195n96; postcolonial remnants, 10, 37, 110, 134, 140, 184n2; the racialized character of, 11, 110; religion as basis for, 176n67; and sense of home, 134–35

commerce, 13, 114, 119–21, 160n30, 180n108

commonwealth: as mechanism for delaying violence, 95–96, 99; commerce as nourishment for the, 120; duality of the subject's status in a, 67, 68; fear as basis for order in a, 94–95; freedom of the subject of a, 9, 93–94; Hobbes's perception of as moveable body, 72, 116–18, 123; the power of over its subjects' movements, 96, 99, 100, 117, 173n42

Communism, 12, 197n121

confinement: as a central technology of Israel's occupation, 33, 193n84; as means of defining socioeconomic boundaries, 181n114, 184n3; as necessary complement to freedom, 6, 9, 11, 77–78, 100–101; as exercise of disciplinary power, 2, 15, 90–91, 107–10, 180–81n110, 181nn113–14; as exercise of discrimination, 3, 11, 73–74, 84–85, 88, 113, 200–201n5; as target of revolution, 12; colonization and, 8, 181–82n117, 199–200n136; revolutions and sociopolitcal movements as not subject to, 118–19, 131–32; self-regulation as, 9, 70–71

consent: appropriation of property without, 111, 177n90; and freedom of movement, 27, 70–71, 72; tacit, 78, 183n128

corporeality: individual as the of the subject, 67–72, 74, 76, 81, 86, 89; laws as a restraint on the of movement, 68–69, 80; and liberal concepts of movement, 25, 81, 89; of rationality, 25, 74–76; of the Hobbesian sovereign, 72, 116, 122; of the liberal subject, 3–4, 16, 62, 65, 188n48. *See also* body

Cresswell, Tim, 10, 145n29

Deleuze, Gilles, 122, 189n60

democracy: democratic spaces, 14, 76, 131; Israel's attempts to reconcile nondemocratic governance with, 22, 142–43n8, 145n37, 149–50n86; liberal, 6, 11, 123, 188n48; moderation in the, 123–24; movement in the *polis*, 91–92; Plato's democratic city, 88, 90–93; and practices of inclusion and exclusion, 142–43n8; reform movements, 197–98n123

deportation: as tool for colonizing states, 183n127; as tool of liberal democracies, 1, 15, 23, 64, 112, 114, 132; camps, 11, 181n113, 181n114

Descartes, René, 4, 62, 80–81, 156n7, 161n10, 162n16, 167n83

desire: as an impetus for movement, 1, 65–66, 68, 92–93; as an impetus underlying reform movements, 129–30, 134; as an object of political regulation, *viii*, 68–69, 78, 94, 96–97, 100, 117; Hobbes on, 65–66, 68, 70, 94, 96–97, 162n14, 167n81; inclination

versus will-based, 164n37; Locke on, 166–67n71; versus self-regulation and reason, 61–62, 77, 107, 165–66n61, 166–67n71
disability and ability, 14, 74, 76, 85
disciplinary power: as tool for normalizing behaviors, 23, 89; as tool of governance, 6, 8, 139, 153n8; condescension as an element of, 33, 37–38, 57; Foucault on, 2, 93, 94, 150n100, 161n7; Israeli military practices of, 21–22, 31–32, 37–38; Locke on labor as tool of, 108; movement as target of, 22, 60, 108, 112; stereotyping the oppressed as "undisciplinable," 5, 32, 34, 50, 55–56; the use of "already-failed" strategies to justify, 22, 33–34, 37–38, 50. *See also* punishment
Dworkin, Gerald, 11, 62, 148n73

education, 33, 74–75, 109, 166–67n71, 174n57, 178n95, 201–2n7
enclosure: as a justification for colonial land-grabbing, 103–5, 178–79n97, 180n104; as a mode of liberal governance, 5, 6, 11, 15, 180n108; as the basis for the sovereign state, 186n18, 186n31, 187n38, 194n92, 194–95n95; the English agricultural Enclosure system, 106–11, 180n107; Israel's use of to control the Palestinian populace, 28; Locke on freedom as derived from, 9, 77, 90, 100–111, 101, 105–6; Locke on rationality and, 109, 178n95, 178–79n97; Schmitt on the as organized space, 105; and unity, 118–19
England: the Enclosure system in, 106–11; philosophical thought in Enlightenment, 65, 81, 121, 180n102; the plight of the poor in Enlightenment, 107–10, 180n103, 183n125, 183n127

enslavement: the slave trade, 3, 11, 111, 121, 132, 199n133; versus freedom of movement, 1, 25, 37, 142–43n8, 175n65, 200–201n5; versus servitude, 70–71
expansion: the blockage of Palestinian, 157–58n13, 193n84; and the concept of balance of power, 119; imperial, 8, 90, 113, 115, 119–20, 122, 176n67; as the movement of collective bodies, 13, 14, 122, 201–2n7
expulsion, 11, 48, 90, 106, 111, 113

Fanon, Frantz, 153–54n14, 194n92, 199n132
fascism, 12, 13, 119, 131, 188n48, 197–98n123
fear: as mechanism of the state, 26, 71, 96, 128, 133; as political technology wielded by the state, 71, 95–96, 100, 171–72n26, 172n34; Cavarero on, 19, 69; Hobbes on, 71–72, 94–96, 171–72n26, 172n34, 173n39; the human will and, 127, 164n37
Feldman, Yotam, 124, 125
fences: law as a "fence" word, 105–6; Locke on as precondition for freedom, 76–78, 101, 105, 110; to regulate movement, 42, 44, 84, 138. *See also* hedges
flows. *See* circulation
Foucault, Michel: on confinement, 108, 180–81n110, 181n113; on emergence of liberal concepts of freedom, 59, 161n8; on idea of the hysterical woman, 73; on powers of the state, 1–2, 63, 143n11, 150n100, 161n7, 186n29, 187n40; on security and movement, 18, 58–60, 93, 160nn29–30; on self-regulating crises, 59; on the self-regulating subject, 8–9, 59, 94, 95, 137
Freeden, Michael, 11, 13, 18

freedom: Arendt on, 1, 14–16, 62, 142n1, 147n67, 171n20, 186n22; Hobbes on, 9, 64–73, 66–68, 94–95, 133, 163n26, 172n35, 186n33; Locke on, 77–78, 77–79, 177nn92–93, 179n100; Mill on, 147n69; negative, 67, 69–70, 77; ordered, 3, 8–9, 58, 89, 95, 112; political, 18, 58, 75–76, 95, 114; positive, 69–70, 169–70n3; rationality and, 74–76, 91, 109–10; will and, 17, 18, 63, 71, 80

freedom of movement: across state borders, 10, 18; as factor underlying revolutionary behaviors, 12–13; as metaphor for freedom of thought, 75–76, 77, 79, 185n6; as exercise of liberty, 16–17, 62–63, 163n26; Arendt on, 1, 62, 131–32, 142n1; as threat, 20, 90, 95, 97, 110, 137; differential, 9–11, 24, 88, 100, 137, 181n113, 181n114; disruptive power of, 159–60n27; freedom of choice as, 18, 148n78; Israel's restriction of Palestinian, 5, 23, 27–28; and liberal idea of physical motion, 4, 17, 37, 58–59, 64, 75, 84–85; of the liberal subject, 3, 58, 61, 63, 93, 95, 97; security concerns as justification for restricting, 18–19, 23, 54, 138, 195–96n100; stability as precondition for, 6, 10, 77, 86, 88, 92, 100–103; volition and, 79. *See also* liberty; self-regulation

Frost, Samantha, 80, 171–72n26, 172n35

Galli, Carlo, 122, 173n42, 184n4, 186n31, 190n64

Gaza Strip; Israeli biases against the Palestinian population of, 31, 49, 124, 155–56n3, 190–91nn74–75; tunnel-based economy of, 191–92n77

gender: as basis for hierarchization, 137, 138; as basis for restricting or forcing movement, 5, 11, 63, 175n65; as topic of sociopolitical conflict, 65, 73–75, 171n24, 201n6; -based discrimination, 2, 3, 84, 138; -based movement, 86, 196n10; and race, 175n65; Westernized symbolism of Chinese foot binding, 7, 74–75, 113, 143–44n16, 144n18, 184n5

globalization: as myth of deterritorialization, 15; antiglobalization movements, 129–30; through colonization, 8, 11, 14, 112; as increased flows of capital, goods, and people, 13, 19, 37, 88, 185n12; of the sea, 114; uneven, biased quality of, 52, 64, 100, 145n35, 175nn64–65; versus tensions that favor barricading, 5, 10, 148–49n84, 187nn39–40

Gordon, Neve, 22, 149n86, 153n8

Gould, Deborah B., 128–29, 196n103

Guattari, Félix, 122, 189n60

Hamas, 149–50n86, 191–92n77

Handel, Ariel, 54, 125, 156–57n8, 191n76

Hardt, Michael, 14, 129

Hass, Amira, 21, 157n9

hedges: the directive purpose of literal and figurative, 6, 78, 88, 100, 107, 166–67n71; Hobbes on laws as, 68–69, 96–97, 179n100. *See also* fences

Hirschmann, Nancy: on the Hobbesian concept of freedom, 69–70, 96, 171–72n26, 174n57; on the Lockean concept of freedom, 75, 104, 165n53, 167n72, 177n84

Hobbes, Thomas: on absolutist governments, 9–10, 71, 95, 119; America as Hobbes's *no man's land*, 97–100, 101, 173nn46–47, 174–75n63; the *Behemoth*, 185n12, 197n117; on civil society, 90, 94–95; commonwealth of, 72, 96, 99–100, 116–17, 187n41; comparisons between Lockean and Hobbesian theory, 78–79, 86, 94, 101–2, 105, 167n74, 167n81; conflation of will and movement in Hobbesian theory, 71, 164n37; *De Cive*, 97, 162n18; on excessive movement, 90, 93–100; on fear as a political technology, 71–72, 94–96, 171–72n26, 172n34, 173n39; on freedom as unimpeded movement, 9, 64, 65–73, 94, 163n26; on freedom as violence, 94–95, 117, 133, 172n35, 186n33; on importance of leisure to achievement of rationality, 99; interest of in movement of the limbs, 65, 82, 92–93, 116; and liberal thought, 70–71, 121, 161n8; on liberty, 66–70, 72, 94–95, 100, 162n18, 163n26, 167n81; on movement as a political matter, 65–67, 86; on movement of political spheres, 8, 10, 14, 72, 115–22, 144n20; political freedom in Hobbesian theory, 94–95; on purpose of law, 68–70, 96–97, 172n34; on rationality, 97–99, 163n35; restrained versus unrestrained freedom in Hobbesian theory, 97–100; on role of consent, 70–72; savages portrayed by, 97, 98–100, 109, 154n15, 173n47, 174n58; on self-regulation, 8–9, 69–71, 76, 93–94, 96; servant as model of subjecthood for, 70–71, 99–100, 163n32, 164m38, 171–72n26; social contract of, 94–95, 116–17, 162–63n21; on the soul as the power underlying movement, 116; sovereign of, 71–72, 96–97, 113–16, 122, 130–31, 164n45, 197n119; state as monopolizer of violence, 94–95, 100, 115–19, 189n60, 190n64, 197n117; and the state of nature, 66–67, 96–98, 162n16, 171–72n26, 174n53, 186n33; tension between the individual and state in Hobbesian theory, 69–72, 94–95, 162–63n21, 164nn41–42, 173n42; on time and the slowing of movement, 90, 95–96, 99, 105; use of images of the body by, 82, 163n33, 187n42, 188n44, 194–95n95; on violence and movement, 94–95, 115, 117–19; war in Hobbesian theory, 117–22, 122–23, 186n31, 190n64. *See also Leviathan*

Hobhouse, Leonard Trelawny, 11–12, 14, 93, 146n43

human rights: Israeli organizations in defense of Palestinian, 24, 29, 150n91; Israeli violations of Bedouin, 201–2n7; Israeli violations of Palestinian, 154n19, 191n75; work of B'Tselem, 23, 191n75; work of Checkpoint Watch (CPW), 38–41, 154n19; work of Disobedient Women, 195n99; work of Gisha, 191–92n77

Hume, David, 61, 183n128

hydra, 115, 130–31, 185n12, 197n117

imaginary lines: as a strategy of political control, 55–56, 106, 125, 137; at Israeli checkpoints, 24, 29–31, 34–36, 39–40, 44, 153n11, 200n3; as settlement boundaries, 106, 125, 137; as tools of discriminatory governance, 39–41, 49–51, 153n14, 195n96

immigration: as a security threat, 10, 19–20, 23, 145n29, 148n84; Blackstone on, 168n89; English enclosure and imperialist policies underlying, 106–7, 110–11, 112–13; forced or induced, 132–33, 175n65, 183n127; and globalization, 114, 169–70n3

Index / 223

Israel: the Bedouin populace of, 3, 201–2n7; and the construction of Palestinian space 190–92nn74–80; "constructive obfuscation" policies of, 47–48, 54–55, 158n15, 192–93nn83–84, 193n87; and democracy, 22, 24, 40, 123, 142–43n8, 145n37, 149n86; general policy of regarding the oPt, 158–59n19, 193n87; justification of continued occupation, 29, 31–32, 35, 38, 40–41, 45, 57; liberal policies and authoritarian behavior of, 36–37, 40–41, 48–51, 133–34, 142–43n8, 145n37, 152–53nn7–8; military actions of against Palestinians, 31, 124–27, 149–50n86, 153n8; perception of Palestinian struggle for independence as aggression, 20, 133, 149–50n86, 159n20, 192–93n83, 194n94; policies of ethnic separation and discrimination of, 52–57, 155–57nn1–10, 157–58n13, 158n17, 175n64; policies of that provoke Palestinian transgression, 32–35, 37–38, 40–41, 55–57, 151–52n5, 154–55n26; "regime of movement" of in the oPt, 20–24, 27–37, 42–45, 52–57, 125, 150–51n100; threat of violence by against Palestinian populace, 36, 56–57, 133, 192–93nn83–84

Jerusalem, 52–53, 156n7, 158–59n19

Kant, Immanuel, 17–18, 61, 75–77, 165–66n61, 166n64, 185n6
knowledge: time as a key to, 38, 68, 92–93, 95, 99; withholding of to exert control, 29, 38, 40, 41, 55–56, 106

labor: and American land rights, 104, 108, 177n90, 182–83n123, 183n125; -based movements for reform, 129, 131; blacks in South Africa, 37; forced as a form of violence, 13, 110, 114, 200–201n5; impact of globalization on, 37, 185n12; Locke on, 108–10; Palestinians in Israel, 22, 28; reconfiguration of through English enclosure, 108, 180n104; slavery, 70, 142–43n8, 199n133; versus freedom, 92, 132–33
land: appropriation of as basis for colonialism, 88, 102–7, 178–79n97; colonial concept of vacant, 78, 101, 102–4, 106, 110–11, 179n98, 189n56; cultivation as basis for appropriation of, 102; English enclosure, 107–10; -grabbing, 104, 106–7, 157–58n13, 158–59n19, 178–79n97; landlessness as vulnerability, 110–11, 181–82n117
law: as a constraint on the actions of the subject, 24, 37, 63, 67–70, 77–78, 81–82, 96; as a shield for the citizen, 40, 41, 49–51; as tool for construing illegality, 29, 40–41, 55–56, 149n85, 183n127, 191n75, 198–99n131; as tool for discrimination, 200–201n5; as tool for obfuscation by the state, 40, 48, 106, 125, 158n15, 158–59n19; Blackstone on liberty of movement, 81–82; the contract, 69, 80, 96–97; Hobbes on the purpose of, 68–69, 96, 118; illegal actions as statements regarding the, 195n99, 198n126; immigration, 1, 19, 168n89; inaccessibility and contradictory quality of Israeli when applied to Palestinians, 38, 40–42, 50, 106, 137; inaccessibility of the for "Others," 40, 50; international, 119, 158–59n19, 189n55, 189–90n63; Kant's notion of the, 166n64; Locke on function of the, 76–78, 102–5, 166–67n71, 177nn90–92, 179n100; of nature,

105, 177n92, 186n31; of reason, 103, 177n90; ownership and settlement as bases for, 88, 93, 104–6, 177n90; Poor Laws (of 1575, 1601, 1834) (of England), 108, 181n113, 181n114, 181–82n117; Schmidt on law as a "fence word," 105, 106; and security, 19; self-regulation and the, 58, 68–69, 96, 165–66n61, 171–72n26, 172n34; stability of the as a precondition for freedom, 40, 76–77, 104–5; suffragist fight for legal equality, 83, 85

Leviathan: Hobbes on colonialism, 167n74; Hobbes on fear, 173n39; Hobbes on free will, 162n14, 163n35, 164n37, 167n81, 172n34; Hobbes on indigenous Americans, 173n47, 174n58; Hobbes on the servant as representing all men, 164n38; Hobbes on the state, 68, 97, 144n20, 162–63n21, 163n33, 173n39, 197n19. *See also* Hobbes, Thomas

leviathan: the political state as a, 115, 117–18, 130–31; violence and war as necessary to the state, 119–21, 123–24

liberalism: as complement to colonialism, 8, 11, 25, 63, 103, 189n57; and concept of freedom, 37, 58–59, 71; and concept of self-regulation, 58, 71, 86, 89, 159n23, 159n26, 166n64; and concept of the "shield of law," 40; conceptual demarcation of 3–4, 11, 61, 62–63; and crystallization of concept of "Other," 63, 88, 168n86, 170n5, 174n54; discursive origins of 9, 58–59, 64–66, 70–71, 80, 161n8; Foucault on, 58–59, 143n11; Freeden on, 11–12, 13, 18; Hobhouse on, 11–12; influence of bourgeois socioeconomic values on, 188n48; and its fiction of universality, 88, 89, 98;

Marx on, 59; mind-body schism in, 25, 73–74, 80–81, 148n76; movement as a pivotal point in liberal thought, 4, 11–13, 37, 59, 62–65, 73–74, 146n43; origins of the term, 144n25; Rawls on, 18, 148n78, 148nn75–76; tensions between order and freedom inherent to, 8–9, 11–12, 18, 58, 86; versus other ideologies, 11–13, 197n123

liberal subject: as an abstraction, 4, 17–18, 61–62, 67, 69, 79–80; as an entity motivated by will, 4, 61, 74, 112; as universal man, 3, 25, 89, 168n86, 175n65; duality of under a commonwealth, 67, 68; entitlement of to protection by the law, 40, 41, 49, 180n108; freedom of under a commonwealth, 9, 93–95; movement as a basic trait of, 4, 23, 25, 50, 58, 62–63, 86; origins of as a corporeal being, 3–4, 9, 89, 93; Palestinians as nonliberal subjects, 25, 44, 58, 62–65, 74, 81–83, 168n93. *See also* subject

liberty: as physical phenomenon, 4–5, 17, 23, 62–68, 71, 74, 82–83; Blackstone's concept of, 81–82, 168n89; civil, 95, 100; corporeal, 65, 67–71; denial of free movement as threat to, 16–17; detachment of from action under the social contract, 80–81, 94–95; fear and, 171–72n26, 172n34; as freedom from impediment, 66–68, 81–82, 94, 166n64; Hobbesian concept of, 64–72, 94–95, 100–101, 118, 162n18, 163n26, 167n81; as the individual's power to act alone, 68, 71, 167n81; Lockean concept of, 77, 79–80, 94, 101, 109–10; Mill's *On Liberty*, 144n18, 147n69, 161n7; as movement, 4, 62–63, 72, 81–84, 121; movement as a threat to, 4, 20, 58, 77, 94–95; natural, 72, 94–95, 100, 163n26, 186n33;

liberty (continued)
  of noncorporeal entities, 72, 118, 121; of the mind, 73–74, 76; Plato on, 90–91; as reducible to individual will and intention, 62–63, 79–80; reliance of on stability, 77, 94–95, 100; republican notions of, 9, 67, 162n18, 164n42; as self-restrained freedom, 6, 58, 62, 71–72, 95, 112. See also freedom
Linebaugh, Peter, 130, 180nn103–4, 183n127, 185n12, 197nn117–18
location: the *demos*, 91–92; home and rootedness, 9, 134–35, 138, 181n114; and movement, 2, 7, 23, 97–98, 175n65; the perpetually changing, 31; the wild "no man's land," 96–97, 105–6, 178n95
Locke, John: advocacy of control of the poor by, 108–10, 180n103, 183n125, 183n127; advocacy of punishment of vagabonds by, 181–82n117, 183n127; America and the American Indian as perceived by, 101–7, 176n79, 177n90, 178n95; on the body-politic, 166n65; comparisons between Lockean and Hobbesian theory, 78, 79, 86, 94, 101–2, 167n74, 167n81; on education, 74–75, 109, 165n56, 166–67n71, 182n120; financial interests of in the American colonies, 173n46, 175–76n66; financial interests of in the American slave trade, 175–76n66; on freedom and reason, 76–80, 102, 177n90; on freedom as movement, 9, 76–80, 90, 94, 102; on free will, 79–80, 167n81; justifications of for colonial land-grabbing in America, 101–7, 110–11, 176n67, 178n95, 178–79nn97–98; labor and industry in Lockean theory, 103–5, 108–9, 177n90, 179n98, 180n102, 183n125;

liberalism in Lockean theory, 161n8, 180n102; on motion, 79–80; on movement, stability, and security, 93, 101, 104–5, 109–10, 182–83n123; personal interests of in the American Carolinas, 175–76n66, 176n75, 178–79n97; on purpose of education, 166–67n71; on purpose of the law, 76–78, 102–5, 166–67n71, 177nn90–92, 179n100; on rationality, 74–75, 102–6, 109, 165n56, 177n92, 178nn94–95; *Second Treatise* discussion of property rights, 77, 103, 178–79n97; *Second Treatise* discussion of restrained freedom, 77–78, 86, 177nn92–93, 179n100; *Second Treatise* discussion of the law of reason, 177n90; self-regulating man of, 90; on the social contract, 102; on tacit consent, 78; on thinking as freedom, 78–79, 102; on time as requirement for rationality, 105–6, 109, 177n92, 182n120
locomotion, 17, 22, 62, 80–83, 84
Lomasky, Loren, 18–20

McClure, Kirstie, 77–78, 166n70
Manning, Erin, 15, 138
Marx, Karl, 13, 59, 120, 160n30
Mayr, Otto, 58–59
Mehta, Uday, 7, 77, 98, 105, 112, 165n53
Merleau-Ponty, Maurice, 81–82, 168n93
migration: expulsion, 11, 48, 90, 106, 111, 113; forced, 110, 146n41, 175n65, 183n127, 199–200n136; global, 100, 111, 148n84
military: as an essential element of colonialism, 8, 122; strategies, 124–25, 149–50n86, 157–58n13, 190–91nn74–75, 192–93n83,

193–94n90; urban layouts that facilitate or impede activities, 124–25, 131, 157–58n13, 187–88n43, 190–91n74, 195n98; violence, 124–25, 149n86, 190n71, 191n75, 199n132; zones in the Palestinian territories, 125, 131, 155n2, 193n84

Mill, John Stuart: on freedom, 17, 147n69; on imperialism, 7–8, 143–44n16, 144n18; on movement of political spheres, 7–8, 14, 17, 63, 143–44n16, 144n18, 161n7; on progress, 7; typology of power of, 17, 63, 161n7

mobility: as hallmark of privilege, 19, 52, 145n35; differential perceptions of, 9–10, 15–16, 22–23, 37, 63, 89, 138; and discrimination, 139, 157n10, 199n133; excessive, 9, 90–91, 107–9, 159–60n27, 181–82n117; feudal immobility, 12, 180n109; gender and, 73–76, 85, 143–44n16, 184n5; globalization as governance of, 10–11, 145n35, 169–70n3; immobility, 96, 105, 125, 127, 145n33, 157n10; liberty as, 62; of citizens as a right, 10, 168n89, 173n42; of colonized space, 125, 127, 183n125, 194n92, 195n96, 199n132, 199–200n136; of states, 115, 119–20, 184n4; and rationality, 75, 109; revolutionary movements and, 12; social, 85, 184n4; tamed and stable, 11, 96, 104, 145n29, 145n33, 162n14, 173n42; versus stagnation, 9, 105, 113, 143–44n16, 184n5

motion: as concrete movement, 73; differential perceptions of, 6, 10, 25–26, 171n24, 186n22; freedom as, 37, 66, 68, 71, 77, 78, 81–82; Hobbes on, 65–72, 94, 96, 118, 162n14, 162n16, 164n44; Locke on, 78, 79–80, 108, 166n65; Merleau-Ponty on, 81; as metaphor, 73, 76; Mill on European political, 7–8; of social and political movements, 13, 16, 66, 113–14, 129–33; of the state, 116–22, 125, 132–33, 144n19, 164n44, 166n65, 187–88n43; physical and scientific, 65–68, 82, 109, 162n14, 162n16, 198n130; politics of, 1, 74, 193n87, 193n89, 194–95n95, 196n104, 201–2n7; rest as the goal of, 170–71n17; sea as boundless, 121–22, 125; self-regulated, 70–71, 112; state as entity that controls individual, 6, 67, 68, 96, 136–37; terror as mpetus for, 19; and thought, 16, 78–79, 81, 164n48, 171n20

movement: as target of disciplinary power, 22, 181n113, 181–82n117, 183n127; knowledge as goal of, 92–93; nonfree, 11, 175n65, 183n127; of sewage, 128, 184, 195n98; Plato's analogy of lingering, 92–93, 110; restrictions on by states, 10–11, 141–42n5, 173n42, 181–82n117, 195–96n100; restrictions on Palestinian by Israel, 28, 39, 55, 125, 137–38, 155–56n2–3, 190–91n74; settlement as, 8, 125; surveillance of, vii–ix, 141–43nn3–6; transgressive, 57, 85, 88, 124, 127

Naveh, Shimon, 124–25, 192n80, 194n94
Nazism, 12, 13, 119, 197–98n123
Neocleous, Mark, 188n48, 197–98n123
Netz, Raviel, 54, 136–37, 157n12
nomadism: colonialist myth of American Indian, 3, 5, 104–6; of state-sponsored war machines, 122, 189n59; state-forced, 183n127, 199n133, 201–2n7; subject-position of the nomad, 11, 13

Index / 227

occupied Palestinian territories (oPt): concealment of knowledge as tool of control, 29, 30, 38, 41, 55–56, 106; enlightened occupation, 22; Israeli attributions of a collective consciousness to Palestinians, 40–41; Israeli discriminatory policies in the, 149n85, 155–56n3, 156–57nn6–10, 158n17; Israeli governance of the, 5, 45, 48, 52–53, 156n4, 158–59n19, 190–91nn74–76; Israel's construction of space via violence in the, 124–25, 149–50n86, 152–53n7, 192n78, 192n80, 192–93nn83–84, 199n132; Israel's control of movement in the, 20–23, 27–28, 32, 46–47, 57, 156–57nn8–10; Israel's logic of separation in the, 45, 52–54, 125, 157–58n13, 158n15, 191nn75–76; the shifting borders of the, 125–27, 156n4, 156–57n8, 193n87, 199n132. *See also* checkpoints; Palestinians

Occupy Wall Street, 16, 144–45n28

Ophir, Adi, 6, 32, 91, 143n11, 170n13, 186n17, 187n38

Oslo Accords, 28, 149n86, 150–51n100, 158–59n19

Palestinians: as a labor force in Israel, 22, 28, 195n99; attribution of a collective consciousness to the, 40–41; construction of as unruly subjects, 29, 31; Beit Furik village, 54–56; camps, 23, 64, 124, 190–91n74, 192n78; Hamas, 149–50n86, 191–92n77; Israeli redefinition of as partial subjects, 38, 50; Israel's policies concerning, 22, 24, 32, 38, 125–26; Israel's rationale of punishment against, 31–32, 33, 42, 55–56, 149–50n86, 151–53nn5–7; military operations of the, 149n86, 155n1; peaceful resistance activities by, 195n97, 195n99; plight of as a colonized people, 26, 28–29, 34–35, 49–50, 57, 150n100, 157n10; population of in the oPt, 21, 31, 156n6; racial discrimination against, 10, 32, 149–50n86, 154–55n26, 155–56nn2–3, 193n84; racial segregation of, 32–38, 46–49, 52–55, 100, 152n7, 155–56n3, 194n92; refugee, 124, 190–91nn74–75; resistance of construed as "terror," 20, 133, 149–50n86; stereotyping of the Palestinian citizens of Israel, 158n17; struggle of for independence, 20, 35, 49, 149–50n86, 152–53n7, 191–92n77; villages, 52, 54–55, 155–56n3, 157n9. *See also* checkpoints; occupied Palestinian territories (oPt)

Pateman, Carole, 102, 173–74n50, 179n98

pauperism, 9, 107–8, 132–33, 180–81n110. *See also* poverty

Plato: criticisms of democratic polis by, 88, 90–93; on movement of states, 8; on political unity, 117, 118, 120; on reason and rationality, 61, 73, 92–93; on time and lingering as essential to knowing, 93, 99, 110

plurality: as a hydra, 115, 130–31, 185n12, 197n117; Arendt on, 15–16, 117, 196–97n116; and unity, 114, 115, 117, 127, 130, 132

polis, 90–91, 92, 93, 118, 176n72

political movements, 12–14, 66, 115, 131, 196n107, 198n125. *See also* social movements

poor: deportation of the, 11, 181–82n117, 183n127; expulsion of indigenous, 11, 48, 90, 106, 111, 113; Locke on labor as

tool to discipline the, 108; Poor Laws, 108, 180n103, 181nn113–14
poverty, 3, 19, 85, 107–8, 180–81n110. *See also* pauperism
power: balance of, 119, 159n24; in colonial relations, 15, 38, 50, 127–28, 189–90n63; and exercise of arbitrariness, 35, 42, 166n64; Foucault on the technologies of, 2, 8–9, 58–59, 63–64, 150n100, 187n40; individual thought as, 78–80, 127; Israeli in the oPt, 22–24, 35, 38, 48, 149–50n86, 153n8; liberty as a power of locomotion, 81; Mill's typology of, 17, 161n7; movement as a grabbing point for exercising, 2, 4, 14, 16–17, 58, 60; of the political system, 2, 4, 60, 63–64, 77, 96–97, 159n22; powerlessness, 85, 92; social and political movements as a means of realigning, 13–16, 115–16, 129–31, 132–33, 185n15, 196n113, 197–98n123; sovereign, 99, 117, 120–22, 153n8, 166n65, 189nn55–60; state and citizenship, 40, 41, 148n75, 180n108; the subject as an element of sovereign, 9, 78; technologies of, 16–17, 30–38, 50, 58–59, 63–64, 136–37, 190–91n74
Procacci, Giovanna, 107–8, 159–60n27
progress, 7, 11, 17, 53, 180n102, 185n5
property: as a basis of freedom, 76, 78, 88, 101, 103, 112, 138; accumulation of, 102, 104–5, 178–79n97; Blackstone on, 81–82; consumption versus labor as tests for ownership of, 103–4, 177n90; enclosed, 104–5, 136; English enclosure system, 107–8, 136; as evidence of rationality, 104–5, 109, 177n84, 177n92, 182–83n123; failure of American Indians to own landed, 103–4; land ownership, 88, 101, 103–4, 107, 138, 177n90; Locke on, 76, 101, 103–5, 109–10; private, 104, 110, 152–53n7; and security, 78, 81–82; and settlement, 103–4, 182–83n123; seventeenth century changes in concepts of, 60; versus subsistence, 103–4, 109, 180n104, 181n113
punishment: of Israeli human rights activists, 41; movement as substitute for race to justify, 10, 139, 149–50n86, 152–53n7; of Palestinians at checkpoints, 31–33, 42, 56–57, 151–52n5

racism: as a basis for constrained or forced movement, 5, 11, 32, 175n65, 200–201n5; against black Americans, 10, 139, 200–201n5; against Palestinians, 10, 27, 32, 41, 154–55n26, 193n84; barriers as tools of, 32, 46–47, 170n5; and colonialism, 97, 106, 128, 174n53, 174–75n63, 184n2, 193–94n90; and creation of nonsubjects, 37, 38, 41, 199n133; discrimination, 3, 139, 141–42n5; enslavement, 1, 25, 200–201n5; and harassment, 27; movement as justification for discriminatory behaviors, 10, 63, 138–40, 149–50nn85–86, 152–53n7; redefinition of individuals as objects, 37, 38, 199n133; segregation, 36, 37, 52–57, 138–39, 151–52n5, 155–56nn2–4, 157n9; separation to prevent unity among the oppressed, 45, 48, 194n94; and social hierarchy, 64, 88, 110, 138, 174n56, 177n84, 186n18; stereotyping and, 158n17; "they know" mantra, 31, 40–41, 57
Rancière, Jacques, 14, 170n15

rationality: as a basis for entitlement to movement, 65, 76, 80, 91; as a product of movement, 74–76, 105–6, 109; as a product of time, 90, 99, 105–6, 109; association of with ability, 74, 76, 98–99, 105–6, 174n57, 177n92, 182n120; as a trait of the liberal, universal subject, 3, 17, 25, 40, 63, 73–74, 97–98; and freedom, 85, 90, 91, 102–3, 105; irrationality, 99, 101–2, 104, 106, 109, 180n102, 201n6; Locke on, 74–76, 102–9, 166–67n71, 177n92, 178n95, 180n102, 182n120; of indigenous or colonized peoples, 98–99, 102–6, 178n95; property and ownership as preconditions for, 101, 103–6, 109, 177n84, 182–83n123; and self-regulation, 76, 77–78, 97–98

Rawls, John, 18, 70, 148n78, 148nn75–76

Rediker, Marcus, 130, 180nn103–4, 183n127, 185n12, 197nn117–18

Republic, 91, 144n19, 170n13

republican liberty, 9, 67, 162n18, 164n42

roads: apartheid, 28, 41, 53–57, 151–52n5, 155n2, 155–56n3; as tools of separation and blockage, 28, 52–53, 57, 157–58n3, 190n74, 192n78

Rogers, John, 65–66, 96

Said, Edward, 87, 89, 153–54n14

savagery: colonized peoples as savages, 9, 97–98, 105–8, 174n58, 174–75n63, 199n133; Hobbes on the excessive movement of "savages," 93–100; unsettled movement as evidence of, 88, 93, 99–101, 173n47, 178n95

Schiller, Friedrich, 61, 71, 85

Schmitt, Carl: on enmity, 118; on Hobbes's America, 97, 105, 173n47, 199n135; on social movements, 12, 131; on the state as an entity capable of movement, 12, 14, 97, 118, 189nn55–56, 198n130

Scott, James, 87, 94, 195n99

sea: as a place of unbound movement, 97, 115, 123, 125, 129, 181–82n117, 189n59; as a facilitator of commerce and of empire, 121–22, 188n51, 189n57, 192n82; as a place of freedom and of violence, 114–15, 121–23, 189nn55–56; *La Monde Diplomatique* map of the West Bank, 125–26

Second Intifada, 124, 152–53nn7–8, 155n1, 155–56n3

security: as a function of the state, 94–95, 97, 99, 143n11, 162–63n21, 193–94n90; as a justification for Israeli limitation of Palestinian movement, 23, 28–29, 191nn75–76; as a means of protecting freedom, 60, 78, 81–82, 90, 133, 169–70n3; as a necessary balance to freedom, 8, 93–95; Foucault on, 18, 60, 143n11, 160nn29–30; freedom as a threat to, 23, 94, 100; Hobbes on freedom and security, 90, 94–95, 96–97, 99–100; Israeli checkpoint apparatus, 30–31, 34, 36, 44, 45–46; Israeli checkpoint strategies, 47, 152n7, 154n24, 192–93n83; Lomasky on, 18–20; movement as a threat to, 19–20, 90, 94, 100; objects as threats to, vii–viii, 18–19; surveillance of movement, vii–ix, 141–42nn3–6; technologies of, vii–viii, 45, 142n6; and the violation of freedom, 133, 138, 142n6, 149–50n86, 158n17, 196n116

sedentarism: and the sedentarization of a populace, 108, 145n33, 180n109, 181n114; as stability, 8, 10, 11, 74, 77, 104

self-regulation: as attribute of freedom and of citizenship, 51, 58–61, 87–88, 89, 94; as attribute only of rational,

230 / Index

liberal subjects, 8, 26, 61, 70, 90, 112; as model of political orders 58, 59, 119, 159nn22–26; Foucault on, 8–9, 59; Hobbes on, 8–9, 70–72, 78, 93–94, 96, 99–100; of one's movement, 5, 70–72; versus transgressive movement, 57; within and among systems, 119, 137, 159nn22–26. *See also* freedom

servant: as self-regulating agent, 70–72, 78, 93–94, 164n38; of Polemarchus in the *Republic*, 91; susceptibility of to being moved involuntary, 91, 107, 184n3

Seth, Vanita, 98–99, 102–3, 171–72n26, 172–73n38

settlement: as precondition for freedom, 103–5; Bedouin settlements-in-motion, 201–2n7; colonial-driven, 107, 128, 134, 176n67, 176n77, 179n98, 199–200n136; and concept of home, 9, 134–35, 180n108; and concept of property, 103, 138; Israeli in the Palestinian territories, 52, 57, 151–52n5, 156n6, 158–59n19, 193n84, 195n97; land-grabbing in colonial America, 101, 128, 178–79nn97–99; separation of Israeli and Palestinian villages, 54–56, 157–58n13, 157nn9–10, 191n76; and social contract, 102, 173–74n50

Skinner, Quentin, 67, 97

slave trade, 3, 11, 111, 121, 132

social contract: and concept of sovereignty, 69, 94–95; the Lockean idea of the, 101–2; settler contract as a, 102, 173–74n50

social movements: and acts of occupation, 132; Arendt on formation of, 15; characteristics of, 128–32, 132, 196n106; early, 131, 197n121; reconciling plurality and unity within, 113–14, 126–27, 130, 197n118. *See also* political movements

soul: as an attribute of nonembodied subject, 17, 73, 147n69, 165n48; as source of movement, 73, 91, 121, 165n48, 171n20, 186n22; as source of power, 17, 91, 92, 116, 147n69

sovereign state: and the technologies of power, 63; as an apparatus of closure, 6, 10, 119, 143nn11–12, 186n18, 187nn38–39; as an artificial person, 69, 72, 113, 115, 116–17, 122; as a source of unity, 117, 118, 130, 197n117; commerce as an essential part of, 120–21; freedom of the subject in, 9, 67–70, 72; power of to dictate a subject's movements, 96–97, 173n42; sovereignty and the state of nature, 67, 72, 102, 118; the subject as an element of, 67, 69, 162–63n21, 164n38, 164n42; as the threat of violence, 69, 96, 150n100, 153n8

space: accessible or common, 14, 115, 130–32, 162n16, 184n4, 185n15, 185n16; colonial American, 97, 101, 105–6, 173n47; confined, 33, 46, 53–55, 136, 162n18, 180n109; demarcated and undemarcated, 24, 39, 41, 44, 56, 90; enclosed, 90, 105, 186n31; fragmented, 21, 28; Lockean empty, 79, 90; locomotion as change in, 81, 82; perception of, 192n80; political, 12, 14, 58, 76, 114, 116, 173n42; power of collective movement to define, 185n16, 198nn125–29; the sea as a free, 189nn55–59; shrinking and oppressive, 21, 36, 66, 139, 141–42n5; state expansion of, 14, 115, 193–94n90; unstable, 8, 29–30, 34, 195n96, 195–96n100; use-value of, 156–57n8, 157n10; violence and, 36–37, 123–27, 157n12, 190n71, 192n80

Index / 231

Spragens, Thomas A., 66, 96, 172n35, 173n42
stability: as a complement to movement, 93, 103, 109, 166n69; as precondition for movement, 11, 138; as precondition for thought and knowledge, 83, 92, 105; as a quality of the liberal subject, 4, 8–11, 112; instability, 13–14, 127; and the law, 40, 76, 104, 157n10, 173n42, 199n132; as the natural order of things, 92–93; and political freedom, 18, 77, 104, 196n116, 198n129; sedentarism, 8, 10–11, 77; sedentarism (forced), 73–74, 83–85, 107–8, 180n109, 181n114
Stanton, Elizabeth C., 183–84, 186
statelessness, 15, 90, 146n41, 198n127, 199n133
state of nature: between sovereigns, 72, 118; as contrary to secure freedom, 94–95; equality of individuals in the, 162n16; man's as defined by Hobbes, 66–67, 68, 96, 171–72n26, 174n53, 189n60; vulnerability of to violence, 95–97, 117, 164n38, 168n90, 172n35, 174–75n63, 186n33
states: ability of to be free or to promote freedom, 87; as demarcated and enclosing territories, 6, 9–10, 60, 119, 143n11, 157n12, 187nn38–39; as dynamic or static entities, 12–14, 72, 114–15, 122, 127–28; modern, 6, 58; nation-, 143n12; power of to separate internal territories, 106, 108; and sociopolitical movements that ignore borders, 118–19; territorial expansion of, 10, 77, 87, 118–19, 123, 127–28
Stoler, Ann, 8, 125, 128, 134–35, 178nn95–96, 193n86
subject: as a product of movement, 3, 14–15, 29, 37, 63; as a product of power relations, 2, 23, 37, 49, 50; as differentiated via the hierarchy of movement, 5, 9–11, 23–25, 37, 57, 88–89, 141–42n5; mechanisms for excluding individuals, 22, 32, 34, 37–41, 50, 88, 137–38. *See also* liberal subject
suffragists, 64–65, 83, 84–85, 139

tacit consent, 78, 183n128
Tahrir Square, 16, 132
terminals: at airports, 10, 11, 44, 146n41, 160n30; as checkpoints, 30, 41–50, 154n24
territory. *See* states
terror, 19–20, 34–35, 133, 137, 191n76
terrorists, 141–42n5, 149n85, 153n13
threat: freedom as a, 18, 20, 88, 92, 100, 110; Israeli perceptions of Palestinians as posing a, 29, 34–35, 149–50n86, 153n13; Israeli use of against Palestinians, 36, 152–53n7; movement as, vii–viii, 4, 5, 18–19, 90, 107–8, 145n29; need to integrate to ensure circulation, viii–ix; power of the state as a, 17; security and, 94, 127, 169–70n3; and socioeconomic perceptions, 9, 128, 137, 180–81n110, 185n12, 200–201n5; stagnation and lack of movement as, 7, 144n18; war as a response to, 118
Tilly, Charles, 129, 196n106, 197n121
time: as an element of rationality, freedom, and security, 90, 99–100, 105, 109, 182n120; as an element of social and political reform movements, 130–32; as product of societal interaction, 172–73n38; as bearer of terror, 19, 42, 95–96, 123; disruptive power of over space, 21; leisure and knowledge, 92–93, 99; and movement, 146n43; robbery of through harassment, 21, 31, 47; and security

surveillance, 141–42nn4–6; and space, 105–6, 156–57n8
Torpey, John C., 6–7, 71, 94, 164n41
tourism, 52, 155n2, 175n64
trade: commerce, 13, 114, 119–21, 160nn29–30, 180n108; commodities and money as life-force of a state, 8, 59, 120; as freedom of movement, 12–13, 121, 184n3; free markets ideas, 18; as large-scale movement, 13, 14, 188n51; markets, and globalization, 19, 37, 180n104; security and, 1–2, 18–19, 143n11; slave, 3, 11, 111, 121, 132; violence, and the state, 120, 121–22, 192n82
transgression: attire as a symbol of, 84–85; and embedded failure, 50, 55; of the imaginary line at checkpoints, 31–32, 33, 40–42, 56–57; movement as, 14, 85, 88, 124, 127
Tully, James, 103, 106
tunnels: as Palestinian political retaliation, 124, 191–92n77; Tunnels Road, 52–53, 155n1

unity: as redistribution of violence, 117–19, 122; as basis of the political state, 12; of the body-politic, 117; destruction of as a restraint on power, 38; function of in social movements, 129–31, 196n106; Hobbesian sovereign as the basis for, 113–14, 118–20, 122, 197n117, 197n119; and plurality, 114; as represented by the political state, 115, 116–17
urban warfare, 124–25, 190n71, 192n78
Urry, John, 171n22, 184n4

vagabondage, 5, 108, 181nn113–14
vagrancy, 3, 5, 99, 107–11, 180–81n110, 184n3; vagrancy laws, 181–82n117, 183n127, 200–201n5

Verdon, Michel, 162n16
violence: as an incentive for movement, 3; checkpoints as microcosms of, 24, 37, 39–41, 153n13, 154n24; disruptive effect of on a space, 36–37; economies of, 198–99n131; Fanon on, 153–54n14; freedom as, 94–97, 114, 116–17, 132–35, 139–40, 172n35, 186–87n33; imperial and colonial, 26, 121–22, 153–54n14, 199–200n136; Israeli against Palestinian civilians, 24, 30, 34–37, 55–56, 57, 124–25, 190n72; military in the oPt, 124–25; moderating of the state, 123–24, 138–39; monopolization of by the state, 6–7, 94, 96, 115, 122, 150n100, 197n117; movement as interchangeable with, 7, 13, 117–18, 121–22, 132–34, 138–40, 188n50; movement of 7, 96, 125, 132, 133, 188n40; nonviolent actions by Palestinians against Israel, 195n97, 195n99; political life and the state as restraints on, 96, 97, 115, 117–19, 172n35; potential for of social movements, 197n118; presentation of as justified, 24, 34–36, 106, 124, 133, 138–39; as product of the induced failure systems of checkpoints, 30, 31, 34, 40–42, 49–50; sea as a place of inherent, 114–15, 121–23, 189nn55–56, 192n82; security as a justification for, 29, 94, 134–35, 138–40, 149–50n86; structural, 48–49, 155n29; threat of by Israelis against Palestinians, 36, 46, 48–49, 127, 136–37, 153n8, 155n29; time as a means of controlling, 95–96, 100; urban warfare, 124–25, 190n71, 192n78; violent resistance as a threat, 35, 132–33, 149–50n86
Virilio, Paul, 12–13, 115–16, 122–23, 188n50, 189n56

walls: as blockages, 131, 138, 199n132; as directive and protective elements, 145n33, 155n1, 169n3, 186n18; Israel's use of to control the Palestinian populace, 23, 27, 44–46, 53, 157n9, 191n76, 194n94; as sites of military motion, 124, 192n80, 195n99

Walters, William, 22–23, 87–88, 145n33, 169–70n3, 181nn113–14

war: as a movement of the commonwealth, 117–23, 159n24, 186n29, 189n60; civil, 95, 186n31, 197nn117–18, 200–201n5; colonial, 120; guerrilla tactics during the Boer War, 157n12; Hobbesian, 119–21, 123, 162–63n21, 189n60, 190n64; the just, 104; Locke on freedom as the opposite of, 166n65; movement and, 8, 120, 144n19, 164n44, 187–88n43; natural liberty as an impetus for, 94–95, 117, 164n38; on the sea, 121, 123, 189nn55–59; as state-dictated movement, 12, 72; urban warfare, 124–25, 190n71, 192n78, 192n80

Weber, Max, 6–7, 94

Weizman, Eyal, 46, 123–25, 156n7, 158n15, 190n72, 192n78

West Bank: as an archipelago in the La Monde Diplomatique map, 125–26; Israeli arguments that the is not an occupied territory, 158–59n19; Israeli biases against the Palestinian population of the, 23, 49, 56–57, 155–56nn2–3, 157–58n13, 157nn9–10, 194n94; Israeli checkpoints on the, 20, 23, 27, 39, 56–57, 151–52n5, 195–96n100; Israeli terminals on the, 48; resistance to checkpoints on the, 195n99

Wollstonecraft, Mary, 64–65, 73–74

women: American suffragists, 64–65, 83, 84–85, 139; attribution of hysteria to, 5; as being enslaved to their bodies, 73–74; the bloomer, 83–85, 168–69n97, 169n101; Chinese foot-binding practices, 7, 74–75, 113, 143–44n16, 144n18, 184n5; the confinement of, 3, 88; discrimination against, 3, 142–43n8, 171n24, 201n6; female attire and physical movement, 83–86; human rights activists, 24, 38–40, 195n99; Locke on capacity for rationality of, 74–75; plight of Palestinian at checkpoints, 27, 46–47; as victims of confined or forced movement, 9, 17, 175n65, 184n3; Victorian attire, 83–85, 168–69n97

Zionism, 129, 134, 185–86n16, 191n76, 198n126

zones: in airports, 11, 146n41; Israeli, 131, 155n2, 156n4, 191n75, 193n84; and movement, 8; sea as a free, 121; unmarked Israeli military, 34, 36, 125

CPI Antony Rowe
Eastbourne, UK
January 21, 2015